Praise for

"A Land We Can Share"

"You're going to love this book! It offers much-needed practical insights into reading for individuals with significant developmental differences. It will help parents, teachers and others make the case that all children and adults have the right to learn to read and also help them to teach reading. Buy it!"

Anne Donnellan, Ph.D.
Professor
School of Leadership and Education Sciences
University of San Diego

"'*A Land We Can Share*' is a book we all *must* share for promoting literacy development of students with ASD. Respectful, insightful, engaging and focused on strengths rather than weaknesses, this is a cutting-edge volume that will move practitioners and parents to a new and more sophisticated level of practice in developing literacy abilities."

Barry Prizant, Ph.D., CCC-SLP
Adjunct Professor
Center for the Study of Human Development
Brown University

"In my work as a psycholinguist and through my experience as a person with Asperger syndrome, I am excited to say. . .finally, an entire book on autism and literacy! I've long suggested the cornerstone of effective autism supports must be a comprehensive understanding of the autistic's literacy and communication skills. Building from that foundation, supporters can more seamlessly design programs that propel their individual students toward self-awareness, problem solving, analytical thought, social understanding, and self-acceptance. Kluth and Chandler-Olcott are to be applauded for understanding that people with autism have good, strong voices that need and deserve to be heard and appreciated. They should be thanked for including instructional strategies that are spot on! '*A Land We Can Share*' is one of the most important books in autism education I have ever had the pleasure of reading."

Liane Holliday Willey, Ed.D.
Senior Editor
Autism Spectrum Quarterly

"Literacy is such an important, and often neglected, area for children with autism. This book is filled with great ideas and suggestions for making literacy a reality for children with autism."

Lynn Koegel, Ph.D., CCC-SLP
Clinical Director
Koegel Autism Center
University of California, Santa Barbara

"A much-needed resource that is informative and engaging, bridging what is known about effective reading instruction and characteristics of learners with ASD to provide educators with inspiring, practical, strengths-based instructional recommendations to build literacy skills. The authors provide a refreshing and positive depiction of ASD that illustrates the importance and functionality of literacy through insightful, rich, personal classroom examples and autobiographical accounts."

Kelly Whalon, Ph.D.
Assistant Professor of Special Education
The College of William and Mary

"This very important book demolishes the 'great wall of exclusion' that has often kept learners with autism segregated from literacy, reading, and language arts activities, the final frontier of inclusion. Filled with clear real-life examples, tools and practices, Paula Kluth and Kelly Chandler-Olcott have built a new foundation that promotes inclusive literacy assessment, development, and learning. If you know someone who has autism as an attribute, buy this book immediately and give it to his or her teacher—it is a must!"

Patrick Schwarz, Ph.D.
Professor and Chair
Diversity in Learning & Development Department
National-Louis University, Chicago

"Kluth and Chandler-Olcott offer practical advice for ensuring all students have access to literacy. *'A Land We Can Share'* delivers on a promise: ensuring that students with autism become literate citizens who use their knowledge of language to participate in real lives. This is a must-have resource for anyone asking themselves, 'How can I ensure that students with disabilities become members of the literate community?' The answers really are here!"

Douglas Fisher, Ph.D
Professor of Language and Literacy Education
San Diego State University

"This is a quintessentially respectful book. Paula Kluth and Kelly Chandler-Olcott have written an accessible, well-researched text that respects the competence of students with autism and the teachers who work with them. [The book] is a welcome antidote to the low-expectation literacy curricula that tend to dominate special education."

Curt Dudley-Marling, Ph.D.
Professor of Education
Lynch School of Education
Boston College

"Kluth and Chandler-Olcott have bridged the complex domains of Disability Studies and Literacy Theory and brought them directly into the Monday morning classroom. This is not only a treatise describing literate possibility for all students, but it is a powerful meditation on rethinking the very nature of autism. Thoroughly researched and full of vivid descriptions and countless well-thought-out examples, this book will dramatically impact classroom instructional practices and the underlying educational theory."

Chris Kliewer, Ph.D.
Professor of Special Education
University of Northern Iowa

"Finally, a book that guides parents and professionals in supporting the literacy development of learners with autism! Yet this is no ordinary methods textbook. Kluth and Chandler-Olcott have skillfully combined their knowledge of autism and reading interventions with a rich tapestry of anecdotes from their own teaching experience and reflections from individuals with autism. The result is a dynamic text filled with practical examples that will motivate and inspire readers to view all individuals as capable, successful literacy learners."

Monica E. Delano, Ph.D.
Assistant Professor of Special Education
University of Louisville

"Jam-packed with easy to implement and practical solutions for addressing some of the most challenging situations facing those teaching literacy to students on the autism spectrum at all levels. Thank you [Paula and Kelly] for helping those special people who support individuals on the autism spectrum in this key area of education."

Stephen M. Shore
Board of Directors for the Autism Society of America,
The Asperger's Association of New England, and MAAP Services

"Literacy is a right of every individual in our society. Through creativity, accommodation, respect, and unconventionality, Kluth and Chandler-Olcott demonstrate how to enable that right."

Morton Ann Gernsbacher, Ph.D.
Vilas Research Professor and
Sir Frederic C. Bartlett Professor of Psychology
University of Wisconsin–Madison

"A Land We Can Share"

"A Land We Can Share"

TEACHING LITERACY TO STUDENTS WITH AUTISM

by

Paula Kluth, Ph.D.

and

Kelly Chandler-Olcott, Ed.D.

·PAUL·H·
BROOKES
PUBLISHING CO.®

Baltimore • London • Sydney

Paul H. Brookes Publishing Co.
Post Office Box 10624
Baltimore, Maryland 21285-0624

www.brookespublishing.com

"Paul H. Brookes Publishing Co.," is a registered trademark of
Paul H. Brookes Publishing Co., Inc.

Typeset by Integrated Publishing Solutions, Grand Rapids, Michigan.
Manufactured in the United States of America by
Sheridan Books, Inc., Chelsea, Michigan.

Cover illustration by Barbara Moran.

Some individuals described in this book are composites, pseudonyms,
or fictional accounts. Individuals' names have been changed and identifying
details have been altered when necessary to protect their confidentiality.

Library of Congress Cataloging-in-Publication Data

Kluth, Paula.
    "A land we can share" : teaching literacy to students with autism / by Paula Kluth and
Kelly Chandler-Olcott.
        p.   cm.
    Includes bibliographical references and index.
    ISBN-13: 978-1-55766-855-4
    ISBN-10: 1-55766-855-8
    1. Autistic children—Education.   2. Language arts.   3. Inclusive education.
    I. Chandler-Olcott, Kelly, 1970-   II. Title.

    LC4721.K56 2008
    371.94—dc22   2007044017

British Library Cataloguing in Publication data are available from the British Library.

Contents

About the Authors

Paula Kluth, Ph.D., is a consultant, teacher, author, advocate, and independent scholar who works with teachers and families to provide inclusive opportunities for students with disabilities and to create more responsive and engaging schooling experiences for all learners. Her research and professional interests include differentiating instruction and supporting students with autism and significant disabilities in inclusive classrooms.

Dr. Kluth is a former special educator who has served as a classroom teacher, consulting teacher, and inclusion facilitator. She works with teachers of all grade levels, from preschool to high school, and in early intervention programs. She also regularly works with family organizations and disability rights and advocacy groups.

Dr. Kluth is the author of *"You're Going to Love This Kid!": Teaching Students with Autism in the Inclusive Classroom* (Paul H. Brookes Publishing Co., 2003); the lead editor of *Access to Academics for All Students: Critical Approaches to Inclusive Curriculum, Instruction, and Policy* (Lawrence Erlbaum Associates, 2003), with Diana Straut and Douglas Biklen, and the co-author of *You're Welcome: 30 Innovative Ideas for the Inclusive Classroom* (Heinemann, 2007), and *"Just Give Him the Whale!": 20 Ways to Use Fascinations, Areas of Expertise, and Strengths to Support Students with Autism* (Paul H. Brookes Publishing Co., 2008), both with Patrick Schwarz. More information about Paula can be found at her personal web site: http://www.paulakluth.com.

Kelly Chandler-Olcott, Ed.D., is an associate professor in Syracuse University's Reading and Language Arts Center, where she directs the English Education program. A former secondary English and social studies teacher, she now teaches undergraduate and graduate courses in content literacy, English methods, literacy and technology, and writing for professional publication. She was awarded a Meredith Recognition Award for excellence in university teaching in 2000.

Dr. Chandler-Olcott's research interests include adolescents' technology-mediated literacy practices, classroom-based inquiry by teachers, content literacy, and inclusive approaches to literacy instruction. With funding from the National Science Foundation, she and several colleagues recently completed data collection for a multiyear study of the literacy demands that reform-based mathematics curricula present for students in urban secondary classrooms. Her newest research project is a literacy intervention situated in an inclusive humanities class in an urban middle school.

Dr. Chandler-Olcott's work has been published by such journals as *English Education, Journal of Teacher Education, Journal of Adolescent & Adult Literacy,* and *Reading Research Quarterly.* She has also co-authored four books, the most recent being *Spelling Inquiry: How One Elementary School Caught the Mnenomic Plague* (Stenhouse, 1999), with the Mapleton Teacher-Research Group; and *Tutoring Adolescent Literacy Learners: A Guide for Volunteers* (Guilford, 2005), with Kathleen Hinchman.

Foreword

Welcome to *"A Land We Can Share": Teaching Literacy to Students with Autism*. You are in for a treat. This book is grounded in the real world of classroom life and builds on the rich stories of people with autism, including several individuals who were once thought so intellectually impaired that they were believed to be permanently illiterate, yet who have managed not only to find their way into the literate world but also to do so with poetry, humor, and even drama. Likely you will appreciate the down-to-earth, practical nature of Kluth and Chandler-Olcott's work, which is filled with helpful frameworks and strategies for creating classrooms brimming with meaningful, varied forms of expression.

The second chapter, "What Is Literacy?," is well named. It offers lessons for teaching about *literacy*, not just literacy in the context of autism, although it does that too. The authors speak to the fundamental importance of framing literacy work broadly, of approaching students with an expectant attitude, of providing multiple opportunities to explore communication, and of bringing technical skill to teaching.

The notion of conveying an expectant orientation toward students is key. Kluth and Chandler-Olcott draw on numerous autobiographical accounts by people with autism, such as Lucy Blackman, Jamie Burke, Tyler Fihe, and Temple Grandin. These individuals describe how their way into literacy came in part because others, usually a combination of parents and teachers, believed they understood far more than they could initially demonstrate and found ways for them to practice literacy. The message is straightforward: Had people not looked for literacy in these individuals, had they not imagined it possible, these learners would have been effectively barred from it.

Openness to a student's possibility has been termed *presuming competence*, as Kluth and Chandler-Olcott explain in the book. From this stance, teachers, parents, and other supporters provide diverse opportunities for expression, expose students to a range of forms of literacy (e.g., symbolic, spoken, artistic/graphic, theatrical), and take on the responsibility of discovering means for students to demonstrate complex thinking. Implicitly, when adopting this framework, a teacher acknowledges that a student's performance does not necessarily correspond neatly with thinking ability, interest, or even effort. That is, the student may be highly intelligent, have enormous interest in the content at hand, and desperately want to participate in literate expression, but if certain conditions impede these intentions, whether the conditions may be neurophysiological in origin or contextual (e.g., a confusing presentation by the teacher, threatening/confrontational style of questioning) or, more likely, both, the ability to perform may be absent. Therefore, finding evidence of literacy skill can prove to be complex and adventurous.

In a world that often seeks one best approach to literacy or, in this case, to autism and literacy, it is refreshing that *"A Land We Can Share"* does not stoop to such reductionist thinking. There is no one best way of teaching reading and writing to people on the autism spectrum. Instead, as with any group, there are multiple ways. Recognition of this guarantees that teaching literacy to children and youth with autism will be inherently interesting, for like all teaching, it involves a combination of detective work (the teacher has to look for clues about when the child engages and with what, or in what situations the student expresses him- or herself and how), creativity to formulate engaging learning situations, analytical acumen to measure change, and constant exploration of strategies.

The one difference between what Kluth and Chandler-Olcott describe for individuals with autism and for most others who are learning literacy is that the impact of certain difficulties (e.g., with decoding spoken language), or of certain strategies (e.g., writing as a scaffold to speaking), may sometimes be more vivid for the person with autism, even an all-or-nothing factor in learning. So a particular student may absolutely require writing in order to speak an intentional sentence (i.e., the student writes out his or her thoughts before or simultaneously with speaking) while another may absolutely need subtitles on a film in order to integrate comprehension of the visual actions with the spoken words.

As multiple examples in this book reveal, teachers will often be called into action as careful observers in order to sort out intentional speech or writing from the automatic, unintended repetitive phrasing that some believe haunts these individuals' efforts at communication. There is much to learn about *reading* the person's ways of engaging the environment, however, and this is just one of the ways in which this book illustrates how important deep knowledge of the student, the subject, and pedagogy is for anyone who seeks to engage in literacy work with people with autism. A student may seem obsessed with a particular subject—for example, butterflies or airplanes—leaving the teacher to figure out how to expand from this highly focused interest to a broader repertoire of expression. A student may seem unresponsive to a series of spoken instructions but be fully capable of accomplishing a complex task when given the same instructions in writing. It becomes the teacher's work to figure out what works for each particular student. *"A Land We Can Share"* is filled with well-described ideas and practices that teachers, researchers, and individuals with autism have found useful.

Many of the authors' examples of classroom practice will be familiar to or at least comfortable for most teachers, not just for those who have extensive background in disability. You will come upon such activities as Reader's Theater, think aloud, and reciprocal teaching, all strategies that have a rich tradition in the broad field of literacy. Oddly, despite the near desperate concern by many experts for the future of children and youth labeled as being on the autism spectrum, professionals in the field of autism and professionals in the field of literacy have had almost no conversations between each other. Happily, *"A Land We Can Share"* breaks that mold.

Much of today's popular writing on autism characterizes the disability as a frightful curse on newborn children and their families. News accounts speak of an "epidemic" of autism and of life with autism as extraordinarily burdensome, both to those so classified and to their families. Readers of this book are likely to experience a huge disconnect between such pessimistic and frightening representations of autism in the news on the one hand and the authors' own perspectives or those of the dozens of people on the autism spectrum whom they quote on the other. The more optimistic, even embracing attitude of the authors toward children and youth with autism does not derive from any Pollyannaish romanticism. Rather, it is the product of knowing and working with people with autism, and of success the authors, parents, teachers, and other researchers have had in imparting literacy through well-documented means. And it is the result of taking seriously the newly emerging literature by people with autism themselves.

Throughout their treatise on literacy and autism, Kluth and Chandler-Olcott carefully avoid speaking for the person with autism. Rather, they give example after example that combine to illustrate barriers to literacy, strategies for overcoming those barriers, and a wide range of writing that has emerged in the new autobiographical autism literature. The only conclusions we can draw from these are that a person with autism is not static, and that there is no such thing as "autistic literacy" or the "autistic mind." There is only complexity. There is only constant change. There is only possibility.

Douglas Biklen, Ph.D.
Dean of the School of Education
Syracuse University
Syracuse, New York

Foreword

Literacy is a way of representing and interpreting the world we live in. Viewed in its broad sense, literacy is more than reading and writing. It refers to a variety of ways in which individuals use symbolic systems—not only oral language and printed words but also pictures, gestures, maps, and electronic images—to acquire knowledge and convey meaning. This perspective of literacy has much to offer for a better understanding of the literacy capabilities of individuals with autism and other disabilities.

In this book, Kluth and Chandler-Olcott provide us with vivid autobiographical examples of the multiple emotional, social, and intellectual aspects of literacy as experienced by individuals with autism. Reading this book reminded me of Christophe, a lively 4-year-old child I worked with many years ago. Christophe's way of communicating was to repeat memorized phrases and to read aloud words he saw in books and environmental print, but without making any apparent connection to meaning. Christophe had taught himself to read at the age of 2, a behavior typical of children now characterized as hyperlexic. Building on Christophe's interest in print—drawing and writing short stories about Christophe's daily routines and things he was interested in—became key to our relationship and to helping Christophe connect print, spoken words, and meaning.

Kluth and Chandler-Olcott draw from three influential theoretical perspectives that are inclusive of all individuals, including those thought to be incapable of literacy learning. Each of these theoretical perspectives, described next, has contributed to new approaches to literacy learning. The *sociocultural perspective* emphasizes how literacy develops in the context of meaningful social interactions with others and provides a framework for how educators can support literacy learning in all individuals regardless of abilities. The *emergent literacy perspective* views literacy as beginning at birth and building on early social, cognitive, and linguistic foundational skills. We now know the importance of supporting beginning language and literacy in infants and toddlers. The Individuals with Disabilities Education Improvement Act (IDEA) of 2004 (PL 108-446), Part C (Early Intervention Program for Infants and Toddlers with Disabilities), for example, recommends the inclusion of early language and literacy outcomes in individualized family service plans. The perspective of *multiple literacies* broadens the definition of literacy to include the many forms of verbal and print symbols—including visual, audio, and digital media—that are an integral part of contemporary human activity. New technologies based on multimodal media have enhanced the communication capabilities and access to print for individuals with significant disabilities.

The Literacy Bill of Rights (Yoder, Erikson, & Koppenhaver, 1996) states that all people, regardless of their disabilities, have a basic right to use print. Kluth and Chandler-Olcott present not only a compelling conceptual framework for the inclusion of all individuals in literacy activities but also practical suggestions of how teachers can make it actually happen in classrooms. The book provides detailed guidelines for assessment and instruction that emphasize flexibility, adaptations, and students' strengths. Teachers will find a broad variety of ideas to support literacy learning in their students, ranging from adapting classroom materials and routines to using visual aids and providing explicit instruction. Instructional strategies are research based and address key components of conventional reading and writing.

Effective interventions need first to address teacher attitudes in addition to knowledge and skills. Kluth and Chandler-Olcott emphasize the importance of teachers having expectations that all individuals, regardless of disability, can learn and engage in literacy activities. In fact, they argue, most individuals with disabilities can become competent readers and writers when offered the appropriate tools and learning experiences.

Second, in order to design and implement responsive literacy instruction, teachers must be willing to learn how their students use literacy to create and convey meaning. Responsive instruction challenges teachers to take the time to observe and listen carefully, and to empathize with and to be open to diverse ways of experiencing the world.

Third and finally, teachers need to be purposeful and intentional in their teaching and be able to make well-informed decisions about which strategies work best for individual students. Kluth and Chandler-Olcott propose the concept of "elastic" instructional models and methods that stretch to accommodate diverse literacy learning and offer teachers specific guidelines and procedures for individualizing assessment and instruction to address children's different characteristics and needs.

Kluth and Chandler-Olcott have combined theory, research, and practical suggestions into a valuable, comprehensive resource for teachers to support literacy learning in children with autism and other disabilities. This book offers a unique, thought-provoking, and authentic perspective that encourages and inspires teachers to ensure that all children are provided with appropriate literacy learning opportunities.

Angela Notari-Syverson, Ph.D.
Senior Researcher
Washington Research Institute
Seattle, Washington

REFERENCES

Individuals with Disabilities Education Improvement Act (IDEA) of 2004, PL 108-446, 20 U.S.C. §§ 1400 *et seq.*

Yoder, D., Erickson, K., & Koppenhaver, D. (1996). *A literacy bill of rights.* Durham, NC: Duke University, Center for Literacy and Disabilities Studies.

Acknowledgments

We thank the many people who aided us in conceptualizing and completing this book, including the many students with autism spectrum labels who have helped us think critically about differentiating instruction, adapting curriculum, and teaching literacy to all. We are especially grateful to Andrew, Dan, Emily, Franklin, Jason, J.P., Matt, Melissa, and Nick.

We are also in debt to the many individuals with autism who have shared their stories through conference presentations, research, and autobiographies, including Lucy Blackman, Tyler Fihe, Gunilla Gerland, Temple Grandin, Kenneth Hall, Luke Jackson, Wendy Lawson, Tito Mukhopadhyay, Jerry Newport, Jasmine O'Neill, Dawn Prince-Hughes, Sue Rubin, Birger Sellin, Liane Holliday Willey, and Donna Williams. In particular, we thank Jamie Burke, a friend, colleague, and teacher, for generously sharing his insights and gifts with us and with others. Stephen Hinkle and Stephen Shore have also been a tremendous help with this book. Their willingness to share their own experiences and their encouraging words, perspective, and direction have been invaluable.

We would also like to express our appreciation to the schools that have welcomed us into their classrooms so that we may teach and be taught. Many educators field-tested strategies with us and entered fearlessly into an exploration of their own practice with students and colleagues alike. We are especially grateful to staff members and administrators from Audubon School in Chicago, Illinois; Greenwich Public Schools in Greenwich, Connecticut; and Mapleton Elementary School in Mapleton, Maine.

Douglas Biklen and Christopher Kliewer initially piqued our interest in this topic with their groundbreaking inquiries into communication, literacy, and inclusive schooling, and they continue to publish provocative, important work in these areas. Doug also serves as Kelly's dean in the Syracuse University School of Education in New York, where he provides important leadership and support for numerous scholars doing cutting-edge research on educational equity for all learners.

We have also drawn extensively on the research of Karen Erickson, David Koppenhaver, and their colleagues. The years they have spent exploring the literate lives of students with significant disabilities have profited not only people with autism spectrum labels but also families, teachers, and other researchers, like ourselves, who have read their studies and tried to extend that work through our own.

Other colleagues who assisted us either formally or informally with the writing of this book include Julie Causton-Theoharis, Marilyn Chadwick, Shelia Danaher, Anne Donnellan, Beth Ferri, Douglas Fisher, Kathleen Hinchman, Patrick Schwarz, Mayer Shevin, Alice Udvari-Solner, and Carol Willard.

Barbara Moran created our fantastic cover art. Barbara, a graphic artist who has autism, spent her childhood in a midwest mental health facility, misdiagnosed as schizophrenic. She is now a successful advocate and artist. We thank Barbara for her enthusiasm and her vision, and we hope that the book cover gets others as excited about her work as we are. Barbara's artwork hangs at the M.I.N.D. Institute at the University of California, Davis and has appeared on the covers of several books, including *"You're Going to Love This Kid!": Teaching Students with Autism in the Inclusive Classroom* (Paul H. Brookes Publishing Co., 2003). Barbara's work is available commercially at http://www.karlwilliams.com/moran.htm.

Support from our spouses, Todd and Jim, helped us find time to write, revise, and confer with each other, often during marathon telephone conferences. Our children—Erma and Willa, Lucy and Quinn—were all born during the 4 years we planned, researched, and wrote this book, and they have graciously allowed us to observe their literacy development, idiosyncrasies, and preferences daily.

Finally, we are grateful to those at Paul H. Brookes Publishing Co. for the time and care they invested in this project. In particular, we extend our very best to Rebecca Lazo who, as always, was patient, helpful, encouraging, and optimistic every step of the way, and to Leslie Eckard, who dealt patiently with our many questions and never failed to include "one more thing" when we asked her to do so!

In addition, permission to reprint the following is gratefully acknowledged:

Excerpts on pages 6, 80, 144 from SONGS OF THE GORILLA NATION by Dawn Prince-Hughes, Ph.D., copyright © 2004 by Dawn Prince-Hughes. Used by permission of Harmony Books, a division of Random House, Inc.

Excerpts on pages 7, 14, 111–112, 132, 144, 147, 168 from Gerland, G. (1996). *A real person: Life on the outside* (pp. 85, 56, 47, 53, 93–94). Used by permission of Souvenir Press, London.

Excerpts on pages 8, 10, 108, 144 from THINKING IN PICTURES AND OTHER REPORTS FROM MY LIFE WITH AUTISM by Temple Grandin, copyright © 1995 by Temple Grandin. Used by permission of Vintage Books, a division of Random House, Inc.

Excerpts on pages 10, 115, 167 from Holliday Willey, L. (1999). *Pretending to be normal: Living with Asperger's Syndrome.* Used by Permission of Jessica Kingsley Publishers, London.

Excerpts on pages 12, 37, 114–115, 122–123, 141, 142 From NOBODY NOWHERE by Donna Williams, copyright © 1992 by Donna Williams. Used by permission of Times Books, a division of Random House, Inc.

Excerpts on pages 16, 147 from *Life behind glass: A personal account of autism spectrum disorder,* by Lawson, W. (1998). Used by permission of Jessica Kingsley Publishers, London.

Excerpts on pages 17, 75–76, 147, 167, 175, 190 from Blackman, L. (1999). *Lucy's story: Autism and other adventures.* Brisbane, Australia: Book in Hand, and (2001) London: Jessica Kingsley Publishers; reprinted by permission.

Excerpts on pages 17, 21, 96, 116, 124, 156, 164 from Shore, S. (2003). *Beyond the wall: Personal experiences with autism and Asperger syndrome* (2nd ed.). Shawnee Mission, KS: Autism Asperger Publishing Company; reprinted by permission.

Excerpts on page 19 from EXITING NIRVANA BY CLARA CLAIBORNE PARK. Copyright © 2001 by Clara Claiborne Park. By permission of Little Brown & Company.

Excerpts on pages 20, 78, 79 from *Life behind glass: A personal account of autism spectrum disorder,* by Lawson, W. (1998). Used by permission of Jessica Kingsley Publishers, London.

Excerpt on page 105 from *Freaks, geeks, and Asperger syndrome: A user guide to adolescence,* by Jackson, L. (2002). Used by permission of Jessica Kingsley Publishers, London.

Excerpts on pages 118, 157, 183 from Mukhopadhyay, T. (2000). *Beyond the silence.* London: The National Autistic Society; reprinted by permission.

To our first reading teachers—
our mothers, Mary Kluth and Gail Gibson

Introduction

Given that we seek the small and manageable, it is no surprise that high-
functioning autistic people, unable to communicate with others above the ringing
swirl, shout across the canyons of reality by writing. . . . There we find a peaceful
world of art and order, a land we can share. Thus, writing was my salvation. I
have said in the past, and I have since heard it repeated by other autistic people,
that written English is my first language and spoken English is my second.
Since I was five years old, I have written all the wonderful and terrible things
that I could not bear to share.
—Dawn Prince-Hughes (2004, pp. 25–26)

We are delighted that you have chosen this book and hope that you will learn as much from reading it as we have from writing it. Like Dawn Prince-Hughes, the poet and anthropologist whose words appear above and served as the inspiration for the title of this book, we see literacy as a powerful force in people's lives—a solace in times of trouble, a means for reflection and communication, a source of comfort and help, and a lever for personal and social change. Although people with disabilities such as autism have not always been offered access to all of these facets of literacy—an issue we take up in more depth in Chapter 2—we see evidence to suggest that this trend is changing, making it possible for an increasingly diverse range of individuals to experience the pleasures, challenges, and satisfaction that Prince-Hughes reports from her literate life. By writing this book, we hope to help others do the same.

To our knowledge, this book is the first to focus specifically on teaching literacy to students with autism spectrum labels. This is not to say that other helpful resources don't exist, as we have both learned a great deal from texts on general teaching strategies for students with autism (Attwood, 1998; Gillingham, 1995; Kluth, 2003; Smith Myles, Adreon, & Gitlitz; 2006; Waterhouse, 2000; Williams, 1996) as well as from those on teaching literacy to students with a range of disabilities (cf., Copeland & Keefe, 2006; Downing, 2005; Keefe, 1996; McEwan, 2002; Rhodes & Dudley-Marling, 1996; Roller, 1996). Given the volume of questions we've both received in the 5 years since we began our research, however, it's clear we're not the only ones who believe that this topic merits a book of its own. Although we doubt that this volume will provide the last word on the subject, we hope that it will serve as a useful resource for practitioners and parents who tell us they need it *right now*. Ideally, it will spark more titles on the subject by others.

Before we define such key terms as *autism* and *literacy* or provide any pedagogical suggestions, however, we think it's important to share some information about our beliefs and the nature of our collaboration. This way, you can evaluate the ideas we advocate within a context. After we offer this background information about ourselves as an author team (please see About the Authors for more information about our individual backgrounds), we'll move to some discussion of our expectations for the book's audience, a preview of its organizational structure, and our rationale for some of the editorial choices we made. We hope this will set you up for a more satisfying reading experience as you move through the rest of the book.

ABOUT US

Paula is an independent scholar and educational consultant. Her primary areas of research, study, and consultation are supporting students with significant disabilities in general education classrooms and differentiating instruction. Paula began her teaching career in a small inclusive school in suburban Chicago, where she supported students with a range of skills, struggles, and strengths. As inclusion facilitator, she was responsible for creating curricular adaptations, collaborating with general educators, co-teaching with colleagues, and providing supports that would promote and facilitate the participation of all learners. Paula also briefly taught students with significant disabilities in a Madison, Wisconsin, high school and acted as an inclusion consultant for an elementary school in Verona, Wisconsin. In each of these instances, Paula had opportunities to learn from colleagues about general education curriculum and instruction. She learned about literacy instruction not from her own preservice teacher education (a professional preparation program focused on the needs of students with "severe and profound disabilities") but from working with colleagues in general education who challenged her to offer a more academic education to her students with disabilities, even those deemed to have the most significant physical, learning, and communication needs.

Kelly is currently an associate professor of literacy at Syracuse University (SU) in Syracuse, New York, where she teaches literacy courses to those preparing to become teachers as well as graduate students returning for further study. Before earning her doctorate, she taught secondary English and social studies in her home state of Maine. This experience included several years at Noble High School, a member of a national network committed to school reform called the Coalition of Essential Schools (http://www.essentialschools.org/). Unlike many secondary schools at the time, Noble offered fully inclusive classes for ninth and tenth graders in English, social studies, earth science, biology, algebra, and geometry. Consequently, Kelly's class lists included a diverse mix of students, with those participating in the school's gifted and talented program working alongside those who had been identified with learning disabilities, Down syndrome, and attention-deficit/hyperactivity disorder. Although Kelly taught only one student with autism during this time, the success she had co-teaching heterogeneous classes in general education classes shaped her beliefs about effective and equitable pedagogy, fostering her confidence that all students can be educated in general education settings if provided with the right supports.

In the fall of 1998, the School of Education at SU, an institution with a longstanding commitment to inclusive education and social justice, hired us as new faculty members—Kelly in the department of Reading and Language Arts and Paula in Teaching and Leadership. We met at a new faculty orientation and immediately struck up a friendship on the basis of our common knowledge of 1970s popular culture, our shared appreciation for the city of Cambridge, Massachusetts, where both of us lived for several years, and our passion for professional sports. Because both of our teaching loads included courses in SU's Inclusive Elementary and Special Education Program, we even had some students in common. We frequently found ourselves discussing all of these mutual interests, as well as our developing research agendas, at a local sports bar, with occasional breaks in the conversation necessitated by important moments in the New York Yankees baseball and Green Bay Packers football games shown on the nearby big-screen televisions. The more we talked, the more clear it was to us that our professional passions intersected as much as our personal ones did—centering on the topic of providing rich, equitable opportunities for diverse learners to develop both academic and personal literacies.

Two years after we met, Paula and several other SU colleagues were in the midst of editing a book on access to academics for all students (Kluth, Straut, & Biklen, 2003), and they asked Kelly to contribute a chapter on inclusive approaches to literacy instruction (Chandler-Olcott, 2003). To prepare for the task, Kelly asked Paula to suggest some books she could read by and about people with disabilities. Among those recommendations were Temple Grandin's *Thinking in Pictures and Other Reports from My Life with Autism* (1995), an autobiography by an adult woman with autism focusing on her unusual gifts as a visual thinker, and Russell Martin's *Out of Silence: An Autistic Boy's Journey into Language and Communication* (1994), an account of how the author's nephew, a boy with autism, learned to use typed communication to interact in powerful ways with his world. Although Kelly had talked with Paula about the literacy-related experiences reported by many of Paula's former students, these two first-hand narratives reinforced even more profoundly her growing belief about the increased necessity of literacy access for people with disabilities. Similarly, Kelly's conviction that insights from such narratives could change literacy instruction for *all* students, not just those with autism, helped Paula to see these books, which she knew very well, as even more important catalysts for educational change than she had previously realized.

Sparked by conversations about these two texts, we decided to conduct a more formal study of how literacy is treated in the burgeoning first-person literature by people with autism. From this inquiry, we hoped to answer questions such as the following:

- What do people with autism spectrum labels who write autobiographies report about their acquisition and development of literacy?

- In the view of people with autism spectrum labels, what aspects of their homes and school communities supported them in developing literacy?

- What instructional practices for supporting students' literacy development might be suggested by the accounts of these individuals?

To that end, we reviewed and discussed 16 book-length autobiographies by people with autism spectrum labels who included material related to literacy in one way or another in their texts. We systematically excerpted all of the data from the larger narratives, and then labeled each piece by category and subcategory (e.g., SCHOOL/attitude toward, READING/early experiences, WRITING/hand-writing) using a coding system we developed. As we began to look across the categories for emerging themes, we saw some trends that validated our previous beliefs (e.g., how written language often helped people with autism cope with their difficulties with speech) as well as some that surprised us (e.g., how families of students with significant disabilities had to fight sometimes to get their child's literacy abilities recognized by others).

Our research underscored Dawn Prince-Hughes' claim that personal writing—diaries, journals, autobiographies, and memoirs—can serve as a "vast resource of knowledge about the diversity and beauty of autism" (2004, p. 31), and we have drawn extensively on these excerpts and insights throughout the book. We have also drawn on personal experiences, anecdotes shared with us by other educators we respect, and the professional literature on autism, literacy, and education.

ABOUT YOU

As we planned and wrote this book, we talked often about who its audience would most likely be. Given our commitment to inclusive education, it probably comes as no surprise that we wanted the book to appeal to as broad an audience as possible. We knew there was a danger in trying to be all things to all people, but we felt it was worth the risk to produce a text that could serve multiple purposes, especially considering how few resources on literacy and autism are available to any of the constituencies who need them.

Because this book is produced by an educational publisher, there is a good chance that you are an educator working in some formal capacity with children in a school setting. If you're an experienced teacher, we hope that you'll find validation here for successful methods that you've used as well as inspiration for new approaches. If you are a student reading the book for a college course, we hope that it will give you confidence about your ability to support all students' literacy development as you begin your career. We hope, too, that you will feel comfortable sharing ideas from the book with more veteran colleagues in your school. (Our students at SU were often pleasantly surprised by how eager their mentor teachers were to hear about the principles and practices these students had learned from participating in an innovative university program.) If you are an educational assistant or another kind of paraprofessional, we hope that you'll find ideas you can adopt and adapt to suit the needs of the students to whom you are assigned. As someone who works intimately with particular learners each day, you should be unafraid to share ideas from the book that resonate for you with the other members of a student's educational team—most notably, the general and special educators with whom you collaborate.

At the same time, we know that you may not be an educator—at least not in the strictest, most formal sense of the word. We are well aware that family members of students on the autism spectrum are among the most avid seekers of information on the planet! In Paula's work as a consultant, she frequently meets parents who are better informed about their children's disability and learning profile than many a teacher, psychologist, or physician. For this reason, we can imagine that you might be a parent or guardian looking for ways to support your child's learning at home and that you might pass along some of the ideas, or even the book itself, to administrators or teachers at your child's school. We hope that you will find our ideas and strategies flexible enough to translate into in-home use. We also hope that you will be heartened by the family-tested ideas we share throughout the text; much of what we have learned about the literacy needs and abilities of individuals with autism has come from their loved ones. So in whatever way suits your situation, please use this text as a tool for communicating with your child's educators. The field needs your wisdom.

Whatever your reason for reading this book, we hope that you will correspond with us about your response to it. We would be interested in hearing from teachers, parents, and others about how these ideas played out in practice. To facilitate that communication, here are our individual e-mail addresses and a URL address for Paula's web site that includes a link for browsers to communicate with her:

Paula Kluth: pkluth@earthlink.net and http://www.paulakluth.com
Kelly Chandler-Olcott: kpchandl@syr.edu

ABOUT THIS BOOK

We've organized this book into informal parts. The first two chapters, "What Is Autism?" and "What Is Literacy?", define and describe the characteristics often associated with autism spectrum labels and explain how we define literacy from our perspective. The second part includes the following chapters: Chapter 3, "Promoting Literacy Development in Inclusive Classrooms," which lays out our vision for the kind of learning environment where our instructional recommendations can best be implemented; Chapter 4, "Assessing Literacy Learning"; Chapter 5, "Focus on Reading"; Chapter 6, "Focus on Writing and Representation"; and Chapter 7, "Literacy Learning for Students with Significant Disabilities: Yes, Those Students, Too." We conclude with a bibliography including a list of references and resources that will help you increase your knowledge base about autism and teaching literacy through suggested readings and web sites on professional experiences and collaboration with families.

ABOUT OUR TERMINOLOGY

Finally, let us say just a few words about some of our other choices as authors.

Throughout the book, we often use the term *autism* to represent all labels on the autism spectrum, including Asperger syndrome, pervasive developmental disorder (PDD), childhood disintegrative disorder, and Rett syndrome. We acknowledge that people with these labels don't necessarily experience them identically; moreover, the labels themselves are not discrete or exact, but it would be cumbersome stylistically to list all of the related labels in every example we provide.

Another choice we need to illuminate is related to how we discuss learners with autism and illustrate their uniqueness without treating them as "other." In some places in the book, the points we are making require us to distinguish the needs of students on the autism spectrum from those of their peers without disabilities. We've struggled to do this (even in the preceding sentence!) in ways that don't position people with autism as deviant from the norm, as this isn't how we see these individuals. At the same time, making the distinction in a more neutral way sometimes requires an awkward turn of phrase. In some cases, we wrote material resembling what you just read—text that distinguishes our target population of learners from those without an autism spectrum label by framing the latter in terms of what they are not (e.g., people with and without disabilities). In other places, we describe students without autism as *neurotypical,* a label we borrow from some people with autism themselves. This is a term that has been circulating on web pages for years and has been made popular by the many sites run by and for people on the autism spectrum, including http://www.autistics.org and http://www.autcom.org. Although we know that this term isn't widely used outside the autism community, we like the way it turns the business of labeling on its head by applying a medical-sounding word to a population that doesn't usually receive such linguistic treatment.

We are also cautious throughout the book in our description of autism itself. Although we sometimes discuss it as a disability, it might be more accurate (and more provocative) to describe it as a dis/ability, which is a presentation of the word used most often in the disability studies literature to suggest that autism and other "disabilities" can be complex and challenging but also, for some, valued and even preferred (Davis, 1997; Garland Thomson, 1996; Shapiro, 1994). Not all people with disability labels view their differences as negative, tragic, or even disabling, including some with physical disabilities (Callahan, 1990; Hockenberry, 1996; Shapiro, 1994), some who are deaf and hard of hearing (Cohen, 1995; Lane, 1999), and those with Asperger syndrome and autism (Grandin, 1995; Hall, 2001; Holliday Willey, 1999; Jackson, 2002; O'Neill, 1999).

Of course, no one lens or perspective will fully explain what it is to have autism, but we did our best in this text to make choices, provide suggestions, and use language that would be easily understood by all and respected by those most closely touched by autism—the people with the label themselves. We hope that we have made the right choices and suggestions and have used the most sensitive language, but most of all we hope that this text will give a wider range of students access to the academic opportunity, social interaction, communication, intellectual curiosity, adventure, and delight that a literate life allows.

REFERENCES

Attwood, T. (1998). *Asperger's syndrome: A guide for parents and professionals.* London: Jessica Kingsley Publishers.

Callahan, J. (1990). *Don't worry, he won't get far on foot.* New York: Vintage Books.

Chandler-Olcott, K. (2003). Seeing all students as literate. In P. Kluth, D. Straut, & D. Biklen (Eds.), *Access to academics for all students: Critical approaches to inclusive curriculum, instruction, and policy* (pp. 69–84). Mahwah, NJ: Lawrence Erlbaum Associates.

Cohen, L. (1995). *Train go sorry: Inside a deaf world.* New York: Vintage Books.

Copeland, S.R., & Keefe, E.B. (2006). *Effective literacy instruction for students with moderate or severe disabilities.* Baltimore: Paul H. Brookes Publishing Co.

Davis L. (Ed.). (1997). *Disability studies reader.* New York: Routledge.

Downing, J.E. (2005). *Teaching literacy to students with significant disabilities: Strategies for the K–12 inclusive classroom.* Thousand Oaks, CA: Corwin Press.

Garland Thompson, R. (1996). *Extraordinary bodies: Figuring physical disability in American culture and literature.* New York: Columbia University Press.

Gillingham, G. (1995). *Autism: Handle with care.* Edmonton, Alberta, Canada: Tacit Publishing Inc.

Grandin, T. (1995). *Thinking in pictures and other reports from my life with autism.* New York: Vintage Books.

Hall, K. (2001). *Asperger syndrome, the universe and everything.* London: Jessica Kingsley Publishers.

Hockenberry, J. (1996). *Moving violations: War zones, wheelchairs, and declarations of independence.* New York: Hyperion.

Holliday Willey L. (1999). *Pretending to be normal.* London: Jessica Kingsley Publishers.

Keefe, C.H. (1996). *Label-free learning: Supporting learners with disabilities.* Portland, ME: Stenhouse Publishers.

Kluth, P. (2003). *"You're going to love this kid!": Teaching students with autism in the inclusive classroom.* Baltimore: Paul H. Brookes Publishing Co.

Kluth, P., Straut, D., & Biklen, D. (2003). *Access to academics for all students: Critical approaches to inclusive curriculum, instruction, and policy.* Mahwah, NJ: Lawrence Erlbaum Associates.

Lane, H. (1999). *The mask of benevolence: Disabling the deaf community.* San Diego: Dawn Sign Press.

Martin, R. (1994). *Out of silence: An autistic boy's journey into language and communication.* New York: Penguin Books.

McEwan, E.K. (2002). *Teach them ALL to read.* Thousand Oaks, CA: Corwin Press.

O'Neill, J.L. (1999). *Through the eyes of aliens: A book about autistic people.* London: Jessica Kingsley Publishers.

Prince-Hughes, D. (2004). *Songs of the gorilla nation: My journey through autism.* New York: Harmony Books.

Rhodes, L., & Dudley-Marling, C. (1996). *Readers and writers with a difference: A holistic approach to teaching struggling readers and writers* (2nd ed.). Portsmouth, NH: Heinemann.

Roller, C. (1996). *Variability not disability: Struggling readers in a workshop classroom.* Newark, DE: International Reading Association.

Shapiro, J.P. (1994). *No pity: People with disabilities forging a new civil rights movement.* New York: Times Books.

Smith Myles, B., Adreon, D. & Gitlitz, D. (2006). *Simple strategies that work! Helpful hints for all educators of students with Asperger syndrome, high-functioning autism, and related disabilities.* Shawnee Mission, KS: Autism Asperger Publishing Company.

Waterhouse, S. (2000). *A positive approach to autism.* London: Jessica Kingsley Publishers.

Williams, D. (1996). *Autism: An inside-out approach.* London: Jessica Kingsley Publishers.

Chapter 1

What Is Autism?

Ray, a student with autism, was educated from second to fifth grade in a facility for students with that label. When he turned 12, his parents pushed their school district to place him in his neighborhood middle school. After several meetings between Ray's parents and educators, a visit to the middle school, and some extended planning sessions, inclusive schooling became a reality for Ray.

It was not, however, a smooth or easy process for Ray, his parents, or the educational team. Staff members questioned their ability to provide appropriate supports for their new student, and they wondered whether Ray would be able to participate in lessons.

Despite these initial concerns, Ray's teachers were committed to his success and therefore devoted time and energy to learn about their new student and to explore adaptations and supports that would facilitate his participation. For instance, when the class discussed The Watsons Go to Birmingham—1963 *(Curtis, 1997), Ray's book club—a group of students reading and discussing the same self-selected text—met on the couches in the corner of the classroom because the seating was more comfortable for him. Ray, as always, brought two copies of the book to the discussion group (one he used for the reading exercise and one he used mostly as a companion or comfort item of sorts). Ray could not read the novel on his own because he had only recently had access to reading instruction. He listened to the book on audiotape to prepare for class. He also worked with a school reading specialist to learn some of the vocabulary words from the story and work on his decoding skills. During their time together, the reading specialist found a short passage from the novel that Ray could read fluently and prepared him to share it with his group. Once in his group, Ray had a hard time waiting for his turn, so his classmates asked him to share his response first, and they used his answer as a jumping-off point for the rest of their talk.*

Portions of this chapter are from Kluth, P. (2003). *"You're going to love this kid!" Teaching students with autism in the inclusive classroom* (pp. 1–21). Baltimore: Paul H. Brookes Publishing Co.; adapted by permission.

Ray's story is an example of how one learner with autism has been successfully included in literacy instruction. His teacher and his peers considered his special preferences (his desire to use more than one book), his classroom environment needs (couches instead of chairs), and his learning differences (speaking first in the group to minimize anxiety). Although these adaptations may seem small, it took Ray's sixth-grade teacher and her special education colleague several months to create the most optimal conditions for his participation. The key, they found, was feeling comfortable with making changes; experimenting with a range of materials and strategies; and, of course, continuously learning about autism and the unique gifts and challenges Ray brought to the classroom. Ray's teachers needed to learn about Ray and his specific needs before they could provide appropriate supports in their lessons.

Ray's teachers are not alone in having to learn quickly about autism. Until the movie *Rain Man* (Johnson, 1988) was released in the late 1980s, few people knew what autism was and fewer still knew someone with that label. Whereas the much-acclaimed motion picture gave the average person a glimpse into this little-understood disability, it also provided Americans with a range of stereotypes about autism and people with that label. Today, due to deinstitutionalization; an increased focus on community living for people with disabilities; and more accurate and varied accounts of people with autism in biographies, autobiographies, magazines, and television, most Americans understand more about what it means to have autism. In addition, the inclusive schooling movement (Fisher, Sax, & Pumpian, 1999; Jorgensen, 1998; Kluth, Straut, & Biklen, 2003; Sapon-Shevin, 2007; Stainback & Stainback, 1996; Udvari-Solner, 1997; Villa & Thousand, 2005), with its increased emphasis on learning about differences in American classrooms and more accurate and varied accounts of students on the autism spectrum in preservice textbooks and courses, has resulted in more practitioners in general and special education learning how to teach students with autism. Furthermore, due to the increasingly prominent place of literacy achievement for all learners in the national political agenda (Allington, 2002; Barone, Hardman, & Taylor, 2004), an issue we take up in more depth in the next chapter, it is no surprise to find educators, administrators, and parents seeking more information about how to help students with autism learn to read, write, listen, speak, view, and represent ideas with symbols in the most sophisticated and satisfying ways possible.

This book is meant to help members of all of these groups support the literacy development of students with autism spectrum labels and characteristics. This first chapter serves a number of purposes beginning with the dissemination of some general information on what students with autism can bring to the classroom. We offer several different understandings of autism and compare and contrast those put forth by medical science with those put forth by individuals with autism themselves. Finally, we describe different characteristics of autism and illustrate how each of these may affect a student's literacy learning.

DEFINING AUTISM

Autism, first described in the 1940s by American psychiatrist Leo Kanner, is one of the most common developmental disabilities. It is 4 to 5 times more likely to occur in boys than in girls, and the U.S. Centers for Disease Control and Prevention (2007) estimates that 1 in 150 children in this country are on the autism spectrum (http://www.cdc.gov/ncbddd/autism/asd_common.htm). As of 2007, no biological markers associated with autism, Asperger syndrome, or other disabilities on the autism spectrum have been determined; therefore, the categories and descriptions that many people use are constructed and culturally reproduced based on the professional judgment and opinion of scholars, researchers, the medical community, and, in some instances, people with these labels themselves. Put more succinctly, these definitions or labels "represent efforts to classify and think about the problems developing children may encounter" (Temple University Institute on Disabilities, 1997, p. 8). In this chapter, we offer several descriptions of autism and share interpretations of the disability from different perspectives. In particular, we explore the medical model of disability and definitions of autism that come from those individuals with the label.

The Medical Model of Autism

According to the *Diagnostic and Statistical Manual of Mental Disorders, Fourth Edition, Text Revision* (*DSM-IV-TR;* American Psychiatric Association [APA], 2000), a reference book designed to provide guidelines for the diagnosis and classification of mental disorders, individuals with autism have "delayed or abnormal functioning" in at least one of the following areas: 1) social interaction; 2) communication; and/or 3) restricted repetitive and stereotyped patterns of behavior, interests, and activities. Specifically, in this model, people with autism are seen as having little interest in making friends, preferring their own company to the company of others, failing to use imitative behavior, avoiding eye contact, seeming unaware of the existence of others, lacking imagination, failing to use symbolic gestures, lacking empathy, and being aggressive and self-injurious (APA, 2000; Powers, 2000).

Another related label that is given to individuals on the autism spectrum is *Asperger syndrome*. Many professionals have described individuals with Asperger-like characteristics as simply having a milder form of autism; others have understood it to be qualitatively different enough to warrant a separate label and, in practice, different supports. In contrast to those with autism, individuals with Asperger syndrome have no clinically significant delays in language or in the acquisition of self-help skills. These individuals are also described as experiencing few or no challenges with adaptive behavior such as eating or dressing (APA, 2000). The essential features of Asperger syndrome, according to the medical model of disability, are severe and sustained impairment in social interaction and, like in individuals with autism, the development of restricted, repetitive patterns of behavior, interest, and activity. People with Asperger syndrome have been seen as demonstrating, among other characteristics, egocentricity, an inability to interact with peers, poor appreciation of social cues, socially and emotionally inappropriate responses, limited interests, and preoccupations.

We believe that there are a host of problems with understanding autism from this deficit-oriented perspective. Donnellan and Leary pointed out that a deficit model is not cautious or generous enough: "For the purpose of diagnosis, behaviors are often described with phrases such as 'prefers to,' 'failure to,' or 'unusual interest in' without specifying what particular symptoms may lead to that impression" (1995, p. 40). These researchers questioned whether an observer, especially one who does not have an intimate knowledge of the child, can know if a child "prefers" to play alone, for example. Perhaps the child who is seen playing alone prefers to play with his sister but is playing alone because she is wearing a lotion or hair gel that bothers his sensory system. Or maybe he is playing alone because he is not sure how to enter the game that the other children are enjoying.

Those subscribing to a medical model of autism tend to view disability through a frame of disease or deficit; see the person with a disability as a constellation of problems; and understand cure, change, or "extraction" of the disability as the ultimate goal of intervention or education. Consider this excerpt from a paper describing Asperger syndrome:

> Although children with Asperger syndrome are frequently noted by teachers and parents to be "somewhat in their own world" and preoccupied with their own agenda, they are seldom as aloof as children with autism. (Bauer, 1996, n.p.)

In this short passage, the author manages not only to outline some of the deficits of Asperger syndrome but also to illustrate that students with autism are, at least in one way, "worse off" than those with Asperger syndrome. Likewise, in the popular guidebook, *Children with Autism: A Guide for Families,* Powers stated that

> [Children with autism] may be extremely apathetic and unresponsive, showing no desire to initiate contact or to be held or cuddled. Indeed when [the child with autism] is held she may stiffen or arch her back as if being held is somehow distressing. The social cues of others—a smile, a wave, a frown—may be meaningless to her. (2000, p. 4)

The Social Model of Autism

We do not subscribe to the medical model and instead, throughout this book, view autism through a social model of disability. That is, we recognize that some people have severe struggles, challenges, and impairments due to their disability, but we also understand that those same individuals may be more or as disabled by the barriers that exist in a society that does not take account of their needs and differences. These barriers may be physical (e.g., seating that isn't comfortable, lights that are too bright), personal (e.g., negative attitudes about people with disabilities), or institutional (e.g., school segregation). In the social model of disability, autism is not seen as tragic, pitiful, or necessarily something to eradicate. Indeed, some (though certainly not all) may view it as an asset or gift.

Some individuals with autism indicate that the most disabling aspects of their lives are the attitudes, perspectives, and actions of those without labels. Many individuals with autism have experienced difficulties that stem from societal and cultural ideas of how people should communicate, interact, move, and behave. Although many individuals with autism share that "it" is real—that they do experience things in different ways, that their bodies are uncooperative or that they have sensory or communication problems—many of these same individuals indicate that autism is, at least in moments, "created" by an inflexible society. Therefore, people may feel more or less challenged on any given day based on whether appropriate supports are provided for them or whether they are expected to communicate, behave, move, or interact in a conventional way.

One individual on the autism spectrum has imagined a world in which autism is the norm and being "typical" is seen as problematic to illustrate the divide between how those with and those without labels often perceive dis/ability.

This world is described on a web site for a mock organization, "The Institute for the Study of the Neurologically Typical." On the site, the tragedy of "neurotypical syndrome" is described in detail:

> Neurotypical syndrome is a neurobiological disorder characterized by preoccupation with social concerns, delusions of superiority, and obsession with conformity. Neurotypical individuals [NTs] often assume that their experience of the world is either the only one, or the only correct one. NTs find it difficult to be alone. NTs are often intolerant of seemingly minor differences in others. When in groups NTs are socially and behaviorally rigid, and frequently insist on the performance of dysfunctional, destructive, and even impossible rituals as a way of maintaining group identity. NTs find it difficult to communicate directly, and have a much higher incidence of lying as compared to persons on the autistic spectrum. NT is believed to be genetic in origin. Autopsies have shown the brain of the neurotypical is typically smaller than that of an autistic individual and may have overdeveloped areas related to social behavior. (http://isnt.autistics.org).

From this humorous and unusual parody, it is clear that there are many varying (and even contrasting) ways to explain what it is like to be on the autism spectrum.

Due to these variances and contrasts, we believe the words and experiences of people with autism themselves should be considered alongside—and in some cases, weighted more than—the words and experiences of the professionals who aim to study and understand them. For these same reasons, medical-model, deficit-oriented descriptions of autism should be questioned and understood in context.

Defining Autism: Insiders' Expertise

From our perspective, one of the best ways to develop an understanding of autism in context, as well as to appreciate the diversity of experience that labels do not reveal, is to read the growing body of literature authored by people on the autism spectrum. These individuals have their own ways of understanding their diagnosis, and in many cases, their definitions and descriptions vary greatly from those put forth by traditional sources such as medical texts and education reports. Here's a sampling of perspectives from both adults and children who have written about their dis/ability:

> Autism isn't something a person has, or a "shell" that a person is trapped inside. There's no normal child hidden behind the autism. Autism is a way of being. It is pervasive: it colors every experience, every sensation, perception, thought, emotion, and encounter, every aspect of existence. It is not possible to separate the autism from the person—and if it were possible, the person you'd have left would not be the same person you started with. (Sinclair, 1993, p. 1)

> Yet I believe autism can be a beautiful way of seeing the world. I believe that within autism there is not only the group—the label—but the individual as well; there is strength in it, and there is terror in its power. When I speak of emerging from the darkness of autism I do not mean I offer a success story neatly wrapped and finished with a "cure." I and the others who are autistic do not want to be cured. What I mean when I say "emergence" is that my soul was lifted from the context of my earlier autism and became autistic in another con-

text, one filled with wonder and discovery and full of the feelings that so poetically inform each human life. (Prince-Hughes, 2004, p. 2)

_____

Autism means having to watch how I feel every second that I am awake. Autism means having challenge [sic] when I leave the room fearing that others will say unkind things about me to other people. Autism means being dateless on weekends as well as constant loneliness, only watching TV on Saturday night. Autism means not being able to fit in on social peer relations. However, autism, in my case, means that I have a calendar memory for birthdays, being articulate and having skills. I, all in all, would rather be autistic than normal. (Ronan, as cited in Gillingham, 1995, p. 90)

_____

I believe autism is a marvelous occurrence of nature, not a tragic example of the human mind gone wrong. In many cases, autism can also be a kind of genius undiscovered. (O'Neill, 1999, p. 14)

_____

I like being different. I prefer having AS [Asperger syndrome] to being normal. I don't have the foggiest idea exactly what it is I like about AS. I think that people with AS see things differently. I also think they see them more clearly. (Hall, 2001, p. 15)

COMMON CHARACTERISTICS OF AUTISM

Although no two students with autism will look, behave, communicate, or learn in exactly the same way, students with this label do share some general characteristics. We believe that knowledge of these common characteristics—and more specifically, knowledge of how each might play out in the context of literacy learning—can be extremely useful for educators seeking to design responsive literacy instruction for individuals with autism. Consequently, we share some of the most significant characteristics, including movement, sensory, communication, social, and learning differences, in this section. After providing a brief definition of each difference, we discuss how they are experienced by people with autism and how each might affect literacy.

Movement Differences

Movement differences describe symptoms involving both excessive and atypical movement and the lack of typical movement. Individuals with movement differences may walk with an uneven gait; engage in repetitive movements such as rocking, hand flapping, or pacing; produce speech that is unintentional; stutter; or struggle to make the transition from room to room or situation to situation. Individuals may experience difficulties in starting, executing, continuing, stopping, combining, or switching movements, thoughts, or postures, and disturbances may range from very simple movements (e.g., raising a hand, pushing a button) to those affecting overall levels of activity and behavior (e.g., completing a task).

Understanding Movement Differences

For some students with autism, even the simplest tasks can be problematic. For instance, Jamie Burke, a young man with autism, has commented on his frustration with not being able to tie his shoes as a young child. This frustration was exacerbated by the fact that his teachers felt the task was not only important but also a measure of his intellect:

> So many things were hard for me to learn. I now think it was so foolish to ask me to learn to tie my shoes. My brain moved into hiding the reason for not being able to do it, but yet my school believed it important mostly as a way to tell you that you are not just greatly smart. (2005, p. 251)

Although all of us may experience minor or subtle movement differences from time to time (e.g., jiggling our feet when anxious, being unable to complete a motor task when we are very stressed out), many people with autism experience significant movement problems on a regular basis. Consider, for example, this description from Tyler Fihe, a young man with autism:

> I never really know when sounds are coming out of my mouth or when my arms need to move or when my legs need to run and jump.... My eyes are unable to move up and down and left to right at will without me moving my head in the directions I'm facing. (2000, p. 1)

Fihe's description of movement problems helps us better understand why students engage in behaviors associated with autism such as gaze avoidance. Taking his perspective, one can understand that lack of eye contact is not necessarily about social avoidance and that, in fact, for many with autism it is a necessary strategy *that helps them* interact with others. Fihe also challenges the notion that all behavior is communication or that all movements are intentional. As he illustrates, to some individuals, movement problems are just problems with movement and nothing more.

According to Donnellan and Leary (1995), atypical movements often mask the competence of individuals with autism who exhibit them, with some observers attributing the movement difficulties to other disabilities or to low cognition. In the classroom, a teacher who is unaware of movement problems might assume, erroneously, that a student who is gazing up at the ceiling or pacing in the back of the room is not attending to a lecture, when in fact, he or she may be behaving in this way without knowing it or perhaps even as a deliberate strategy to *enhance* attention. Paula had a student, for instance, who had a hard time sitting for teacher-directed instruction. Too much quiet time in his seat made him uncomfortable, but he was often very interested in the teacher's long presentations. During these longer lectures, it was not unusual for this student to flap his hands, rock back and forth, and even jump in the air. To respond to the young man's need for movement, the teacher allowed him to stand at a lectern, pace in the back of the room, or even take notes on the chalkboard when she was presenting information.

Gunilla Gerland pointed out another way that problems with what she calls "automatization" can cause students on the autism spectrum to be misunderstood by their teachers:

> The funny thing is that when you do everything as if it was the first time (which is the case if you have poor automatic motor skills) you usually do it better or more neatly than other people—this makes it even harder for others to understand that you have a problem with this. (1999, n. p.)

Teachers who are not aware of the extraordinary effort and concentration required for some people with autism to suppress, control, or channel their movements may wonder why their students do not consistently perform well when faced with physical tasks such as drawing recognizable images or operating a computer with efficiency.

Movement Differences and Literacy

Students with movement problems may have a range of struggles with literacy instruction, especially in classrooms with rigid expectations for student behavior. For instance, many students with autism have a difficult time sitting in a chair or at a desk to read, write, or listen for a sustained period of time. It may be challenging for them to signal their desire to enter into a classroom discussion if they cannot conform to the conventional method of raising one's hand to be called on by the teacher. And they may find the physical motions associated with reading—from tracking print with the eyes to turning the pages of a book—to be difficult to perform or to coordinate with other movements.

Imagine, given these issues, the difficulties presented for students with autism by one of the most common of literacy activities: the teacher read aloud. A daily occurrence in most elementary classrooms, though somewhat less prevalent in secondary schools, this structure typically requires learners to listen to the teacher while they sit quietly, often as a tightly clustered group in a carpeted area, with student interruptions sanctioned only when they are related to the story and signaled by a raised hand. Unless the teacher accepts more than one way to participate, the norms of such an instructional event are likely to be violated by the rocking, hand flapping, or involuntary speech that many students with autism may demonstrate in these kinds of settings.

Handwriting presents another particularly significant struggle (Grandin, 1995; Hall, 2001; Mukhopadhyay, 2000; Shore, 2003). As Temple Grandin, a woman with autism, described, having poor penmanship may cause not only academic problems but also general frustration and angst:

> I was the last person in my fourth grade to get the penmanship award. This was a big deal to the children because when the penmanship was good enough, the teacher designated you as "scribe" and you were given a set of colored pencils. I didn't care so much about the "title," but I coveted the colored pencils. I tried very hard and still I was last to qualify. . . . Learning math was even more difficult because I had a British teacher, Mr. Brown. He was a very proper Englishman and made the class do the math problems with a fountain pen. We had to rule the plus and minus signs and be ever so neat. It was bad enough trying to understand math but having to be neat besides was impossible. No matter how hard I tried, my papers were splattered with ink. (1995, p. 37)

Anecdotes like Grandin's are about more than the difficulties of meeting a fussy teacher's expectations for neatness because students' lack of facility with letter formation and the other physical aspects of writing can often interfere with their fluency—the ease with which they compose—when they try to transfer their ideas to paper. We share some ideas in Chapter 6 about strategies for supporting student writers both physically and cognitively.

Although many students with autism in today's classrooms are freed from some of their handwriting woes by the availability of word processing software

(Temple Grandin attended school at a time when personal computers were unavailable in schools), such technologies are not available for all students or for all literacy-related tasks. Authors who write about their more recent school experiences, still lament handwriting as a particular challenge given the physical manifestations of their disability.

Sensory Differences

People with autism tend to have unusual sensory experiences. They routinely report differences in hearing, touch, smell, sight, or taste. Individuals may report that they are too sensitive or not sensitive enough in any one (or in more than one) of these areas. In other cases, students may have difficulty interpreting a sense.

Understanding Sensory Differences

Jared Blackburn, a man with autism, described how *sensory differences* can cause discomfort and frustration for those who experience them:

> One common effect of these heightened senses is that autistic people are vulnerable to sensory overload with continued low-level bombardment. This may also result from too much emotional or social stimulation. Autistic people may become overloaded in situations that would not bother (or might even entertain) a normal person. When overloaded, autistic people have trouble concentrating, may feel tired or confused, and some may experience physical pain. Too much overload may lead to tantrums or emotional outburst. (1997, n.p.)

Students with sensory problems may experience anything from slight discomfort to annoyance to distraction to the full sensory overload that Blackburn describes. Touch and proximity can be challenging for individuals with autism. It is not uncommon for these individuals to avoid being touched, to be able to tolerate only some types of touch, or to use touch in unusual ways (e.g., to be connected to or to learn about a person or object). One student we know, for instance, could not abide being touched softly. If the teacher brushed his hand or tried to guide him somewhere by lightly grasping his shoulder, he screamed as if in pain. If she gave him a firm handshake or clapped him on the back instead, he did not appear to be negatively affected and, in many cases, seemed to welcome these less gentle interactions. Other people with autism appear to find certain kinds of pressure on their bodies to be soothing. Schwarz (2006), for instance, tells a story about a student with autism who loved to be "squished" in between the gymnastics mats in his school. And Hall (2001) reported that his "jammie days," those spent reading in a sleeping bag that tightly enclosed his body, were among his favorites.

Autism also affects some individuals' hearing perception. Students may be bothered by sounds that teachers cannot even detect, as Tyler Fihe, a young man with autism, reported:

> I hear things that many people can't hear. For example, I can be in one room of the house and hear what my mother is saying on the telephone even when she has the door shut. There are also certain sounds that are painful to listen to like the microwave, the telephone ring, lawnmowers, leaf blowers, the blender, babies crying, vacuum cleaners, and my mom's VW [van] when it just starts up. (2000, p. 1)

As Fihe pointed out, a person with autism may experience anxiety over a range of noises and sounds, including those that may appear benign to the average person. For instance, an individual might be completely distressed by the sound of a crayon moving across a tablet or frightened by the hissing of a radiator. Many people with autism also have trouble understanding conversation or verbal directions if they have trouble processing sound.

Individuals with autism also may be affected by visual sensitivities to certain types of light, colors, or patterns. As Liane Holliday Willey, a woman with Asperger syndrome, described, visual sensitivity not only can have a negative impact on the person's sensory system but also can cause the individual to become fearful or anxious in general:

> Bright lights, mid-day sun, reflected lights, strobe lights, flickering lights, fluorescent lights; each seemed to sear my eyes... my head would feel tight, my stomach would churn, and my pulse would run my heart ragged until I found a safety zone. (1999, p. 26)

It's important to note, however, that people with autism do not always experience sensory differences in a negative way. In some cases, their heightened awareness of sensory input can be a positive attribute or a source of enjoyment. For instance, the writers of many of the autobiographies we've read report particular strengths in visualization that they link to their autism. As one of the most articulate authors on this subject, Temple Grandin, wrote:

> I think in pictures. Words are like a second language to me. I translate both spoken and written words into full-color movies, complete with sound, which run like a VCR tape in my head. When somebody speaks to me, his words are instantly translated into pictures. ... I value my ability to think visually, and I would never want to lose it. (1995, p. 19)

Other individuals can appreciate and discriminate among auditory data:

> Fine things happened when I mixed my voice with the monologues and original oratories I wrote. I would play with my voice, working it, pushing it to reach new tones and pitch, different volumes, and a myriad of rhythms. I enjoyed the feeling my voice left on the ear, the way it resonated in my throat and the sensation it created as it slipped past my lips. My voice did as much as my thoughts to choose the words I would put in my work. I would search long and hard to find words that tickled, words that had smooth textures, and words that warmed when I spoke them. I knew I had written something great when I found words that looked, sounded, and felt good. (Holliday Willey, 1999, p. 36)

And Echo Fling, a mother of a young man with Asperger syndrome, shares that her son, Jimmy, has a sense of smell that is not only remarkable but also incredibly useful in certain situations. One day, Fling explained, neighborhood boys were playing together with *Star Wars* figurines. Each boy had brought his own set of characters to add to the game. When it was time to go home, however, the boys were troubled by the fact that they didn't know which figures belonged to which boys—all of the characters had gotten mixed up in the play scenarios. Fling's son solved the problem quickly: "Jimmy held each one up to his nose, took a quick sniff, and immediately told the other boy 'this one is yours'" (2000, p. 146). Jimmy also appears to use his sense of smell as a way to find connection and comfort.

Fling reported that as a child, her son would approach her from behind and wrap his arms around her neck to take a sniff of her hair. When she asked him what he was doing, he would reply, "I'm remembering you" (2000, p. 147).

Sensory Differences and Literacy

Although the previous examples from Grandin and Holliday Willey point out that sensory differences experienced by students with autism are not always problematic, many of those differences do indeed position such students to struggle with typical literacy activities and the materials employed in them. For instance, some students have a hard time focusing on classroom technologies such as overhead projectors, televisions, or computers because they are bothered by flickering lights and cursors or distracted by the machine's hum (a sound most students in the class will not hear at all). In addition to having problems with computers themselves, students may also struggle with certain web sites they are asked to access, especially those with flashing text, cluttered pages, extraneous sounds, or many different colors. And teachers should be aware that certain bulletin boards or other visual displays might be distracting for some learners, particularly if those areas are highly disorganized or cluttered.

These learners may balk at using materials such as paste, glue, and correction fluid that are common revision tools in a classroom writing center because of how those things feel on their skin or because of the way such items smell. They may also resist some of the most common classroom materials such as books or papers if those materials have an unusual or bothersome texture, appearance, or odor. One high school student, for example, resisted a teacher-imposed research project because it required him to compare and contrast popular culture today and in the past by examining both current magazines and those from the 1950s and 1960s. Because the teacher had been storing the old magazines in her basement, they had a musty smell. The learner with autism was so bothered by both the smell and the ever-so-slightly damp feel of them that he could not participate until his teacher made copies of the pages he selected to study.

Sensory differences can also create complexities for students with autism related to classroom discussion. These learners may struggle to listen to the teacher and take notes, especially if there is excessive or unusual background noise or if the teacher's voice is difficult for the individual with autism to process and tolerate (e.g., a new voice, an unusually loud voice, a voice with unusually high or low pitch). Some students may find it uncomfortable to participate in whole-class discussions of an assigned reading because of the difficulty in predicting and sorting out whose turn it is to talk from so many different contributors. In situations such as these, a teacher may interpret a student's lack of participation to mean lack of comprehension or preparation when the student's reluctance is actually rooted in sensory discomfort.

Finally, the touch and proximity difficulties cited above can make it problematic for students with autism and related labels to engage in cooperative learning activities such as literature circles (Daniels, 1994) or peer editing groups (Maifair, 1999) that have become common in many literacy classrooms. These learners may be uncomfortable when asked to face other students while sitting in a peer-led, small-group discussion or when asked to interact with others physically in an informal drama activity such as a pantomime. They may struggle to confer with other students about drafts of their writing if required to sit very close to each other. In each of these cases, learners may need supports such as adapted rules, seating changes, or choices of how to participate in order to pursue the activity comfortably.

Teachers also need to be aware of how attending to sensory differences can help them understand, see, and develop students' literacy skills. Many students with autism, for instance, may smell their books (Fling, 2000). Jimmy, the young boy with the *Star Wars* figure-sniffing abilities, gave similar treatment to his reading materials. His mother recalls that even as a baby, her son would open a book, hold it up to his nose, and "take in a deep breath." According to Jimmy's mother, "My husband once said that Jimmy took the term 'sticking your nose in a book' to whole new heights" (2000, p. 145). Others on the spectrum have reported needing to feel their learning materials before using them. And Donna Williams shared that she has even "tasted" materials as a way of getting, in some way, connected to them and to the act of literacy:

> When I was ten [years old] a typewriter was left in my room. I smelled it, licked it and tapped at the buttons. I felt its texture and the sound it made when touched, its shiny surfaces and its rough ones. I explored its mechanisms and its systems, fragment by fragment. I typed onto the roller, strings of letters and patterns of letters. The roller became indented and covered with overlays of letters. I worked out how to put the paper into it and typed strings of letters and then patterns of letters. (1992, p. 241)

Williams goes on to note that, over time, the typewriter unleashed the poet in her:

> By the time I was eleven [years old], I had typed lists of words running down the page and the words jumped back at me with imagery and feel to them in a way written words that had come from other people, never had. These had come from my own context from somewhere within me, beyond my conscious mind. By the time I was twelve, those lists had begun to look like poems. By thirteen, those poems were waterfalls falling out of my fingers. (1992, p. 242)

This excerpt is important in that the mainstream literature on autism portrays the behavior of licking and smelling objects as inappropriate and purposeless. In Williams's account, conversely, we see these behaviors as important to her understanding of the typewriter and its function. Other authors with autism have also illustrated the importance of using all of their senses in learning new things.

Communication Differences

In addition to movement and sensory differences, students with autism may experience *communication differences*. Some students use few or no spoken words. Others can use their voices reliably, but their speech may have unusual intonation or pacing. Still others use speech in ways that seem idiosyncratic or are difficult to interpret. For instance, some students can recite all of the words from a song or videotape but cannot ask for a glass of water when they are thirsty. Other students can use only a few familiar words or expressions such as "My name is Ted," or "How are you?"

Understanding Communication Differences

Because of the portrayal of people with autism in media contexts such as *Rain Man*, the communication difference many people in the general public associate with autism spectrum labels is *echolalia,* the repetition of words, phrases, and expressions heard from others. There are two types of echolalia: instant or immediate echolalia, in which a student may say, "Good morning, students," immediately after hearing his or her teacher say it to the class; and delayed echolalia, in which a student repeats something said minutes, days, or even weeks before. One of our favorite examples of the latter comes from Paula's teaching of Phin, a fifth-grader who knew that Paula lived near Wrigley Field in Chicago. During their year together, he often greeted her by asking, "How are the Cubs doing?" When Paula saw Phin years later and asked him how he was, he said, "The Chicago Cubs" a few times and then asked, "How are the Cubs doing?"—indicating that he wanted to make a connection with her.

Phin is not alone in his meaningful use of echolalia. A number of authors report that echolalia can, at times, be quite functional (Gillingham, 2000; Grandin, 1995; O'Neill, 1999). That is, when some individuals with autism cannot control or access all of the speech they need for a given situation, they "borrow" words or phrases that they can control and access for a variety of reasons and purposes. Susan Stokes (2001), an autism consultant, offered this example to illustrate how one student used echolalia in a purposeful way:

> A student with autism became upset with his teacher over completing a task. He then verbalized loudly, "Go to hell, lieutenant!" His parents reported that he had been watching the movie *A Few Good Men* (Brown & Reiner, 1992) quite frequently. This movie contains this exact same utterance in the emotional context of anger. This child with autism was unable to spontaneously generate language to communicate, "I'm upset and I don't want to complete this assignment," but could pull forth an echolalic utterance which he had processed in the context of the emotional state of anger. (2001, pp. 70–71)

Similarly, one mother we know reported that her son often puts records on the living room stereo and subsequently will turn to anyone else in the room and ask, "Do you want me to leave you alone?" (something he often hears from his family members). The family has grown to understand that this statement means "Leave me alone, please."

Others have noted that echolalia can be very relaxing and pleasing at times (Grandin, 1995; O'Neill, 1999). For example, Jasmine Lee O'Neill, a woman with autism, recounted that her echolalia can bring her "a peaceful inner feeling":

> In those who speak, they will often talk to themselves, chatting away about almost anything, and echoing tunes, phrases, or words that sound pleasing to them. The sounds of certain words can roll about deliciously and provide auditory stimulation. Even in completely non-verbal autistics there is a rare child who makes no sound at all. Each child picks and utters key noises to himself. (1999, p. 25)

Of course, "extra" speech can also be a hindrance, and many individuals with autism have reported the frustration of speaking words they don't need, want, mean, or, in some cases, realize they are speaking (Jolliffe, Lansdowne, & Robinson, 1992; Kluth, 1998; Rubin, Biklen, Kasa-Hendrickson, Kluth, Cardinal, & Broderick, 2001). For example, Sue Rubin, a woman with autism who uses both speech and typed communication, shared that having *some* speech can be frustrating, particularly when that speech is unpredictable and difficult to control:

> When I use speech alone I sometimes mean what I say and other times I don't. My awful echolalia is . . . an example of movement [problems]. I say a word or sound and am unable to switch it off or change to a different sound. (Rubin et al., 2001, p. 421)

Unfortunately, teachers sometimes view speech differences such as echolalia as intentional attempts by students to disrupt the classroom. Learners who struggle with speech are sometimes blamed for saying inappropriate things or for not trying hard enough to "speak the right way." Some people who use language in unusual ways may even be assumed to be incompetent or, in some cases, acting in intentionally bizarre ways. For instance, a teacher who hears a student repeat, "The sky is falling, the sky is falling" for weeks after the class reads *Chicken Little* might assume that the student is not smart enough to know that his speech sounds silly. But people with autism such as Therese Jolliffe often report that they have little or no control over their speech:

> I sometimes know in my head what the words are but they do not always come out. Sometimes when I really need to speak and I just cannot, the frustration is terrible. . . . I usually end up giving up in despair, and terrible it feels too. When I get like this, no amount of trying to do anything about it makes a difference. (1992, p. 14)

Clearly, speech is a primary issue for those on the autism spectrum. Language use can be a challenge as well. For instance, Gunilla Gerland related that she often gave literal answers to questions, confusing her communication partners:

> My attitude to questions was quite concrete. "Can you . . . ?" I answered with a "Yes" which meant, "Yes, I can . . ." But that it should also mean "I will" or "I shall . . ." was a totally alien concept to me. If I said "I can," then I meant just that and nothing else. So the effect of my "Yes" to the question "Can you tidy your room?" was not the required one. I didn't at all understand why [my parents] were so cross at me. (1996, p. 85)

Likewise, one of Paula's former students often became frustrated when students would talk about "laughing their heads off." It frustrated him to the point that he would shout out, "Your head is still on and you know it, so stop saying it isn't!"

Finally, students may also struggle with the pragmatics of communication. Wendy Lawson, for instance, reported that making eye contact could be very uncomfortable (and not especially helpful as a communication tool):

> How much easier is it to hear someone if you can't see his or her face. Then words are pure and not distorted by grimaces and gestures. I can listen better to the tone of someone's voice when I am not confused by the unwritten words of their facial expressions. (1998, p. 97)

Her words are echoed by Jasmine Lee O'Neill, who offered similar advice and insight:

Autistics often avoid eye contact, so don't assume you're being ignored or treated rudely if you're not looked at directly. . . . Gazing directly at people or animals is many times too overwhelming for the autistic one. Eyes are very intense and show emotions. It can feel creepy to be searched with the eyes. (1999, p. 26)

Other concerns related to pragmatics shared by people with autism include difficulties with knowing how to enter or exit a conversation; how to adjust the conversation for different partners (e.g., talking differently to a child from how one might speak to an adult); how to read a communication partner's communication cues and respond to them; and how to stay with a topic, switch topics, and moderate turn taking.

Communication Differences and Literacy

Perhaps no other characteristic of autism has the potential to affect literacy learning more than differences in communication. Students with autism who have communication problems may not be able to demonstrate what they know or participate in typical ways in many of the literacy activities common in the general education classroom. For example, students may struggle to answer teacher questions, ask questions of their own, share their writing, or read aloud.

Even students with mild communication problems can be affected. Some students may read and understand a story, for instance, but fail to respond correctly to comprehension questions on an exam or during a discussion. This gap between the quality of thinking and performance can be due to a variety of factors such as an inability to produce reliable speech at all, a need for more processing time than the communication event allows, and/or a difficulty in producing responses on demand. Students may have difficulty participating in oral reading, class discussions, peer-to-peer interactions, and writing exercises without adaptations. Communication differences will also create problems for assessing literacy skills and progress. Students with autism will, in most cases, struggle to show teachers what they know and can do.

From our perspective, some of the most interesting and insightful material on communication differences and how they play out in the classroom comes from autobiographical writing by Donna Williams. In *Somebody, Somewhere: Breaking Free from the World of Autism* (1994), she described how she approached a college instructor for feedback after feeling uncomfortable about her oral contributions to class:

"Tell me to shut up if I'm being annoying," I told one of the lecturers. "Your comments are most welcome," she said. "They get people thinking. They add life to the class." I either spoke one-to-one or addressed my comments to no one in particular, so I had no way of measuring the degree to which I dominated the class. When I spoke, there simply was no class, there was only a topic or a sentence that had triggered a comment, and people around me who happened, by coincidence, to be there. One of my classmates, Joe, singled me out as a sparring partner. His comments were fueled by an ego that needed constant victories. My comments were fueled by a fight to stay on track, to make connections, and to comprehend something. (1994, p. 74)

Although Williams's teacher was sensitive and secure enough to put a positive spin on her unconventional ways of participating in discussion, Williams's comments about her peer, Joe, and the way he baited her in class remind us that these differences exhibited by people with autism aren't always perceived in the same way by teachers or peers.

Social Differences

People with autism report a range of *social differences,* including difficulty reading faces or body language; shifting attention between auditory and visual stimuli (Grandin, 1999); and observing others to pick up social norms, rules, and rhythms of personal interaction. Students on the spectrum may also have unique social abilities that help them cope and even thrive in certain situations. For instance, some learners, especially older students, are acutely attuned to social rules and like to follow etiquette to the letter. This focus on "the right thing to do," while often viewed as a deficit, can also be viewed as a social gift.

Understanding Social Differences

It is often reported that students with autism are not interested in social relationships. Although some individuals with autism do report that they need time alone or that they find particular social situations challenging, some of these same individuals also claim that they crave social interaction and friendship. It is common for a person with autism (as it is for many "neurotypicals") both to struggle with and to desire social relationships (Lawson, 1998). In fact, some individuals with autism claim that being with people isn't challenging but that the "things" that accompany being with people make building friendships difficult. For instance, a high school student, Mary Kathleen, loves to be with her friends but has a hard time figuring out the rules of conversation; therefore, she finds parties to be very stressful and unpleasant. Another learner we know, Theola, values the relationships she has with her sisters, nieces, and nephews but cannot tolerate the noise and commotion of family gatherings.

Other students may find social situations difficult because they lack the skills necessary for success with typical social interactions. For instance, individuals with autism may not be very good at reading subtle social signals. Most people understand that when a person at a party yawns or begins putting on his coat, he is signaling that he is getting ready to end the conversation and go home. Likewise, most people realize that when a colleague greets another in the hallway and asks, "How are you today?" she isn't looking for a long, honest, and detailed response but rather for a pithy and predictable, "Fine. How about you?" For some individuals with autism, reading these signs is difficult. Wendy Lawson, a woman with autism, illustrated how the requirements of even the most basic and common of social situations can be puzzling:

> "Can I buy dessert now?" I asked. We were at McDonald's, my favourite eating place, and my main meal was over. "Wendy, you don't have to ask my permission to buy dessert," my friend said. "You are an adult; you can do what you want." But that is how it is. Due to being constantly unsure of required behavior, I always ask my friends what needs to happen next. Some actions are routine and I understand what is required, but others are always changing. (1998, p. 100)

Students with autism may also struggle socially because those around them do not understand their attempts to be social or to interact. For example, Donna, a student with autism, often ripped paper from her notebook, crumpled it into a ball, and tossed paper at her classmates. Students reprimanded Donna for this behavior and told her repeatedly, "Donna, you don't throw garbage at your friends."

When Donna's mother was told about the behavior, however, she gasped and laughed. She then explained that Donna was imitating her older brothers. When they wanted to play with her, they folded paper into little balls and pretended to shoot baskets through hoops they made with their outstretched arms. In Donna's house, play could be initiated by throwing paper in someone's direction; the correct response in that situation, of course, was to arc one's arms to make a "basket" for the shooter. From Donna's perspective, she was behaving perfectly appropriately; it was her classmates who lacked social awareness!

Lucy Blackman, a young woman with autism, emphasized the importance of realizing the different ways students initiate social contact and interaction:

> For me, successful "social" contact depended on someone else interpreting my own signals. Some of my attempts at communication were fairly conventional, as when I put my arms up towards a person with my hands stretched up because I desperately needed to be picked up or lifted over an obstacle. However Jay [her mother] noted that if I turned my hands outward when I put my arms up to her, I was asking for a boost for a somersault, rather than some help in climbing up. If she interpreted wrongly, things could get very noisy. (1999, p. 11)

Stephen Shore found that such struggles and social misunderstandings are less common when people are sensitive but direct; he pointed out that he often needs more social information than others and often must ask for it explicitly:

> When dealing with emotionally charged situations with other people, I find it helpful if others can say exactly what they mean along with creating a feeling of safety and trust. If this happens, I feel freed from the concern of having to create an appropriate response. Some phrases that I keep in my response repertoire for these situations include, "What can I do to make you feel better about this?" or "Look, I sense that you have some strong feelings about _____. Can we talk about it?" While having an algorithm or method for handling these types of situations helps, it does not approach the facility others off the autism spectrum seem to have for these emotionally charged situations. (2003, p. 110)

Shore emphasized that some people on the autism spectrum need to analyze social situations as if they are problems to be solved. For them, participating in a social interaction is like playing a game without knowing the rules or the objective. The social demands of making small talk or walking into a party can create stress, anxiety, and panic. They often feel as if everyone else knows the social secrets necessary for success that they do not. For these reasons, it can be very helpful to teach students with autism explicitly and directly about the demands of various social situations.

Social Differences and Literacy

Stephen Hinkle, a man with Asperger syndrome, has shared that his social differences and the isolation that those differences caused led to difficulties in comprehending literary texts:

> All fiction books are about relationships and when you are isolated and when you don't have social support, you don't learn about or understand social relationships. This makes it hard to understand the characters in books. (Personal communication, June 16, 2005)

Stephen's observation captures perfectly the intersection between social life and literacy. Social skills, interactions, experiences, and abilities are integral to a literate life. Teachers must be mindful of gaps that may occur in literacy learning because of challenges with social competencies and skills. If students struggle to read body language in the "real world," they will likely also have a hard time understanding what an author intends to convey by having a character roll her eyes or cross her arms over her chest or purse her lips. If an individual struggles with inferences and hidden meanings in language as it is used in everyday interaction, symbols in literature will undoubtedly be challenging to learn without explicit instruction.

Another social challenge some students may find is the design of literacy instruction itself. Whereas students with autism need to communicate and interact with peers in order to maximize their learning, some of the structures that teachers engineer for these purposes can be challenging for students accustomed to working individually or on predictable tasks. For instance, many teachers now use reader-response approaches that promote students' exploration of personal meaning (Probst, 1988). Many of these approaches also happen to encourage student-to-student collaboration. Although such instructional activities are beneficial for students with autism (as they are for most learners), teachers may need to think about them in new ways in order to maximize participation for all. When these students participate in cooperative activities around literature—for example, the book clubs described at the beginning of this chapter—they may have a hard time waiting their turn to speak, thinking on their feet, or interacting with people they don't know well. In addition, the unstructured nature and the open-ended format can be difficult for some students. Adaptations that allow students to prepare material in advance (and, for some, to rehearse engaging in the actual structure) will be helpful for many learners on the spectrum.

Finally, we believe it is critical to note that many individuals with autism can and want to expand their social competencies and experiences but need certain supports in order to make that happen. For instance, Kelly's mother, an elementary school principal, shared a story of how one of her students was able to communicate the conditions that helped him work with others most comfortably. Rick, a fourth grader with autism, developed a support plan for himself that included a reward of volunteering as a reading tutor in a third-grade classroom when he met particular goals. (That he chose this option instead of his other choice—working on the principal's computer independently—challenges the stereotype that students with autism necessarily prefer solitary or adult-centered activities.) When another teacher invited him to work with her second graders, however, Rick declined, telling Kelly's mom that he thought he'd be better off working with one class at a time and with a teacher he knew better than the second-grade practitioner. Rather than seeing his refusal as an indication of his lack of social skills, we interpret it as a strength; Rick knew the boundaries of his comfort zone and could articulate to others what kinds of social participation would work for him.

Learning Differences

Along with the movement, sensory, communication, and social differences we have discussed here, students with autism may learn differently than do peers with more typical profiles. On the one hand individuals on the spectrum struggle in areas ranging from perception to memory to comprehension. On the other hand, some people with autism also have very impressive intellectual and creative abilities. Although it is certainly a myth that all people with autism have some special or "savant" skill, some individuals do have exceptional and, in some cases, extraordinary abilities in learning and performance. Common areas of exceptionality include mathematics (Mont, 2001; Newport, 2001), art (Bissonnette, 2005; Park, 2001), and foreign language learning (Hays, 1996; Smith & Tsimpli, 1995).

Understanding Learning Differences

In the family memoir, *Exiting Nirvana* (2001), Clara Claiborne Park describes the incredible abilities of her daughter, Jessy. As an adult, Jessy is a successful and extremely talented artist. As a child she demonstrated abilities in many different areas including computation, memory, vocabulary, and spatial relationships:

> Colors were easy. Numbers, even arithmetical processes, were easy. They were there in her head already, waiting for names. The year she turned nine we sat together as I filled sheet after sheet with rows of renditions for valentine heart-candies, things she knew and liked. They could be counted, grouped in twos, threes . . . fives . . . nines . . . which could themselves be grouped: three groups of nine heart-candies clearly made twenty-seven. Or I drew circles and divided them into halves, thirds, fourths, fifths—fractions! Or I added pentagons and hexagons to the triangles and squares she'd recognized before she was three. With her still rudimentary speech she asked for the series to continue: "Seven sides? Eight sides?" Heptagon, octagon, dodecagon—she learned those words as soon as I spoke them. . . . Two years later she would spend hour upon hour in solitary, not to say compulsive, multiplying and dividing. We watched her cover sheet after sheet with divisions by 7, 11, 13, 17, 19, identifying primes and prime factors, happy in a world of numbers. (2001, p. 14)

But these abilities can, in some ways, be understood as secondary to her talents in the world of art. Park's stunning paintings (http://jessicapark.com/index.html) have been featured on many national news programs, and there is a waiting list to purchase a piece of original artwork from her. Park explained how an attention to detail has made Jessy's art special and how the art itself (or the act of creating art, perhaps) appears to make some difficulties disappear:

> What's an obsession in psychiatry becomes in art the exploration of a theme. We encourage her to paint these sources of delight. They make her painting not a task but a pleasure, and infuse it with the surreality of her secret world. Though people buy her paintings, there's one she hasn't wanted to sell. It's up in her room, a rendition, in lovely pastels, of the two best things in all of New York City, marvelously come together in the atrium of the World Financial Center: the Merrill Lynch bull and the logo of Godiva chocolates. Through her own script is that of an unusually neat third-grader, the elegant lettering is perfectly reproduced, with her unerring hand and eye. Godiva, Merrill Lynch. The very words make her smile. (2001, p. 15)

Another learning difference that might make students with autism stand apart from others is their attention and focus. While students with autism are often accused of perseverating or obsessing on certain objects or topics, some people with autism see their ability to focus intently as a gift. Wendy Lawson, for instance, sees her habit of carefully observing nature as something to cherish, not as something to correct:

> Glancing at the ground as I walked along, I noticed some movement at my feet and saw the last exit moments of a cicada crawling out of a hole in the ground. I watched this creature transform before my eyes from a dull brownish-green bug into a beautiful bright green and gold, singing creation. The process took only one and a half hours. I have since heard that people thought my standing in the heat for one and a half hours to watch an insect was a crazy thing to do. I think it is they who are crazy. By choosing not to stand and watch, they missed out on sharing an experience that was so beautiful and exhilarating. (1998, p. 115)

While Lawson understands her abilities in attention and learning as "exhilarating," others may find their differences a challenge. People with autism have reported a wide range of learning problems, including struggles with memory, processing, and expression. Although many of these learning problems associated with autism are assumed to be problems with intellect, they are remarkably similar to the types of struggles reported by individuals with learning disabilities (Gilroy & Miles, 1996; Mooney & Cole, 2000; Smith & Strick, 1997). Donna Williams characterized some of her processing differences as "sorry, wrong address" moments, or "misfires":

> Messages can be sorted inefficiently so that they are related badly. This is like putting a call through to the wrong number or the next door neighbour's house instead of your house. These are what I call "misfires." Some examples of these in my own life have been where I've come up with words or names that have a similar shape, pattern or rhythm to one I am trying to recall without being similar in meaning. I've had this trouble with names such as Margaret and Elizabeth because they seem to have the same feel and seem similar to me. . . . In the same way, I've said things like "I want my shoes" when I meant "I want my jacket" and been surprised to get things I apparently asked for. (1996, p. 89)

And Sue Rubin, a woman with autism, reported that she has significant problems with memory:

> I have a deficit in my thinking and I don't know if it is common in autism or is just unique to me. When I remember events, I can't tell if they really happened or I imagined them. I can actually picture events in my mind and I am sure they are real until someone points out that they couldn't have happened. Awash in embarrassment, I realize that I imagined the event. I even worry about imagined events that I think really happened. Waking nightmares may be a good description. Lasting problems can result from this. The problem with my memory does not affect my schoolwork. I learn what is in my books, what the professor says, and what everyone says in class. I admit I still have problems with assignments. I need someone to write them down for me because I cannot recall them. Assume my forgetting assignments is much worse than normal people's forgetting. (1998, p. 3)

In instances like the ones Rubin and Williams report, teachers may assume that a student does not give a correct answer or respond to a direction because he or she is incapable of understanding the task. In many instances, it may be that the student does not perform because of how the information is presented or heard.

Learning Differences and Literacy

From the descriptions just discussed, one can imagine the types of classroom struggles students with these profiles might encounter in literacy instruction. Students' struggles with remembering and organizing information can be especially detrimental in secondary school, where there is an expectation in many subject areas—social studies and science, for example—that students will gain a good deal of content knowledge from assigned reading in comprehensive textbooks, often without much teacher support (Vacca & Vacca, 2005). We've come to believe that this expectation is unreasonable for most learners (many students *without* disabilities need explicit modeling and scaffolding from their teachers about how to make best use of difficult content-area textbooks), but it is particularly onerous for students with autism who have difficulties with information retrieval.

Students with learning differences associated with autism may also encounter difficulty staying focused when teachers use another common instructional delivery method, the lecture. Tyler Fihe, a young man with autism, vividly illustrated why this might be the case:

> I also have a hard time controlling my thoughts when someone is not helping me focus. You see my mind is very active and thoughts jump around like popcorn being popped. I have very interesting thoughts. It's just that they keep firing off so fast that it's hard to stop them unless someone helps to focus my attention on something. You can imagine how hard it is to get anything done with a roller coaster mind without any clear destination. (2000, p. 1)

Students who share Fihe's profile are often aided during lectures when their teachers present material that is clearly organized, break down information into smaller parts, supplement their talk with visual aids, and check understanding frequently by requesting some kind of student participation. When these supports are not provided, some learners with autism may find it difficult or impossible to focus on the lesson.

The autobiographical literature written by people with autism suggests that they often see the world in ways that are hard for people who are considered neurotypical to imagine—and that these differences in perception influence their learning in powerful ways. The following vivid example of these difficult-to-predict learning differences comes from Stephen Shore:

> I remember being very upset about being introduced to the spelling concept of dropping the "e," if one exists, at the end of a word when one adds the suffix *–ing*. My concern over the letter was so great that I talked about it during a counseling session with a psychiatrist that I was seeing at the time. He drew the letter of concern and let it fall to the floor. I had to go rescue it. I truly felt bad for this letter that was cast aside and dropped to the floor. It was much easier for me at that time to imbue this inanimate object with feelings than people because humankind is full of unpredictable emotions that can be difficult to decode. It was as if the object had feelings of its own. Even now, when I see an object damaged I feel badly for it. (2003, p. 57)

We think it's likely that Stephen's elementary school teacher wasn't constructing the same meaning during this spelling lesson that Stephen was! For us, this is a classic example of how learners on the autism spectrum may view an instructional activity using a different lens than learners who are neurotypical might use. Such learning differences don't mean that learners like Stephen should be excluded from spelling or other literacy instruction—far from it—but they may have to learn more than a simple rule to be successful.

Another learning difference that teachers may not understand well is a student's tendency to "perseverate" on certain materials or activities in an unusual way. Examples of this might include a student carrying or refusing to part with certain objects, attending to certain aspects of materials in atypical ways such as flipping through the same two pages of a book over and over again, stacking papers repeatedly, or spreading video boxes on the floor in a pattern (J. Burke, personal communication, July 8, 2005; Hughes, 2003; C. Tashie, personal communication, October 13, 2006; Williams, 1992). Although some of these behaviors might reflect movement problems or sensory differences, for some students they are part of the learning process. Unfortunately, not all observers will perceive these behaviors as learning related or literacy related, as this story from researcher Pat Mirenda demonstrates:

> "Why is Stanley sitting over there stacking blocks instead of listening to the story?" I asked. This was my second visit to Stanley's kindergarten, and I was still trying to understand the classroom expectations and rules. "Oh, he can't sit still during story time and he doesn't seem to understand the stories, anyway," his teacher replied. "We decided he would benefit more from one-on-one instruction to improve his fine motor skills." "But I just saw him yesterday looking at a book about fire trucks for more than 10 minutes at recess. He seemed really interested in that," I countered. "Oh, well, yes, he has this thing about fire truck books, but all he really does is 'stim' on the pictures. We try to discourage him from that," she explained. "He's not really a reader." (2003, p. 27)

Mirenda goes on to share how so many learners are left out of literacy opportunities because of how we, in education, have traditionally understood autism, literacy, and behavior. She reminds us to observe carefully how students learn as well as to remember that individuals with autism often have very different or unusual ways of knowing, learning, and demonstrating what they know.

CONCLUDING THOUGHTS

There is no question in our minds that some of the differences associated with autism can present complex challenges for students and their teachers in negotiating literacy instruction. The more practitioners, students, and families know about how the characteristics of autism may influence literacy development, the more readily they can identify those challenges if they arise, reducing frustration for all involved and increasing the chances of student success. The vignette of Ray's book-club participation in the beginning of this chapter reminds us that this process can take time and will likely require patience on everyone's part before the right mix of approaches is found.

Ray's story also reminds us, though, of the rich instructional possibilities that open up for all learners, including but not limited to those with autism, when their teachers know them intimately—recognizing both their strengths and needs—and plan curriculum and instruction rooted in that intimate knowledge. Ray benefited greatly from the opportunity to respond to literature, interact with peers, and share his background knowledge with his teachers—but he wasn't the only one to benefit. Ray's peers without disabilities gained a fresh perspective on both the literature they were studying and the potential of people with disabilities from their shared book-club membership with him, and his teachers learned more about their craft as they experimented with supports and adaptations to meet Ray's needs.

It's important to note, however, that the adaptations that worked for Ray might not work for other learners who share his label. As we mentioned at the beginning of this chapter, students on the autism spectrum vary widely; each one comes to the classroom with unique abilities, interests, and learning profiles. Ultimately, it is far more important to learn about these *individual* students with autism than to learn about autism itself. It is also important for those who would support the reading, writing, and communication of students with autism to learn about literacy. We take this topic up in our next chapter.

Chapter 2

What Is Literacy?

Dear Ms. Clinton,
I wanted to send you a copy of the report I did in social studies. I am 13 years old
and I am also autistic. I go to [Western Junior High] School and I am attending
regular classes. This is the first reoport they let me do becuase they did not think
I was smart. I read and write and communicate with facilitated communication,
reasearch shows that autistic people are very capable when they are given a
chance. . . . [1] (Kluth, 1998, p. 86)

In 1996, middle schooler Michael Ward, a former student, research participant, and collaborator of Paula Kluth's, sent this letter, along with an essay he had written on The Gettysburg Address, to First Lady Hillary Clinton in an effort to raise her awareness of autism (Kluth, 1998). Three years earlier, when Michael began attending the elementary school where Paula taught, few people would have expected him to create such a complex piece of writing or to seek such an influential audience for it. At that time, he exhibited a number of the characteristics associated with autism that we profiled in the previous chapter, including movement differences and largely echolaliac speech.

Michael's mother, Raquel, fought for years to get teachers to understand that her son was capable of learning. Michael had demonstrated literacy abilities at home since he was quite young, and Raquel was desperate to cultivate his skills. Her observations in his classrooms over the years revealed that students were usually working on functional tasks or not engaged in learning at all. She expressed particular frustration at visiting him in a segregated special-education set-

---

[1]In the places in which we feature typed communication, we have not edited the individual's communication in order to illustrate both how typed communication can look and feel different from speech and to help the reader see how integral literacy development is to communication for many students using alternative and augmentative communication (AAC).

ting when he was nearly 10 years old and seeing only materials and activities appropriate for young children:

> I kept pushing them like, "Don't you teach reading? How do you know these kids can't read?" The teacher would take a very simple, *See Dick Run* [book] and make copies of it and that's how they read. . . . They would sit and she would read that book. . . . They did "stretch and bend" [exercises] and nursery rhymes and circle time. (Kluth, 1998, p. 70)

Although Michael's individualized education program (IEP) from this classroom contained some objectives such as writing his name that were related to literacy and academic learning, most of the plan concerned the acquisition of functional skills such as using a napkin, preparing a snack, and pushing the correct button of a vending machine.

Raquel, who staunchly maintained that Michael could do more academic work, eventually moved him to Paula's school because of its commitment to inclusion, and Michael showed slow progress in social skills, spelling, and vocabulary. He did not make his most impressive strides as a literacy learner, though, until he learned facilitated communication, an augmentative communication technique. As Michael gained greater control as a typist, he produced texts ranging from essays and math solutions to e-mail and poems. He felt that written communication allowed him to express himself in ways that speech did not ("WHEN I AM GIVEN A CHANCE I DO HAVE ALOT TO SAWY . . . . WHEN I TALK ONLY THE TGHINGS TAHT ARE TOP OF BRAIN ASRE COMING OUT"), and he sought out opportunities to communicate through typing in and out of school.

Although Michael's letter to Mrs. Clinton represented an academic highlight for him, his educational career included more trials than triumphs once he moved from middle to high school. Although he was enrolled in numerous general education courses, many barriers—most notably, the slow pace of his communication method in an environment privileging quick responses—still prevented him from full participation. And he wasn't always placed in inclusive environments. He began ninth grade, for instance, in general English but was transferred after only a few weeks to a special education class because of teacher concerns that the volume of writing was too taxing for him. Asked about the switch, his inclusion coordinator, Ms. Hanson, shared that his time in general English was "frustrating" to her because they had to spend so much time on writing, an area that, in her view, would never be one of Michael's strengths. The coordinator went on to say:

> Writing English papers, is that going to ever be a piece of his life? . . . When it takes me two weeks to produce a paragraph with him, I don't think so. But there [are] lots of other things he has strengths in. That's what I'd like to focus on. (Kluth, 1998, p. 95)

Writing, however, was exactly what Michael wanted to focus on. Two years earlier, when the team updating his IEP asked for his input, he expressed a desire to become a published author, asking for more opportunities to write and to read what he called "significant articles" that could serve as models for that writing. Unfortunately, he struggled throughout the remainder of his high school education to convince his teachers—including those such as Ms. Hanson, who provided him with a good deal of support in other areas—that his program should include greater emphasis on print literacy.

We share Michael's story at length here because we think it reflects some key themes we take up in the rest of this chapter, including the astonishing gains that many learners with autism can make when offered responsive literacy instruction and the difficulties those learners often face in obtaining access to such instruction. It also demonstrates what we see as the urgent need of that instruction for students without reliable speech because they are the ones whose abilities are most likely to be underestimated—and whose social, academic, and employment opportunities are most likely to be constricted without reading and writing to help them compensate. For all of these reasons, we used Michael's experiences to launch this chapter, which subsequently reviews trends in literacy research and instruction for students with autism spectrum labels; describes how recent policy debates and legislation are influencing K–12 literacy instruction for all learners, including those with disabilities; and concludes with an overview of the perspectives about disability, literacy, and learning that guide the rest of this book.

LITERACY RESEARCH AND INSTRUCTION FOR STUDENTS WITH AUTISM

Struggles such as Michael's to have his literacy-related aspirations recognized by his teachers have been the norm rather than the exception for students with autism spectrum labels. Numerous authors (Hedeen & Ayers, 2002; Kasa-Hendrickson, 2005; Kliewer & Biklen, 2001; Kluth, 1998; Koppenhaver & Erickson, 2003; Mirenda, 2003; Ryndak, Morrison, & Sommerstein, 1999) have documented these learners' exclusion from literacy-focused activities. These exclusions occurred sometimes because learners were perceived as being incapable of benefiting from literacy instruction, other times because their communication or movement differences were perceived as disruptive to other students, and occasionally because literacy was not viewed as an educational priority for the learner. One compelling example of limited access to literacy instruction comes from a 7-year study by Ryndak and colleagues of a young woman (Melinda) with "moderate to severe disabilities" (1999, p. 6) who received services in both a self-contained classroom and in inclusive environments. When Melinda was in the segregated classroom, her parents were told that her IQ was low and that she would never learn to read above the second-grade level. These expectations translated to less-than-progressive practice in the classroom, with her mother reporting that her teachers "wouldn't teach her anything—wouldn't give her opportunities to learn anything" (1999, p.11). In this setting, Melinda, not surprisingly, did not progress as a literacy learner:

> I saw the same red plaid phonics book come home four years in a row. They were all only half used, starting on page one every year. . . . Reading was a misery, an absolute misery. They started her in DISTAR [a highly scripted program providing direct instruction in reading], and she would hit 75, which was the wall for her. Then they'd push her back to 50. They'd just keep trying the same reading program over and over again until she learned to try to escape from reading. (1999, p. 11)

When students with autism have had access to literacy instruction, it has most often focused on the acquisition of high-frequency sight words needed for basic communication (Marshall & Hegrenes, 1972; McGee, Krantz, & McClannahan, 1986) or on the development of so-called "functional" literacy skills such as reading bus schedules, making lists, and following recipes (Erickson & Koppenhaver, 1995; Porco, 1989). Although some teachers have challenged these norms, many students with autism are still engaged in copying text, completing worksheets, or memorizing sight words on flash cards while peers enjoy stories, drama, or discussions.

Unfortunately, the research on literacy for students with autism has been, for the most part, as narrowly focused as the experiences offered to learners with these labels. According to Koppenhaver and Erickson (2003), the literature has historically been clustered in three domains: 1) sight-word learning; 2) hyperlexia (a precocious ability to read words that is often accompanied by difficulties in understanding and using verbal language); and 3) validation of facilitated communication by individuals whose other means of communication are unreliable. No matter how one views the progress that has been made in these three areas, taken together they represent only a tiny fraction of what practitioners need to know in order to support full and equitable participation in literate communities by students on the autism spectrum.

For this reason, we're glad that researchers in the past few years have begun to explore a broader range of issues related to how students with autism learn to read and write, with these investigations often set in richer and more authentic contexts than was previously the case. Rita Colasent and Penny Griffith (1998) published one of the first studies of this kind to come to our attention. Their intervention involved a teacher reading three fiction books about rabbits to middle school students with autism. These students were subsequently engaged in related literacy activities such as drawing pictures in response to the stories and answering comprehension questions about them. Before the study, these students had been exposed only to a curriculum of functional life skills. Their speech was largely echolalic, and their scores on several standardized reading tests ranged from a low of "untestable" to a high of Grade 3. Yet they bloomed when given opportunities to listen to and discuss stories on the same theme, with all of them demonstrating the ability to "state a title, state their favorite character, and describe their personal feelings" after listening to the target texts (1998, p. 416). Furthermore, all three wrote longer passages and longer sentences, using more sophisticated vocabulary, after interacting with the three stories than they had in the context of their past instruction.

We found this study to be provocative for several reasons. Despite the fact that these students had received no reading instruction before the study began—their individualized education programs included no reading goals and labeled them as "essentially nonreaders" (Colasent & Griffith, 1998, p. 415)—they had clearly developed some important skills related to literacy that no one noticed or valued prior to the project. They were able to develop these skills further as a result of lessons that we would not classify as "special" interventions or strategies; instead, they were simply given opportunities to engage in literacy activities common in many general education classrooms. The more we talked about this research, though, the more questions we had, such as

- How had these students' abilities and skills been overlooked prior to the study?

- Why did their diagnosis of autism construct them as "nonreaders" who were therefore unable to benefit from literacy instruction?

- What might they have been able to do if provided with a steady diet of rich literacy experiences, not just a 2-week intervention?

The idea for this book emerged, in no small part, as we sought to answer those questions. Since we were introduced to what we fondly came to call "the rabbit study," we discovered other research reporting important gains for students with autism when their educational programs were infused with more attention to literacy. Koppenhaver and Erickson (2003), for example, introduced literacy supports such as a wide range of reading materials, an electronic writing center, and a sign-in routine into a preschool program that had included little attention to emergent literacy in the past. After 4 months of the intervention, which also featured print-based interactions in the play center and during singing time, these researchers reported "dramatic changes" in focus and duration for independent book explorations by the 3-year-olds with autism they studied (2003, p. 284).

In addition, Schlosser and Blischak (2004) investigated the effects of three different kinds of feedback on spelling development for four boys, ages 8 to 12, all of whom had a diagnosis of autism and no functional speech. Although different methods appeared to be more efficient for individual children depending on their learning preferences, all four children met their spelling goals with each type of feedback, suggesting that, if given the opportunity, students with autism can learn to spell well under a variety of instructional conditions. And in an experimental study involving 20 high-functioning adolescents with autism spectrum labels, O'Connor and Klein (2004) compared three different methods of promoting reading comprehension while the students negotiated a number of different texts written at the sixth-grade level. They found that deliberately cueing the students to consider the referents for the pronouns that they encountered in the texts—a literacy skill with which students with autism often struggle—led to statistically-significant gains in post-reading comprehension for more than half of the students. Their work suggests that teaching students with autism explicit strategies to monitor their comprehension—and to repair it when it breaks down—may be very promising.

Another provocative study comes from researcher Susan Gurry, who documented the literacy journey of an 8-year-old boy, Tom, in collaboration with the child's mother, Mary (Gurry & Larkin, 2005). At the beginning of their work, Tom's language skills clustered around the 2.0–2.5 year range; he spoke in three- to four-word sentences, and he perseverated on several words. He did not use prepositional phrases in his speech and did not attempt to draw, scribble, or write his name.

In the first intervention she designed with Gurry, Mary attempted to teach Tom to recognize his name, common words in his environment, and letters of the alphabet, all using discrimination trials. Over a semester, even with school support, Tom experienced no success. Then, Mary suggested a second study in which she would work with her son daily, engaging him in many age-appropriate activities such as reading predictable texts and creating big books related to their shared experiences. They also played games and shared fun summertime activities as Mary verbalized their actions, surroundings, and experiences.

Over the course of the summer, Tom began to exhibit emergent reading and writing skills. He memorized a few predictable books and began scribbling with a pencil and paper while verbalizing, "This says Tom." When reading out loud to him at bedtime, Mary sometimes hesitated before reading the next word in a familiar text. Although he appeared not to be listening, Tom often provided the correct word. He also demonstrated beginning book knowledge by holding the text correctly, opening it to start the story, and turning the pages at the appropriate times. For this young man, the most powerful and effective learning approaches appeared to be immersing him in daily activities with language; allowing him plenty of exposure to and interaction with print, including predictable text; and providing him with opportunities to scribble and attempt to form letters.

As varied as these studies are in terms of their participants' ages, diagnoses, and severity of communication impairments, all of them suggest what is possible when the previously ignored (or worse, previously discounted) literacy capabilities of children with autism are carefully nurtured in print- and language-rich environments. Our own professional experiences square with these published results in that we have observed, heard, and read about numerous individuals with autism who were able to thrive as literacy learners when appropriate scaffolding was in place for them. In some cases, these supports looked very similar to the kinds offered to the vast majority of students in inclusive environments; in other cases, students with autism needed more significant adjustments to be made based on their learning profiles. We discuss these ideas in more depth in subsequent chapters.

AN INCREASED NATIONAL FOCUS ON LITERACY

In the past few years, we have seen a sharp increase in the number of questions we're asked about literacy development for students with autism—and we believe that this is no accident. Although the inclusive schooling movement and proactive efforts by parents have heightened interest in the topic, trends in public policy, including the work of several blue-ribbon commissions and the passage of new pieces of education-related legislation, have also led to greater attention to literacy instruction in general, especially in Grades K–3.

The best known and most influential of the blue-ribbon commissions was the National Reading Panel (NRP), convened by Congress in 1997 to review the research literature on teaching children to read. Among its 14 members were psychologists, cognitive scientists, education professors, business leaders, and school personnel (though some criticized the make-up of the committee for the underrepresentation of this last group). Conducting its inquiry over a 2-year period, the panel restricted its review to studies conducted with K–12 students that were experimental or quasi-experimental in design, that focused on reading in the English language only, and that had been published in a refereed journal. Although the panel's final report (National Institute of Child Health and Human Development, 2000a; available in its entirety at http://www.nationalreadingpanel.org) reviewed findings on a variety of topics, including, for example, teacher education and reading-related computer technology, the areas of focus most frequently associated with it are the following five components of reading: 1) *phonemic awareness*: the ability to hear and identify sounds in spoken words; 2) *phonics*: the relationship between the letters of written language and the sounds of spoken language; 3) *fluency*: the capacity to read text accurately and quickly; 4) *vocabulary*: the words students must know to communicate effectively; and 5) *comprehension*: the ability to understand and gain meaning from what has been read.

Unlike the work of many commissions, the NRP's report attracted widespread attention in the literacy community and beyond. Its publication ignited debates among literacy scholars about panel members' methods, the scope of their inquiry, and their conclusions, and the report also spawned a plethora of commercial programs and professional resources that used the panel's language and areas of focus in their promises to improve literacy achievement.

The report's influence became even greater when George W. Bush was elected President in 2000 and made the passage of an education bill a top priority. The new administration vowed to emphasize reading improvement, at least in the primary grades, and they drew on the NRP findings as well as on a model emphasizing phonics instruction that had been implemented in Bush's home state of Texas. As Bush explained to the media during his first campaign, his focus on reading was intended to end social promotion for students and to address inequities between low- and high-performing schools and students.

In January 2002, Bush claimed success for this agenda when he signed the No Child Left Behind Act of 2001 (NCLB; PL 107-110), a reauthorization of the Elementary and Secondary Education Act of 1965. Reading First, the portion of NCLB dealing with literacy, used a good deal of material from the report of the NRP, citing it explicitly and taking definitions from it for many key terms. According to the official NCLB web site, Reading First made funds "available for state and local early reading programs" that provide "systematic and explicit" instruction in the five components of reading identified by the NRP report. In addition, Reading First placed a premium on what its authors called "scientifically based" reading instruction, defined in the legislation as research applying "rigorous, systematic, and objective procedures to obtain valid knowledge relevant to reading development, reading instruction, and reading difficulties" (http://www.ed.gov/policy/elsec/leg/esea02/pg4.html).

Like many other people involved in education, we have followed the debates about the NRP report and NCLB with interest as well as trepidation. On one hand, we are glad to see a national focus on the problem of helping *all* children learn to read proficiently. One aspect of NCLB that we like is its requirement that schools and districts examine disaggregated achievement data for students with disabilities, among several other categories. Although we're not big advocates of the standardized tests that are used to measure this achievement (more on this in Chapter 4), nor of the punitive sanctions that accompany students' poor performance, we do appreciate that the law requires a spotlight to shine on all students' learning, not just those who lack a label.

Like NRP member Tim Shanahan (1999), we also welcome the suggestion that instructional approaches for all students, including those identified with disabilities, should be grounded in the best and most current information we have about what works. (If this were always the case in schools, we think there would be a lot less of the impoverished "functional literacy" curricula described at the beginning of this chapter.) Researchers have generated some important insights about how literacy develops, as well as what instructional approaches support that development, and we believe that all students, including those with autism spectrum labels, will benefit if their teachers' practices are informed by the research base on the five components of reading—phonemic awareness, phonics, fluency, comprehension, and vocabulary—emphasized by the NRP and by Reading First. We think these components are so important, in fact, that we chose to organize a large portion of Chapter 5, the one focused on teaching reading, around them.

At the same time, neither the NRP report nor Reading First has been without critics. Scholars like Stan Karp have pointed out that the NCLB legislation has produced a backlash for many special education students:

> In special education classes across the nation, NCLB is pressuring teachers to substitute an inappropriate focus on test-taking skills instead of serving the individual needs of the students in front of them. Some states, like Oregon, have given special education parents the right to determine when their children are ready to take state assessments, but under NCLB the federal government makes the choice for them. As a result, special ed students in some schools find themselves being blamed for the school's poor AYP [Adequate Yearly Progress] results and for putting "good schools" on "the list." (2004, p. 56)

Numerous prominent researchers in the field of literacy have charged that NRP members excluded seminal studies using qualitative or case-study methodologies from their review by employing an overly restrictive definition of research. They have also argued that both the report and the NCLB legislation define literacy too narrowly, with an exclusive focus on reading print texts and little attention to writing and other forms of representation (Allington, 2002; Cunningham, 2001; Pressley, 2002; Pressley, Dolezal, Roehrig, & Hilden, 2002). Although such moves have potentially damaging consequences for all learners, we think that their impact is especially grave for students with autism, whose participation may be difficult to obtain or interpret in the kind of experimental studies privileged by current federal guidelines for scientifically based research (it's worth noting here that almost none of the studies cited in the NRP included students with severe disabilities as participants) and whose communicative competence may be overlooked by observers working from a narrow definition of literacy.

OUR THEORETICAL COMMITMENTS

Our own definitions of literacy are considerably broader than those inscribed into law by NCLB, and the work that we do with K–12 learners and their teachers is grounded in a different set of theoretical perspectives. These include a disability studies-informed perspective on participation by people with disabilities in educational contexts known as *presumed competence* (Biklen, 1990; Biklen, 2005; Biklen & Burke, 2006; Kliewer, Biklen, & Kasa-Hendrickson, 2006) and a sociocultural theory of literacy that we and others call *multiple literacies* (Alvermann, Hinchman, Moore, Phelps, & Waff, 1998; Gallego & Hollingsworth, 2000; O'Brien, 2003; Purcell-Gates, 2002). In the section that follows, we lay out the key tenets of both of these perspectives.

Presuming Competence

In his decades-long work on inclusion, communication, self-determination, academic access, and literacy (Biklen, 1990; Biklen, 2005; Kliewer & Biklen, 2001; Kliewer, Biklen, & Kasa-Hendrickson, 2006; Kluth, Straut, & Biklen, 2003), Doug Biklen has explored the concept of competence and the possibilities available to students when teachers and others working with learners reject deficit models of disability and, instead, look for student abilities. Biklen described his philosophy in this way:

> In its simplest articulation, presuming competence means that the outsider regards the person labeled autistic as a thinking, feeling person. This is precisely the stance that every educator must take—failing to adopt this posture, the teacher would forever doubt whether to educate at all, and would likely be quick to give up the effort. Aside from the optimism it implies, another benefit of the presuming competence framework over a deficit orientation. . . . is that when a student does not reveal the competence that a teacher expects, the teacher is required to turn inward and ask, "What other approach can I try?" (2005, p. 73)

Such a question, Biklen pointed out, "refuses to limit opportunity" and casts the person who asks it "in the role of finding ways to support the person to demonstrate his or her agency" (Biklen & Burke, 2006, p. 167). In his emphasis on agency and voice for the person with an autism label, Biklen and his collaborators remind us that the obligation of the teacher, researcher, or other advocate who presumes competence "is not to project an ableist interpretation of something another person does but rather to presume there must be a rationale or sympathetic explanation for what someone does and then to try to discover it, always from the other person's perspective" (Biklen & Burke, 2006, p. 168).

Most learners—that is to say, most without significant disability labels—receive informal, and later formal, support for language and literacy development from their parents and teachers that does presume competence. Both the parent who takes an infant's babbling as evidence that she wants a particular toy and the teacher who invites a first grader to "label" her drawing with a scribble make their moves based on a belief that these children are meaningfully engaged in forms of talking and writing, even in the absence of much direct evidence to support these assumptions. Considerable evidence suggests that these expectations, and the interactions that stem from them, *create* the possibility for children's language development, rather than simply respond to existing potential (Weaver, 1994; Wertsch, 1986). For students with autism labels, the opposite is often true; the "medical model" understanding of such a label can erode the basic optimism that many educators have about children's potential. The lack of that optimism generally translates into a lack of expectation and opportunity that becomes a self-fulfilling prophecy.

One mother Paula recently met shared a story of how her young son was perceived as illiterate even after she videotaped him identifying words and concepts on flashcards and interacting with books in his bedroom. Because he was largely nonverbal, had unusual ways of moving and behaving, and scored in the "mentally retarded" range on a standardized test, his educators told her that he was unable to profit from literacy instruction (and documented this finding on his IEP).

Those subscribing to a model of presuming competence resist both the ideology and the practices—exclusion and denial of educational opportunity—employed by these educators. Instead, as Biklen and Burke explained:

> Educators must assume students can and will change and, that through engagement with the world, will demonstrate complexities of thought and action that could not necessarily be anticipated. Within this frame, difficulties with performance are not presumed to be evidence of intellectual incapacity. (2006, p. 168)

Not only does such an orientation challenge educators to provide rich, intellectually engaging instruction for all learners but also it challenges the prevailing discourse of NCLB and the high-stakes testing associated with it: that no student achievement exists unless and until it can be documented with performance above an arbitrarily determined score on a standardized test. Instead, an educator presuming competence assumes that if students do not demonstrate traditional achievement, then the assessment approach to indicate a given student's achievement has perhaps not yet been found. The search for such responsive, individualized assessments must therefore continue.

Although Biklen and his collaborators have applied the idea of presuming competence to literacy in a number of publications (Biklen, 2005; Biklen & Burke, 2006; Kliewer & Biklen, 2001; Kliewer, Biklen, & Kasa-Hendrickson, 2006), the construct can be applied to any domain of learning, both in and out of schools. We can imagine, for instance, the usefulness of math teachers presuming competence on the part of secondary students in inclusive classrooms or workplace supervisors presuming competence on the part of adult workers with disabilities. Because Biklen's model is a generic one, we have combined it with another body of literature—socioculturally oriented theories of literacy—for more discipline-specific power. More specifically, we have found the theory known as multiple literacies to be a useful tool in illuminating the possibilities of presuming competence where students' reading, writing, speaking, listening, and use of other forms of representation are concerned.

Multiple Literacies

Literacy has traditionally been constructed as the ability to read and (more recently) to write print text (Graff, 2001). Narrow conceptualizations of these abilities, however, position those who struggle with conventional literacy tasks, despite any skill they may show with media texts or oral language, as illiterate, at risk, incompetent, or even lacking in intellect (O'Brien, 2001). Such models continue to be manifested in the standardized tools used to assess student ability and progress, certain classroom practices such as ability grouping, and even, some might argue, in the work of the NRP.

Scholars and practitioners have become interested in understandings of literacy that are contextualized and linked to a student's identity and agency (Barton, Hamilton, & Ivanic, 2000; Street, 1995). Paulo Freire, the father of liberatory education, saw literacy as reading both the "word" and the "world" (Freire & Macedo, 1987). For him, "reading" referred to the ability to manipulate any set of codes and conventions—the words of a language, the symbols in a mathematical system, or images posted to the Internet—to live satisfying lives, have more personal power, and address inequities in society.

Similarly, the theory known as *multiple literacies* asks educators to value a wide range of literacy skills and abilities that students may bring to the classroom and to acknowledge that individuals can demonstrate these skills and abilities in ways that might not be measurable or even easily observable. In this model, teachers understand literacy as a broad and complex set of behaviors. Consider this definition from Edwards, Heron, and Francis:

> An ideological model of literacy expands the definition of literacy from the ability to read and write to the practice of construing meaning using all available signs within a culture, including visual, auditory, and sensory signs. . . . To become literate, then, students must develop a critical awareness of multiple texts and contexts. . . . This involves an ability to understand how social and cultural ways of being and understanding affect how meaning is construed and conveyed. . . . (2000, p. 1)

According to these authors, students demonstrate literacy when they act out a scene from a favorite movie, page through a book, have a conversation, listen to the teacher read a poem, illustrate an idea, tell a joke, or show a peer how to use their communication board or sign system. Students who are fantastic storytellers, who improvise their own rap songs, who can navigate a new online environment with ease, who communicate needs without words, and who understand the unwritten codes and policies of institutions are all demonstrating important literacies.

Recognizing such abilities, skills, and behaviors as literacies is especially critical when teaching students who do not follow a typical developmental sequence of literacy because they are often seen as being unable to profit from academic instruction related to reading, writing, speaking, and listening. When teachers expand their understanding of literacy, however, they can build on the skills that students do have to craft learning experiences while stretching their current capacities. For example, if a student's interest in designing comic books is seen as literacy-related (something that is not always the case in classroom settings), the teacher can use this experience to teach the student new vocabulary or literary devices that can be used to make the books more interesting and complex.

Another example of honoring unique kinds of literate competencies comes from Paula's first year of teaching. One of the students in her school, Jay, was fascinated with Eric Carle's picture book, *The Very Hungry Caterpillar* (1969). Every day, Jay, who did not speak, came into his classroom, grabbed the book from the classroom library, threw it on the floor, rotated it 360 degrees, flipped through the pages (often when the book was turned upside down), licked or pressed his cheek to the cover, and stared silently at each illustration. Although some of Jay's teachers found these behaviors bizarre and problematic, Jay's general education classroom teacher, Ms. Knight, saw Jay's actions as purposeful, complex, and literacy-related. She therefore made efforts to enhance his skills and knowledge by asking the school librarian to bring other books by Eric Carle into the classroom and slowly introduced Jay to new pictures, plots, vocabulary, and characters. She then asked Jay's mother to identify literacy-related behaviors she saw at home. When Jay's mother told Ms. Knight that her son often sat in his red beanbag chair when he wanted a story, Ms. Knight bought a red beanbag chair for the classroom and shared this "story signal" with other teachers and students so they could respond when Jay wanted to read. Ms. Knight also introduced Jay to the felt board and told him the caterpillar story using this tool. Because Jay was a kinesthetic and tactile learner, he was instantly drawn to the board and began creating his own stories with the felt objects and characters.

Clearly, embracing multiple literacies means that notions such as ability grouping and reading readiness—the belief that "there is a set of cognitive, motivational, and intellectual skills that children must possess before they can benefit from instruction in reading" (Smith, 2002, p. 526)—must be rejected. Scribbles can then be seen as meaningful, stories can be "told" with gestures, and a computer-generated drawing can be viewed as no less important than a piece of writing. Students won't need to demonstrate certain kinds of literacy competence before being invited to participate in curriculum and instruction in general education classrooms; learners won't be expected to develop, behave, and learn in the same ways; and individual differences in learning will be supported and appreciated. Rejecting linear models of literacy development also means that teachers will come to know their students as complex thinkers and capable learners. Teachers will look for gifts in every student and become talent scouts in their own classrooms; value diverse ways of interacting with materials, expressing knowledge, and communicating; and embrace the uniqueness of their students and the skills they bring to the classroom.

GUIDING PRINCIPLES

From our perspective, presuming competence and multiple literacies are highly compatible frameworks whose combination allows us to see an ever-increasing number of learners as capable of literacy learning and to recognize that many behaviors that may have been previously dismissed should actually be seen as evidence of literacy. These lenses in tandem help us not only to value the participation and interest of a student with autism who is flipping quickly through a dictionary but also to consider that he may be *reading* the dictionary, even if he can't provide us with "proof" of that learning at this point in time.

With ideas from both frameworks in mind, we conclude this chapter with discussion of three principles about literacy—or more properly, literacies—that undergird the pedagogical approaches we recommend in all subsequent chapters of this book. These principles are as follows:

1. All literacies are valuable.

2. All literacies are social.

3. All literacies are functional.

All Literacies Are Valuable

Similar to Stephen Phelps, we believe that the full range of literate behavior in which people engage "is much more complex, dynamic, and sophisticated than what is traditionally encompassed within school-sanctioned literate activity" (1998, p. 1). Considerable research, including that by members of the influential New London Group (1996), makes a compelling argument that schools' narrow focus of certain kinds of print literacy is increasingly anachronistic, especially given the importance of multimedia composition with digital technologies in the world of work. High-stakes testing has exacerbated this problem because it tends to privilege traditional forms of discourse (e.g., the five-paragraph essay or multiple-choice questions about a short passage) in no small part because they are efficient and economical to score on a large scale. Until schools acknowledge and value a wider range of literate competencies, we believe that students from dominant groups (e.g., Caucasian students, native speakers of English, those without disabilities, those from middle- or upper-class backgrounds) will be more likely to achieve school success than those from other groups, regardless of how many laws are passed or how many tests they are given.

In pointing out that academic literacies have been overemphasized in Western culture, however, we don't intend to suggest that we see these ways of thinking and communicating as unimportant. We value them, as others do, because they have currency and power in our society; and we hope to offer wider access to them by helping all students to use their skills, interests, and experiences in the service of school-based projects. Donna Williams provided an excellent example of how this kind of bridging between individual students' passions and academic literacy might take place. As Williams explained in a memoir, the willingness of one of her high school teachers to negotiate greater topic freedom and a later deadline for a project on the American civil rights movement made all the difference in her engagement:

> I told my teacher that what I wanted to do was a secret, and she agreed to extend my due date as I enthusiastically informed her of the growing length of my project. I had gone through every book I could find on the topic, cutting out pictures and drawing illustrations over my written pages, as I had always done, to capture the feel of what I wanted to write about. The other students had given her projects spanning an average of about three pages in length. I proudly gave her my special project of twenty-six pages, illustrations, and drawings. She gave me an A. (1992, p. 81)

We are convinced that more students would find success within traditional school genres, such as was the case with Williams and her report, if they were allowed to investigate topics holding personal interest for them.

In addition to the traditional types of school literacy illustrated by Williams's project, we also care deeply about what Gallego and Hollingsworth (2000) called *community literacies,* ways of knowing and communicating that are associated with membership in particular cultures and communities, such as speaking a dialect or participating in a call-and-response pattern in church; and *personal literacies,* ways of knowing and communicating that individuals adopt and adapt based on their individual needs and styles, such as their preferred approaches to studying or favorite methods for selecting fiction.

In recent years, we have learned a great deal about both kinds of literacies from researchers who have gone beyond the schoolhouse door to investigate how young people read, write, and communicate through their membership in church congregations (Knobel, 2001), gangs (Moje, 2000), community-based organizations (Blackburn, 2003), and online networks (Chandler-Olcott & Mahar, 2003). Studies like these revealed how students who were seen as "struggling" or "at-risk" literacy learners in school often engaged in complex and sophisticated literacy practices elsewhere, with some of their out-of-school activities requiring skills that overlap considerably with those associated with academic success (Burke, 2002). This mismatch between how some students were positioned in the classroom and how they were seen by others in their lives often made school seem irrelevant or insignificant to them, and some reported disengaging from school out of frustration and/or self-protection. Consequently, we feel that privileging learners' school literacies over other kinds is just as restrictive, and just as potentially dangerous, as privileging the kind of narrowly focused, medical-model definition of autism that we critiqued in Chapter 1.

All Literacies Are Social

A good deal of the conventional wisdom about literacy in our culture emphasizes individualistic images of reading and writing such as the reclusive (often starving!) novelist in a garret and the bookworm who rejects physical activity and friendship to read inside on a sunny day. These stereotypes are further underscored by an emphasis in school settings on *independent* production and interpretation of written text. For example, plagiarism, the borrowing of another's work without proper citation, is considered one of the most serious violations of the academic integrity policy at most post-secondary institutions. But as anyone knows who has ever tried to teach students how to credit and cite ideas from other sources, these issues can be cloudy in practice.

The sociocultural theory to which we ascribe actually helps us to see why these issues are so complex. In this view, literacies are learned through social interaction with others, including but not limited to interaction with "distant mentors," Vera John-Steiner's (1987) term for the authors from whom readers learn. These theorists go on to say that what counts as literacy in one classroom at a particular time is shaped by local culture as well as social institutions, hierarchies, and cultural norms (Lewis, 2001). It is difficult from this perspective, therefore, to identify all of the influences on the production of a written text, regardless of whether that text was composed by a single adult with no identified disabilities or by a child with autism who needs assistance from a communication partner to type.

Take this book, for instance. In addition to the obvious social nature of co-authorship (one of us wrote the first draft of each chapter before e-mailing it to the other for additions, revisions, and deletions), many other aspects of the text bear the marks of social processes: Our tone was borrowed, in part, from professional development sessions we attended during our K–12 teaching careers that we felt were successful; our beliefs about literacy, dis/ability, and inclusion were forged during countless conversations with colleagues over lunch, via e-mail, and at conferences; our sense of how to organize the text was internalized after reading dozens of other books for teachers, only some related to the topics we were writing about. We joked near the end of our process that we could no longer tell where Paula's ideas stopped and Kelly's started; in reality, though, it's even messier than that. Indeed, some of the theorists we admire might argue that there were NO new ideas in this text per se—that the act of writing is a recombination of previously existing ideas and forms in a hybrid way, rather than the generation of something completely new (New London Group, 1996), and that this is generative and important work, not something for which we should apologize. In fact, Mikhail Bakhtin, a key figure in social theories of literacy, pointed out:

> The word in language is half someone else's. It becomes one's own only when the speaker populates it with his own intention, his own accent, when he appropriates the word, adapting it to his own semantic and expressive intention. Prior to this mo-

ment of appropriation, the word does not exist in a neutral and impersonal language (it is not, after all, out of a dictionary that the speaker gets his words!), but rather it exists in other people's mouths, in other people's concrete contexts, serving other people's intentions: it is from there that one must take the word, and make it one's own. (1981, pp. 293–294)

In addition to being learned and defined through social interaction, literacies can serve as tools for connection, communication, and community building. Rich examples of these kinds of social literacies can be found in Denny Taylor and Catherine Dorsey-Gaines's award-winning ethnography, *Growing Up Literate* (1988). In this book, the authors follow four families in a poor, urban neighborhood, examining their views on and uses for reading, writing, speaking, and listening. The researchers found that parents whose demographics had led many educators to dismiss their potential to support their children's learning were not only able to influence and support their children as they learned to read in school but also they were able to model important literacy skills associated with living in poverty. For example, parents had to master literacies such as navigating the policies, rules, and codes of social agencies in order to locate and receive services for their families, and they passed on these competencies to their children.

Moreover, although the young students in the study were often labeled by their teachers as "struggling literacy learners," out-of-school data revealed that the children were developing important literacy skills. For example, families encouraged literacy through sociohistorical reading, defined by Taylor and Dorsey-Gaines as "reading to explore one's personal identity and the social, political, and economic circumstances of one's everyday life" (1988, p. 173). Texts they used for this purpose included *Ebony* magazine, school yearbooks that family members read and re-read, writing done by family members or friends, and newspaper clippings related to the family or the community. One mother wrote pieces of her life story to share with her daughter, thus creating a text that prompted togetherness and provided a historical record of family life.

Another example of social literacy is illustrated in Diane Parker's (1997) book, *Jamie: A Literacy Story*. Jamie, a young girl with physical disabilities associated with spinal muscular atrophy, came into Parker's classroom and inspired her to teach differently as well as to understand literacy in new ways. At one point in the story, Parker sees that holistic, student-centered approaches to teaching literacy aid Jamie in learning more about her own life, abilities, and needs as well as in forging relationships with other students and her teacher. At one point in the story, Jamie shifts from being a follower to a leader as she serves as director of an informal performance of *Swimmy* (Lionni, 1963), a popular children's picture book. According to Parker,

> Jamie gradually took on the roles of announcer, director, and performer. She invited the class to watch when the play was ready, made announcements at appropriate times, prompted the big fish when it was time for him to eat the smaller ones, and animatedly "swam" her part in her little chair. I couldn't believe that this confident leader was the same quiet girl I had met only a few short months ago! Literature was empowering her to reach far beyond herself. (1997, p. 22)

Through her experiences in this classroom, Jamie also connected more intimately with her own family. Parker recalls being impressed with the progression of her pupil's reading skills, but she was even more touched and encouraged by the interactions Jamie and her parents had around a family literacy journal. Jamie's mother, Laurie, captured the richness of such an interaction focused on a book about divorce:

> Jamie knows that [certain relatives and family friends] are divorced. . . . When Jamie was asked about how she would feel if her parents got divorced, she said, "You almost did, remember?" We talked about a situation and I had to explain that couples argue from time to time but that doesn't mean they want to get divorced. She was almost three years old at that time and she recalled an argument her parents had. Interesting! (1997, p. 47)

At the end of the school year, Laurie shared how the family literacy journal had enriched their home life and how both parents had seen Jamie grow and demonstrate competence in ways they had not imagined. Laurie further vowed to save the journals as "keepsakes" because the document honored memories and marked special accomplishments. Tangible products like these make it easier to see social literacy processes that might otherwise be invisible.

All Literacies Are Functional

When we first proposed this book, several reviewers of the prospectus suggested that we devote more attention to *functional literacy*—a term generally used to refer to a level of reading and writing that enables people to function adequately in social and employment situations. In their book, *Teaching Students with Moderate to Severe Handicaps*, Hamill and Everington outline some of the characteristics of functional curricula:

> [One] aspect of functional curricula is the deemphasis on academics (Weaver, Adams, Landers, & Fryberger, 1998). Many functional curricula guides stress decreasing academic instruction as students get into the middle and secondary grades (Kokaska & Brolin, 1985). When academics are addressed, a "functional academic approach" is used. This represents a departure from the standard academic curricula and emphasizes only "survival" curricula (Clark, 1994). For example, this approach would imply teaching only those reading vocabulary words considered essential (sign for rest room or danger) or the minimal mathematical skills necessary to survive. (2002, p. 9)

Although we value practical uses of literacy and provide some suggestions in this book about how to foster them where appropriate, we feel that the kind of narrowly focused curriculum described in the textbook passage has been grossly overemphasized for students with disabilities. Although this way of supporting learners dominated the literature in the 1980s and was viewed by most at that time as progressive, changes in technology, evolving understandings of disability, advancements in augmentative communication, and even insights from collaboration between general and special educators have resulted in a new set of best practices that ask educators to value academic curricula for students with disabilities and to consider the limitations of the functional curriculum as it has been implemented (Jorgensen, 1998; Kluth, Straut, & Biklen, 2003; Pugach & Warger, 2001).

The theory of multiple literacies, more than any other lens we have, gives us a principled way to frame our objections to narrow conceptions of functional literacy, because from a sociocultural perspective, *all* literacies are functional. This is so because in this view, reading, writing, and talking are always meant to get particular work done for particular purposes in particular communities (Gee, 1996). These purposes differ, of course—people don't read a novel when they belong to a book club for the same reasons that they read the instructions for their new digital camera—but each is important in its own right.

Literacy instruction that deals only with practical living skills, then, gives students certain kinds of tools they can employ in their lives, and correspondingly, opens up membership in certain communities that use those tools. Predominantly focusing on such literacies, however, limits students' access to other tools and closes down membership in other communities. Too often in schools, an emphasis on functional literacy causes teachers to reject classroom practices that would not only serve to connect students to peers but also help them learn new competencies, especially those associated with communication and social interaction, in context. It is not uncommon, for instance, to see students, especially those with more significant disabilities, pulled out from scheduled literacy activities in the general education classroom to work on reading recipes or on reviewing flashcards. Such emphasis paired with learning in isolation often fails to inspire students to grow their literacy skills at all—even those related to so-called functional literacy!—and they certainly decrease the chances that students will master forms of literacy tied to aesthetic or expressive purposes.

Some might argue that students with the most significant disabilities won't "need" these kinds of literacies in their future, but our commitment to presumed competence makes us skeptical of such an assumption, especially given the existence of numerous narratives about and by people with autism (Blackman, 1999; Martin, 1994; Mukhopadhyay, 2000; Sellin, 1995) who demonstrated sophisticated literacies long after the possibility of this kind of literate development on their part had been dismissed by others.

Furthermore, it has been our experience that students with autism often need a rigorous, responsive curriculum to keep their bodies in check and their attention focused. Sue Rubin has shared in many different forums, including Rubin, Biklen, Kasa-Hendrickson, Kluth, Cardinal, and Broderick (2001), that she learns best when she is challenged and engaged by her teachers with the richest material they can devise. If the classroom is disorganized or expectations are too low, her own difficulties with behavior can surface, not because she intends for this to happen, but because a lack of intellectual engagement allows unintentional behaviors including echolalia to come out.

This is quite similar to what Birger Sellin, a German man who communicates only with an augmentative communication device, has described. Like Rubin, Sellin was seen by others as incapable of profiting from an academic education, an assumption that is belied by the poetic discourse of the memoir in which he discusses his need for rich intellectual stimulation:

> *I can find no way out of this circle*
> *one solution is intellectual discussion in the family*
> *like over the last few days*
> *that did me good*
> *I have to think about it afterwards and that makes me*
> *calm. . . .*

but I can hardly help myself
I am always getting into that pattern of unthought
I am a stereotypical fool. (1995, p. 205)

Rubin and Sellin challenge traditional notions of functional literacy in that they ask us to consider intellectual engagement for learners as necessary for feeling comfortable, keeping their bodies organized, and, well. . . functioning!

Others have found that the literacies that had the biggest impact on their lives were those that helped them solve problems or learn about topics that interested them. One young man we know was so afraid of Halloween that he was unable to get through October each year without constant counseling and attention from his parents. But when his sister began reading him self-help books on phobia, his life changed dramatically and he began employing strategies he learned from the books. After this incident, his mother begged teachers to expand his literacy curriculum, stating, "Curt needs to learn about more than grocery shopping. To really 'function,' he needs to read everything—literature, humor, science, you name it. It's a big world" (M. Heggen, personal communication, June 20, 2006).

CONCLUDING THOUGHTS

It is indeed a big world, and literacies of all types are among the most important tools individuals have at their disposal to make sense of it and to act on it. If we have been thorough in our work in this chapter, it should be clear that we do not see literacy as a single, stable "thing" to be identified, assessed, or transmitted to others. Nor do we see it as a rigid set of subskills to be mastered in sequence, one by one. Instead, we hope that you understand literacy to be multifaceted and inextricable from thinking, interacting, and communicating in particular social contexts, for particular goals and purposes. We also hope that our explanations of, and commitment to, frameworks such as presuming competence and multiple literacies demonstrate that all students with autism spectrum labels should be viewed as capable of literacy learning.

Although we feel strongly that traditional ways of understanding—and therefore teaching, assessing, and researching—literacy have hurt students with autism spectrum labels, we feel equally sure that new and expanded conceptualizations can improve classroom practice for them. If teachers increasingly understand all literacies as valuable, social, and functional, learners will get increased access to academic curricula, appropriately challenging instruction, and inclusive environments—all conditions we feel will help students to be seen by others, and to see themselves, in the most capable and complex ways.

In this world that we imagine, there will be no need for Michael Ward to write to a public figure like Hillary Clinton to convince her of his literacy competence or to argue that societal expectations should be higher for individuals who share his label. Those expectations will already be in place: policy makers and community leaders will recognize all students' potential to use powerful literacies—not just those measured by standardized tests—to improve their own lives and the lives of others, and teachers will view their role in students' literacy development as challenging, no doubt, but also as rewarding and doable. We turn in the next chapter to discussion of specific strategies for creating and sustaining the inclusive classrooms that will make these visions a reality.

Chapter 3

Promoting
Literacy Development
in Inclusive Classrooms

Respect comes with love and understanding each kid's abilities and the desire to teach so therefore teachers must have a desire to teach everyone. They must real-ize that their dreams are not ours. Ask us what we will need to be an independent person later in our life. Teach good skills in a respectful way. Conversations with me will tell you if I'm happy. (Burke, 2005, p. 250)

Jamie Burke, then a 13-year-old boy with autism, shared this eloquent message when he was asked to speak to a university class in education about his ideal school environment. In addition to sharing insights like these with future teachers, Jamie's accomplishments over the past few years include writing and narrating a documentary film (2002), graduating from high school, serving as a guest speaker at several academic conferences, meeting with New York Senator Chuck Schumer about an autism-focused bill before Congress, and matriculating as a student at Syracuse University. Each of these accomplishments required Jamie to use written literacy in sophisticated ways, especially because his speech was unreliable and echolalic until fairly recently, when he began to experiment with reading his own typed communication and found that this approach helped him learn to develop increasingly more control over his oral language.

These examples show Jamie to be an exceptional person—bright, articulate, and thoughtful. What is just as striking about his story for us, however, is that his gifts were nurtured through the efforts, over a 15-year period, of a remarkable team of educators—including teachers, speech-language pathologists, occupa-tional therapists, and his parents—committed to inclusive schooling. He began his educational career at a preschool known for its commitment to serving a wide range of students, including those with severe disabilities, in inclusive settings. When he moved into the public school system, he was a member of general education classes for his entire K–12 career, during which he participated in a typical academic curriculum with carefully-designed supports. According to his mother, inclusive schooling was a crucial part of her son's academic success in general and his speech breakthrough more specifically, as she explained when asked by a researcher to comment on his growth:

> I think that being in a classroom where everybody is reading, speaking, and I think the use of overheads, seeing print and not have everything read to the class, but a big visual display. . . . I'm thinking too, probably his drive to be like the other students, that's such a huge motivator for him. (Broderick & Kasa-Hendrickson, 2001, p. 22)

Clearly, inclusive schooling has the potential to support literacy development at high levels, among other goals, for students with autism. This didn't happen for Jamie just by accident—as it would not happen by accident for other students who share his label. Instead, the members of his team, especially his teachers, needed to commit to, and then enact, a number of principles about literacy pedagogy for students with diverse learning needs. The purpose of this chapter, consequently, is to share what we think those principles should be with regard to literacy as well as to provide concrete examples of how they might play out in classroom communities in which students with autism are members. First, however, we discuss our working definition for inclusive education so that you will be clear about what we do and do not mean by that phrase.

For us, inclusion is about more than where a student is placed for instruction in the school setting; instead, it's a way of thinking that permeates all aspects of teaching and learning. In a previous book, Paula argued that, although "every inclusive school will have a different look and feel" (2003, p. 24), the following components are essential:

- *Committed leadership*: Administrators articulate a vision, build support for it, and provide resources and support so that it can be enacted.

- *Democratic classrooms*: Teachers and students see themselves as collaborative partners.

- *Reflective teachers*: Teachers' systematic inquiry and self-critique drive change.

- *Supportive school culture*: The environment for learning is safe, positive, and supportive of high achievement for all.

- *Engaging and relevant curriculum*: Teaching and learning activities reflect and draw on students' wide range of interests and talents.

- *Responsive instruction*: Teachers provide differentiated support grounded in their ongoing assessment of individual learners' needs.

In a chapter on the philosophical foundations of inclusive secondary schools, Fisher, Sax, and Jorgensen (1998) echoed several of these ideas, including the importance of administrative vision and leadership, but they also spoke to school organization more specifically. According to these authors, schools with a commitment to inclusion eliminate tracking and group heterogeneously as much as possible; design pedagogy for students with disabilities within the context of general education reform; use time creatively through innovative school scheduling; infuse social justice issues, including a focus on disability, through the curriculum; and demand that general and special educators share responsibility for the learning of all students, including those with disabilities. Although neither Paula nor Fisher and colleagues refer to literacy instruction explicitly, they provide a useful overview of the broader philosophical underpinnings of inclusion for our work as educators. Now, however, we turn to the heart of this chapter—a discussion of the principles that we believe should guide inclusive literacy practices, given the commitments and beliefs about autism and literacy that we shared in Chapters 1 and 2.

PRINCIPLES FOR PROMOTING INCLUSIVE LITERACY PRACTICES

Our readers might be interested to learn that an earlier draft of this portion of the chapter was titled "Developing Habits of Mind for Inclusive Literacy Instruction" because we firmly believe that a teacher's belief system—and even more specifically, a teacher's orientation toward his or her students—is a powerful predictor of success in diverse classrooms. We revised the focus, and therefore the subheading, of the portion a bit because we wanted to emphasize the link between teachers' habits of mind and what they *do* (after all, it's not enough to espouse certain beliefs about inclusion or social justice if those ideas aren't enacted in classroom practice), but we still think it's important to consider how teachers' beliefs and habits of mind shape the practices in which they engage and the outcomes that their students achieve.

To that end, the rest of this chapter is organized around seven principles for promoting inclusive literacy practices that we see as the foundation for all of the instructional suggestions we make in subsequent chapters. The principles are as follows:

1. Maintain high expectations.

2. Provide models of literate behavior.

3. Elicit students' perspectives.

4. Promote diversity as a positive resource.

5. Adopt "elastic" instructional approaches.

6. Use flexible grouping strategies.

7. Differentiate instruction.

In the pages that follow, we discuss each of these principles in turn, explaining why we see each as essential to engagement and achievement for all literacy learners, but especially for those with autism spectrum labels. For each principle, we discuss the research base that supports it, and then we provide examples of what it might look like in practice.

Maintain High Expectations

High teacher expectation has long been recognized as critical to student achievement in general (Brophy & Evertson, 1981; Feldman & Theiss, 1982; Gaddy, 1988), but more recent work has underscored its importance where literacy is concerned (Allington & Johnston, 2002; Au, 2000; Ladson-Billings, 1994; Richards & Morse, 2002). For instance, in a large-scale study of fourth-grade teachers from four states, a research team led by Allington and Johnston (2002) found that the assumption of all students' literacy potential was among the key beliefs held by the most exemplary teachers, including those who taught in inclusive settings. And in a recent review of research, Gurry and Larkin (2005) argued that the success of literacy learners with developmental disabilities depended on having teachers who see them as capable of learning to read, regardless of the challenges they face and the time it might take. This research and our own experiences suggest that a key element in inclusive environments that promote literacy is a teacher who believes that all students can learn and who implements practices in order to make this expectation become a reality.

One of the best ways to enact this expectation from our perspective is to be systematic about asking reflective questions such as the following about each student in your care (Kluth, Straut, & Biklen, 2003, p. 11):

- Under what circumstances does this student thrive?

- What gifts/skills/abilities does this student have?

- How can I help this student find success?

- What prevents me from seeing/helps me to see this student's competence?

- How does this student learn?

- What does this student value?

- How and what can I learn from this student?

We suggest taking notes about your responses to each question and then using those notes to inform your instructional decisions. The positive orientation of these questions is especially important when planning for students with autism spectrum labels who are often understood and described within a deficit model. It's possible that you may need to enlist help from other people in answering these questions with any degree of depth or certainty. In fact, we strongly recommend asking significant people in a student's life (e.g., a parent, a paraprofessional, a close friend) to share their answers to some or all of these questions. Combining information from multiple perspectives will increase the chances that your expectations for the student's growth in literacy will be high while remaining grounded in his or her personal reality.

A specific tool that can be used to gather strengths-based information about learners is the Strengths & Strategies Profile, developed by Paula and her colleague, Michele Dimon-Borowski (Kluth & Dimon-Borowski, 2003). This tool consists of two related lists that provide positive and useful information about a single learner. One list contains a student's strengths, interests, gifts, and talents. The other list answers the question, "What works for this student?" and contains strategies for motivating, supporting, encouraging, helping, teaching, and connecting with the learner. The Strengths & Strategies Profile can be used any time for any purpose. We have used the profile in curriculum planning, at IEP meetings, and as a communication tool for teams who are helping a student make the transition from teacher to teacher or school to school. See Figure 3.1 for a completed profile that might be used as a model.

Once you have established high but reasonable expectations for an individual student, it is crucial to think through how you can help that student meet these expectations in the context of your classroom. Allington and Johnston's (2002) case studies showed that exemplary literacy teachers enacted their expectations for students in specific, observable behaviors such as the following:

- They held students accountable for doing their best possible work, sometimes requiring them to revise or spend more time on a literacy-related task than they originally specified (or in some cases, more time than students desired!).

- They didn't permit students to opt out of literacy-focused activities based on students' lack of self-confidence.

- They prohibited the students from putting themselves or others down.

- They provided many models and demonstrations of what high-quality work in literacy would look like and what strategies might be used to produce it.

Provide Models of Literate Behavior

When a teacher explicitly models his or her enthusiasm for literacy, students often find it infectious, making it easier for them to engage in learning. We think this is particularly important for individuals whose labels have prevented them from being seen as literate in the past because exclusion from typical classroom activities deprives students of literate models as much as it denies them meaningful opportunities to use literacy themselves. Students with and without autism will profit from interactions with a teacher who is excited about reading, writing, and sharing ideas and who wants to spread that excitement. For this reason, we advise you to talk with students extensively and authentically about what, how, and for what purposes you read and write yourself. Whenever possible, model for your students how you approach the literacy tasks you assign them in class as well as how you interact with genres such as posters, e-mails, letters, and greeting cards from your life outside of school.

To make sure that you are attracting a range of learners with these demonstrations, be sure to show them *all* of the ways you read, write, listen, speak, and represent ideas, including some that you might previously have taken for granted. Model the ways in which you use literacy-related adaptations to access text or to communicate and share ideas. PowerPoint presentations are one form of augmentative and alternative communication. If you incorporate these presentations in your classroom, students may be interested in knowing how you construct them (e.g., what decisions you make about organization, how you incorporate visual material, how you edit the files). If you ever listen to books on CDs—say, while driving in your car or exercising at the gym—this practice could be helpful to share with your students, both because it shows how literacy is interwoven into your daily life and because it emphasizes the idea that listening to books is an option that all readers might choose for a variety of reasons, not just a "crutch" for struggling readers. If you use study or learning aids such as highlighter markers, Post-It notes, or graphic organizers, students will benefit from hearing about how these tools help you meet your personal goals, whether you hope to master a new scrapbooking technique or improve your classroom practice. In all of these cases, your literate models will help students get to know you better as what

Strengths & Strategies Profile

This form can be used as an attachment to a positive behavior plan or as a communication tool for teams who are transitioning a student from teacher to teacher or school to school. A student's team (e.g., teachers, family, therapists) should work together to fill in this form. Ideally, each list should contain NO FEWER than fifty items.

Mischa's strengths, gifts, interests, and talents

- Can count to 100
- Can read around 100 words
- Likes to stack books on her desk
- Is very neat and tidy
- Can pour her own drink
- Keeps her desk area tidy
- Likes to have her back rubbed
- Can solve simple addition problems
- Knows how to use a calculator
- Likes to have responsibilities
- Fascinated by watches, especially big faces
- Can start her morning routine w/o help
- Enjoys doing class jobs (e.g., lunch money)
- Is loving
- Likes to look at animal magazines
- Knows left from right
- Knows how to use her CD player
- Loves the Dixie Chicks
- Can read her "All About Me" book
- Likes to be a leader
- Energetic
- Likes to hear people talk like Donald Duck
- Likes to watch siblings play sports
- Likes to show family photos to friends
- Improving in comprehension
- Can show others how to use her CD player
- Loves to trace and write numbers

- Can read 2 picture books to her sister
- Can stay "on the job" for 10 minutes at a time
- Can put her shoes on without support
- Likes to run on playground & be chased
- Likes to organize things by color or size
- Loves Mega-bots and creates neat stories with the characters
- Knows how to play 4 computer games
- Is knowledgeable about birds, especially hummingbirds
- Loves to sing folk songs, especially by Peter, Paul, & Mary
- Exceptional memory, knows birthdays of all classmates
- Is cooperative
- Is a peacemaker
- Cares about others
- Loves movies about animals and Donald Duck
- Shares her things
- Can prepare her own snack
- Very polite
- Sweet personality
- Seeks out affection
- Likes to play games with numbers
- Carries number magnets around classroom
- Loves Dora the Explorer
- Is self-confident

What works for Mischa? Effective strategies

- Giving her genuine and gentle encouragement
- Telling her when she is doing something right
- Using a calm and gentle approach
- Whispering instead of using a firm voice
- Giving her lots of choices

- Pre-teaching difficult lesson content
- Asking her opinion
- Giving her responsibilities
- Letting her use a pencil grip
- Using humor
- Letting her work with friends (especially Ava Rose)

Figure 3.1. Example of a Strengths & Strategies Profile. (From http://www.paulakluth.com. The authors wish to thank Michele Dimon-Borowski for her help with brainstorming these items.)

- Letting her call home if she seems stressed out
- Letting her use her red pens
- Letting her sit on the floor when she asks to
- Showing her instead of telling her
- Letting her take the spot at the end of the line
- Explaining EVERYTHING in detail
- Writing things down. She sometimes responds better to written "speech"
- Using visual information (charts)
- Giving her time to work on her own (don't over-support)
- Telling her something about yourself. (She likes to hear about her teachers' children and dogs.)
- Asking her to "read" to other students
- Giving her previews; if you are taking a field trip, tell her about it
- Encouraging her to "do her positive self-talk" if she seems frustrated
- Letting her review her "recess choice" book before going on the playground
- Having her start the day by looking at her favorite farm magazine
- Letting her "read" more than one book at a time; she often puts 2 side by side
- Allowing her to occasionally do her math problems on the chalk board
- Letting her send e-mail to friends (helps her work on her writing skills)
- Asking her to help with organizing things (e.g., straighten book shelves)
- Challenging her with hard questions related to her areas of interest (farm animals)
- Giving her opportunities to share her "All About Me" book with friends

- Letting her circle the table before she takes a seat
- Showing her where to work; sometimes likes to know exactly where her work space is (you can tape it off to show her)
- Helping her to change topics by bringing up special interests
- Taking a break; may need to take little "safe spot" or relaxation breaks
- Using Dora the Explorer to interest her in activities (e.g., give her math problems about Dora)
- Using photographs to interact with her
- Letting her help to teach a part of a lesson (she likes to help the teacher)
- Giving her a squishy toy to play with during whole-class work (rubber ball)
- Giving her time to respond (several seconds) to verbal questions
- Giving her breaks to move around
- Letting her choose where she wants to sit (floor, desk, back couch)
- Letting her choose one item on a test or worksheet to omit (calms her down)
- Giving her headphones for music during independent work
- Singing Peter, Paul, & Mary or Beatles songs during times of stress
- Letting her smell lavender; she loves the smell
- Allowing her to hum and rock; she can work for long periods of time when she is allowed to hum and rock in her chair a bit
- Writing the steps or directions on a chalkboard (w/ pictures) if she seems confused.
- Humming to her when she is stressed

Vygotsky (1978) called "the more capable other" (i.e., the more experienced person responsible for scaffolding and supporting their learning) and these models also offer students an insider's glimpse at strategies they can adopt for use themselves.

It is important to remember, however, that you are not the only person who can model literate behavior for students, nor should you be. If one of the messages you hope to communicate to learners is that different literacies are useful and powerful in various contexts, including but not limited to school, then you'll find there's a great deal of utility in inviting other people to serve as literate models for your students, including peers, family members, other professionals in the school, and community contacts. You might invite people from each of these groups to make presentations in class about their literate lives and, perhaps, teach students how to interview them and record their responses. You might help students develop surveys about literacy habits and preferences to be administered in the school building, their homes, or neighborhood institutions such as the mall or church. Not only will initiatives like these boost the number of literate models to which your students have ready access but also interaction with community members has the potential to diversify that pool of models in terms of race, ethnicity, socioeconomic status, disability, and primary language spoken—identity markers on which the teaching force often differs markedly from its K–12 student populations (Latham, 1999).

We urge you not to limit the scope of your efforts to provide literate models to those who can come in person to the classroom, however. One clear theme of our autobiography-focused research is the positive impact that reading about others with disabilities can have on students' lives (Gerland, 1997; Jackson, 2002; Shore, 2003; Williams, 1992). Such texts help individuals with autism realize that others have faced the same challenges they do and present healthy, multidimensional portraits of people with disabilities who are reading, writing, and communicating in sophisticated ways, from poetry (Blackman, 1999; Mukhopadhyay, 2000; Prince-Hughes, 2004) and visual art (Bissonnette, 2005) to academic textbooks (Grandin, 1997) and music (Shore, 2003).

One of our colleagues had remarkable success using autobiographical literature as a teaching tool. The teacher, who worked with Tim, a young man with significant disabilities, began reading him *A Real Person*, an autobiography authored by Gunilla Gerland (1996). Before he was introduced to this book, Tim was able to remain seated for no more than 15 minutes at a time for *any* activity, let alone reading. When he listened to Gerland's book for the first time, however, Tim sat rapt for more than 45 minutes. The teacher reported that she had never seen him sit so still or so quietly, and she interpreted this behavior to mean that he was interested in and understanding the text. She then chose other books to read to the young man and found that Tim had a similar positive reaction to other texts she chose, especially those related to autism and disability studies.

The team took this breakthrough and used it to both educate people about autism and to include him in his high school. The first step of the process was to bring Tim into the school library so he could enjoy books, as other students his age did, in a comfortable social setting. Then the team invited peers without disabilities to read to Tim so they could both fade the presence of an adult; get Tim acquainted with peers; and, through the shared reading activity, teach these students both about Tim and about autism itself. Ultimately, the experience was so successful that Tim's peers began asking to borrow the books to share with others, and when the sociology teacher learned of the reading activity, she invited Tim to visit her class and launched a unit on autism.

In addition to reading traditional print materials by and about people with autism, a multiple literacies perspective suggests that students might use digital technologies such as electronic mail, discussion boards, or chat rooms to query people with disabilities as well as their caregivers and collaborators about how literacy fits into their lives. Students might also be interested in exploring the web sites of individuals with autism to get insights into how people with this label use their literacies and how they represent their ideas and their lives. This can be powerful for students with disabilities because they need a range of role models that includes people with similar diagnoses, but this is not the only benefit. All students, with or without labels, could benefit from exploring these web sites or from interacting with a disability rights advocate, a teacher in an inclusive preschool, or a lawyer working on civil rights legislation, among others, about their literacies. Teachers who broker these kinds of connections, as well as share their own literacies openly and honestly, create classroom environments that invite literate participation by everyone.

Elicit Students' Perspectives

One of the messages we try to communicate clearly in our work with preservice teachers around inclusion is that all instructional decisions have costs and benefits, and that even the most research-based and teacher-tested approaches benefit some students while disadvantaging others. Although we regularly recommend, for example, that teachers use cooperative learning structures because many learners benefit enormously from social interaction with their peers, we know that a few students—sometimes more than a few—in every class find these structures inefficient, frustrating, or even intimidating. Those students need something different as learners, and it's important to keep in mind that the "something different" they need may, in turn, work poorly for a whole new subset of the original class. The only way to sort out these tensions, and to ensure over time that the same students don't get disadvantaged again and again, is to be systematic in eliciting individual students' perspectives on your teaching and their learning and then using that data to inform our decisions, to vary our instructional approaches just as systematically. Although it is risky for teachers to assume on the basis of limited evidence that they know how their literacy pedagogy is being construed by any student population, it is particularly dangerous to do so with those on the autism spectrum because of what Biklen (2005) calls the "big disconnect": the impossibility of understanding what a person with autism is thinking and feeling from observation alone. For this reason, teachers in inclusive classrooms need a deliberate strategy for triangulating data on student perspectives on literacy, teaching, and learning from multiple sources.

The most successful practitioners of inclusive schooling that we know build a range of quick and informal data-gathering methods into their regular classroom routines. They make a special effort to use approaches that generate information about every single learner, rather than overgeneralizing from the public comments of a vocal few. Some teachers ask students to use their initials or to choose a card to indicate their preferences for small-group activities, texts, or discussion topics as part of the sign-in procedure for entering class. Others gauge individual student understanding during a whole-class activity by asking individuals to indicate with a gesture (e.g., thumbs up, down, or level) how comfortable they're feeling with a skill that's just been introduced. Still others use a Four Corners approach that asks students to move to the place in the room that best represents their response to a question (e.g., "Go to the back left corner if the person you identify with most in this story is Wilbur"). Because these approaches allow students to convey information with limited writing and gestures and only simple movements, they can often be adapted for learners who struggle to produce extended text.

In addition to these techniques, teachers committed to inclusive schooling can benefit from simply listening to students. Individual conferences during instructional time—for example, a few minutes per student scheduled on a rotating basis during times when members of the class are regularly working independently or with peers—can provide one structure for this listening to occur. Although conferences such as these are most commonly associated with the teaching of writing (Anderson, 2000; Calkins, 1991), they can be used to probe students' understanding and support their acquisition of new skills in other areas of literacy. According to Calkins (1991), conferences typically require teachers to engage in three processes: interviewing (listening carefully to students to determine where they are with their reading and writing), deciding (figuring out what to focus on instructionally), and teaching (providing brief, targeted instruction to the individual student). During the interview portion of a student conference—the part most directly related to eliciting students' perspectives—consider asking one or more of the following questions:

- General
  —How's it going in this class for you?
  —What would you like to tell me about this assignment?
  —What are you best at in this class?
  —What would you like to work on as a learner this _____ (week, project, unit, quarter, year)?

- Writing
  —Tell me how this piece of writing is going for you. What are you hoping to say with it?
  —What problems have you faced as a writer with this piece?
  —What do you think has been your best piece of writing this quarter? Why?
  —What would you like to work on next as a writer?

- Reading
  —Tell me about the _____ (e.g., novel, comic book, poem, newspaper article, web site) you're reading.
  —Who else might like to read this _____ (e.g., novel, comic book, poem, newspaper article, web site), and why?
  —What have you learned about yourself as a reader during this _____ (week, project, unit, quarter, year)?
  —What would you like to read next?

Figure 3.2 includes a graphic organizer that third-grade teacher Joanne Hindley (1996) developed for recordkeeping associated with literacy conferences. We like the way its first column emphasizes students' strengths, as well as how the third column frames learning something new as a collaboration between teacher and student.

If you commit to scheduling individual literacy conferences periodically with your students, you might also consider adopting a student-centered method of eliciting information described by Pam Michel in her book, *The Child's View of Reading*. According to Michel, the "listening question" is "a style of interviewing" used by teachers or researchers whose "objective is to have a conversation . . . rather than to conduct a question-and-answer exchange" (1994, p. 24). The interviews Michel conducted with first graders for the research reported in the book

What Does He/She Know?	What Does He/She Need to Know?	How Can We Go About This?

Figure 3.2. Sample form for conference recordkeeping (From *In the Company of Children* [p. 110], by Joanne Hindley, ©1996, with permission of Stenhouse Publishers.)

rarely included direct questions; in fact, some of her most successful exchanges included very few questions at all. Once she opted to spend 10 minutes swinging in silence with a shy boy rather than querying him, and the move paid off the following day when he initiated a rich exchange with her about a book he was reading. Because of her sensitivity and patience, Michel's study included rare information about young learners' perspectives on reading; she learned, for instance, that a number of children defined reading as a physical activity associated with a school routine: "Reading is when we take our pencils and come up front" or "In reading we put Xs in the boxes" (1994, p. 139). Although the classroom she studied did not include students with autism, we learned recently that a range of other disabilities was represented among the student population—a piece of information that reinforces our conviction that her "listening question" can be a powerful tool for those teaching literacy in inclusive settings.

In addition to data gathering during typical school activities, teachers may discover new ways to support students' literacy development by creating hybrid spaces (neither academic nor personal but a blend of both) for social interaction. When Eileen Yoshina-Grant, a colleague of Paula's who teaches fifth grade, formed an "anyone-is-welcome" poetry club, she learned a good deal about her students' perspectives from their conversations with each other and with her, but she learned just as much, perhaps more, from the poetry they wrote. Likewise, when Donna Mahar (2003), a collaborator of Kelly's, opened her middle school English classroom during lunch to students who shared an interest in games and cards inspired by Japanese animation, she aided a group of otherwise disparate— and in some cases, disenfranchised—students in forging connections with each other while expanding her own ideas about what should count as literacy in the classroom in light of the strengths and interests they revealed.

Some teachers also find it helpful to tune into students as they socialize with each other or pursue self-selected activities of importance to them (being careful, of course, to position themselves as people who are interested in students' lives as they are lived publicly, not as eavesdroppers). Teachers who participate in casual conversations at recess, hang out in hallways during passing times between periods, or attend extracurricular events such as concerts, gallery showings, and games can learn about students as whole people, not just students in a grade or discipline, and these insights can inform literacy instruction in some powerful ways. These types of informal observations and interactions can be especially valuable for teachers who have students with limited or no means to communicate formally. Watching and "listening" to these learners in social or unstructured times can yield helpful information about students' abilities, nonverbal communication strategies, and preferences.

Position Diversity As a Positive Resource

Recently, one of us read with dismay a grant application for a project to be implemented in a large urban school district that framed a large "influx" of English language learners as a "burden on a district already struggling with literacy." We frequently read and hear similar statements made about including students with disabilities in general education classrooms. Although we understand to a degree where the authors of such statements are coming from (district leaders with a new population of students with any label will need to think about how they recruit and allocate resources to help those students be successful), we think such language choices reveal a different orientation on diversity in classroom settings than the stance typically held by teachers who promote inclusive schooling. From the former perspective, diversity and difference are troubling variables to be managed and minimized; from the latter—the stance that we personally hold—diversity is a resource that both individuals and communities of learners can call on to reach higher levels of engagement and achievement (Craviotto, Heras, & Espindola, 1999; Ladson-Billings, 1994; Nieto, 2000). Where literacy is concerned, a student population that is diverse on such variables as race, ethnicity, gender, linguistic status, sexual orientation, religion, socioeconomic status, and disability can lead to the following positive outcomes:

- A wider range of literacy skills and strategies developed in home and community contexts to adopt and adapt for academic tasks

- A wider range of background experiences for the group to call on when reading and responding to literature

- Increased opportunities for students to serve as tutors and develop a greater awareness of what they know and can do well as literacy learners

- Increased opportunities for students who struggle with literacy to be tutored by peers as well as supported by their teachers

- Increased opportunities for students to use assistive technology, augmentative communication, and other types of specialized supports and adaptations

- A greater awareness of differences that exist in the world beyond school, where people are rarely sorted and segregated from each other on the basis of narrow bands of ability

Teachers can capitalize on these differences among students by using approaches that highlight them publicly. For example, Harvey shared the story of one primary school in Denver where every member of the school community has an area of expertise (AOE):

> These AOEs range from a first grader's knowledge about cheetahs to a custodian's expertise in quilting. AOEs are displayed prominently in the school's corridors, so school community members know where to go for specific information. People in the school, adults and teachers alike, are expected to set aside some time each year to teach their AOE. (1998, p. 15)

This strengths-focused practice reminds us of a teacher who used a cooperative structure called Match Game to showcase the talents of one of her students, Marn, a young woman with autism who was interested in trains. During a unit on transportation, Marn created one set of cards that contained concepts, words, and phrases related to trains. On the other set of cards she wrote the corresponding definitions. One card, for instance, had the phrase, "run-through" written on it. The definition of run-through, "a train that generally is not scheduled to pick up or reduce (set out) railcars enroute," was written on another card. Students had to find matches for terms and phrases that were, in most cases, completely new to them. Students had fun learning the new lingo and were impressed with Marn's expertise in this area. According to the teacher, the game was the first time students in her classroom had to go to Marn to get help and information, rather than the other way around. This experience changed students' perceptions of their classmate and it gave Marn the courage to share more of her specialized knowledge with others. In addition, all students became interested in the activity and were anxious to take a turn designing their own set of cards for the group (Udvari-Solner & Kluth, in press). In addition to verbal definitions, students were encouraged to incorporate visual images and graphics into their cards to make them more accessible and interesting to everyone.

Other teachers we know have taken a similar approach to literacy in the classroom, posting charts on the walls that identify which students to call on for particular kinds of expertise or encouragement (e.g., "George is good at identifying run-on sentences, so ask him to proofread your writing for that" or "May-Li really likes being read to, so she'd be glad to serve as an audience while you're practicing your fluency"). If you make students' potential contributions visible in these ways—and then schedule time during class for peers to make these connections with each other—you will undoubtedly build community among the group as well as create a diffuse network of assistance in the classroom rather than making students dependent on a single helper (you!).

In our experience, the potential presence of students with autism in a class is too rarely presented to teachers as an enriching experience for all involved, and yet many teachers we know who have had students with that label in their classes see those times among the highlights of their teaching careers. Kelly's aunt, Mary Caron, a general education teacher who has had a number of students with autism spectrum labels in her fourth-grade classroom, insists that she became a better teacher for everyone because these students' presence forced her to be more reflective and deliberate about her everyday choices than she would have been otherwise. In a chapter on inclusive early literacy instruction, Koppenhaver, Spadorcia, and Erickson (1998) made a similar argument when they described how, for one student given an autism spectrum label, a teacher made modifications to her writing instruction that she planned to continue using the next school year, even if she did not have students with disabilities or such labels.

Employ "Elastic" Classroom Structures

Elsewhere, Kelly wrote about "elastic" instructional frameworks: models and methods of instruction that stretch to accommodate diverse literacy learning needs without requiring students to be labeled or segregated from each other (Chandler-Olcott, 2003). Such frameworks allow students who are very facile or experienced with an aspect of literacy to develop skills at increasingly higher levels while simultaneously allowing students who lack certain skills or experiences to acquire them at their own pace. Without a range of such structures in their repertoire, teachers often end up teaching to the perceived "middle" of their classes, thereby failing to support or to challenge a large number of students who don't fit that profile. Structures that don't stretch much—whole-class oral reading of a single text, for example—have the potential to be disastrous for students on the autism spectrum because many of these students present skills that would be located on the extreme outskirts of a developmental continuum, regardless of whether these are deficits (e.g., profound struggles with oral reading fluency) or strengths (e.g., an unusual ability to remember where on a page they've encountered particular words). For this reason, rigid, one-size-fits-all structures are likely to frustrate or bore students with autism (although, in fairness, we must point out that we don't think they work very well for students without autism, either).

In our experience, the following classroom structures used to promote literacy are particularly elastic and therefore appropriate for inclusive settings: literacy workshops, partner reading, book clubs, and learning stations. Each of these provides opportunities for students to practice literacy skills in meaningful contexts at an appropriate pace and level of difficulty. We've chosen to profile these structures here rather than in subsequent chapters because each of the structures has the potential to promote multiple facets of literacy simultaneously. Book clubs, for instance, allow students to practice turn taking, which helps improve their comprehension of literary texts (something we discuss in Chapter 5), and sharpen their notetaking abilities (discussed in Chapter 6). In the rest of this section, then, we describe each elastic structure and explain why we think it is likely to support the needs of learners on the autism spectrum in inclusive classrooms. At the end of this chapter, we also cite sources for further reading so that you can find more detailed information about how to implement each structure in your own practice.

Literacy Workshop

Literacy workshops, sometimes called reading–writing workshops (Allen & Gonzalez, 1998; Hindley, 1996; Lattimer, 2003; Roller, 1996), are a framework that typically divides a block of literacy-focused instructional time into three predictable chunks:

1. A whole-class mini-lesson led by the teacher on some aspect of reading or writing that she feels will be useful for all students to consider (5–15 minutes)

2. A work session when students read self-selected texts at their independent reading level, write about their reading responses, and/or confer with peers and their teacher about their learning (30–50 minutes)

3. A whole-class debriefing session when students read their writing aloud for

peer feedback, make text recommendations to others, or reflect on their strategy use during the work time (5–15 minutes).

Some variations of the workshop model place very few constraints on what individual students choose to read or write, especially when the learners in question are inexperienced, disengaged, or poorly skilled (Allen & Gonzalez, 1998; Roller, 1996). Other versions embed the structure within a thematic unit requiring students to read different books on a common topic such as coming of age or prejudice (Robb, 2004) or within a unit of study requiring students to read and write in a specified genre such as memoirs or editorials (Arnberg, 1999; Lattimer, 2003). Regardless of these differences in emphasis, the key elements that make a workshop distinctive are time in class for students to engage in meaningful reading and writing; a provision for some student choice about topic, text, and/or response options; and opportunities for feedback from peers and teachers (Giacobbe, 1986).

We see literacy workshops as elastic because they allow all students, not just those identified as needing extra help, to read texts at different levels and, in many cases, on different topics. They also create opportunities for teachers to confer with individuals and small groups to provide instruction at the point of need. Evidence from a multiyear study of a literacy workshop for struggling readers, many of whom had been labeled with disabilities, suggested that such an approach not only improves students' literacy but also repositions children as competent who had previously been seen as incapable of achieving high levels of literacy:

> Because children are variable the classroom accommodates variability. Choice is the mechanism for accommodation. When children choose their activities within a structured environment, they are able to choose tasks consistent with their abilities and interests. Thus, there is no need for them to be "disabled." Rather than view children as capable or disabled, workshop classrooms assume that children are different, that each child is unique and has unique interests and abilities, and that difference is normal. (Roller, 1996, p. 7)

Partner Reading

We use the term *partner reading* to refer to any instructional approach that pairs two readers around the same text so that they can support each other in making meaning as they work through it. Partners are usually seated side by side to facilitate quiet talk between them, and they may choose to read the text silently or aloud, depending on their own comfort level and the teacher's preference. One of the best-known articulations of this approach is Short, Harste, and Burke's (1995) Say Something strategy, which has the following steps:

1. Students are paired with each other (either by teacher recommendation or by student choice).

2. The partners choose or are assigned a common text (e.g., a book, a poem, a short story) that both can read at about the same pace and with about the same degree of comprehension.

3. The teacher designates several stopping points in the text, or the students agree on those points themselves (e.g., after every paragraph, at the end of each subsection, after every page).

4. The partners alternate reading if they are reading orally or read each section at the same time if they are reading silently.

5. At each stopping point, students converse with each other about what they are thinking about the text (in other words, they "say something" before moving on).

Because this approach allows teachers to select texts at students' reading levels as well as to match them with peers who have similar strengths and needs, it allows for all members of a diverse class to practice active, social reading at the same time and in the same way, thus differentiating instruction without visibly positioning some learners as more or less successful than their peers. It also integrates reading, listening, speaking, or using augmentative or alternative communication in one meaningful activity. See Table 3.1 for adaptations that can be made to the Say Something strategy.

Buddy reading, a variation on the previous approach, generally takes place in cross-age groupings, either in multiage classrooms or in programs allowing interaction between students in different grades in the same school (Chandler & Gibson, 1998; Samway, Whang, & Pippitt, 1995). In these cases, an older student is paired with a younger student. Each partner either practices a book ahead of time to read to the other during his or her session or takes turns reading a shared text in much the same way that the Say Something strategy requires. Although the cross-age reading partnerships described in the literature have taken place most commonly in English language arts classes, this need not be the case. Kelly spent a semester a few years ago observing middle school science students reading biology-focused books with their second- and third-grade partners, all of whom gained valuable reading practice, increased their motivation to read, and reinforced discipline-specific vocabulary through their weekly interactions.

Cross-age partner reading is elastic because less skillful readers on either side of the partnership, with their teacher's help, choose texts that are easy and interesting to them, and then practice them as many times as needed in order to read them fluently. More skillful students will appreciate the chance to choose the texts they share, too, but they can also be helped to plan their buddy reading sessions to model a particular reading strategy (e.g., predicting, questioning one's way through the text, creating mental images) for their partners—a task that Kelly and her mother, then a reading teacher, found to be both motivating and cognitively challenging for learners who were already fluent readers (Chandler & Gibson, 1998).

We see partner reading as potentially beneficial for students with autism for a variety of reasons, regardless of whether the partner is a same-age peer or a younger child. First of all, either type provides far more reading practice for individual learners than whole-class or small-group approaches would allow (there's only so much air time to go around in a class or group), and we know that many learners with autism need more reading practice than they typically get in school (especially for older students who no longer have "reading class"). In one Chicago public school in which students in Grades K–8 are educated together, Luis, a seventh grader with autism, and a few of his peers who like working with small children eat their lunch with first-grade students and spend 15 minutes reading favorite stories to them. This is a nice service-learning experience for all of the older students and an authentic opportunity for Luis to become more fluent in his reading.

Table 3.1. Say Something: Adaptations for diverse learners

Say Something can be used with non-text material. Students may be partnered with one student examining text on a topic and the other examining visual media (photos, pictures). At an agreed upon time frame (e.g., after examining the materials for 3 minutes), students can stop and "say something."

Students may also be paired with readings on the same topic but at different reading levels. At the stopping points, students share what they have gained from their own specific reading.

Say Something can be implemented with one person in the partnership reading aloud.

For students who read at a different pace, the student who completes the reading first can write down her say-something comment while her partner completes the reading.

Both students can keep a running list of comments and questions that have been generated and use them during the class discussion. This list can also assist the teacher to assess student accountability.

From Udvari-Solner, A., & Kluth, P. (2008). *Joyful learning*. Thousand Oaks, CA: Corwin Press; reprinted by permission.

Partner reading can also be easier than larger cooperative groups for learners with autism to negotiate socially because it requires students to read cues from body language and tone from only one person at a time. If students are encouraged (or in some cases even required) to work with the same partner over time, their comfort level with each other will likely increase, making it easier for them to negotiate procedures for choosing texts, taking turns, and sharing ideas. That greater comfort has the potential to lead to more efficient and deeper learning, of course, but it may also lead to an increased sense of social acceptance and belonging for kids who might otherwise feel alienated in a large-class setting—outcomes that, to our minds, are just as important when we think about what makes a structure elastic.

Book Clubs

Book clubs—also known as literature circles, book groups, or student-led reading discussions—have the potential to increase students' ownership over their reading; help to create a positive and collaborative climate in classrooms; and provide a low-risk learning environment for students who might otherwise be marginalized. Although there are some variations in how these groups are organized, we like the following list of characteristics from O'Donnell-Allen (2006, pp. 1–6):

1. They are made up of small groups of readers.

2. They meet on a regular basis.

3. They engage in systematic discussion.

4. They discuss books (and other texts) of the members' choice.

5. They use a variety of open-ended response methods (e.g., journal entries, graphic organizers, Post-its with notes on them) to prompt extended discussion.

7. Their membership varies according to the desired configuration.

Book clubs can be implemented in a variety of disciplines (though they are most closely associated with English language arts classrooms) and they are appropriate for all ages, even for those in kindergarten (Hill, Johnson, & Noe, 1995).

Although a key aspect of book clubs is that they are led by students, teachers and other significant adults such as parents, community members, and other school staff can and often do participate in the discussions. This participation allows these adults to both model their own literate thinking and, occasionally, to help keep the group on track or steer the discussion in some way. When Kelly taught secondary English, she had a good deal of success with inviting various members of the school community to be members of book clubs with students. In one notable example, the school nurse joined several groups of 10th-grade girls reading *Make Lemonade* (Wolff, 1993), a young-adult novel about teen pregnancy and parenting, and students reported that her contributions to the conversation helped to make the issues "more real" to them (Chandler, 1996). The key in these instances is to make it clear to all involved that the role of the adult members is not to facilitate the group's discussion—that's part of what students need to learn to do for themselves—but rather to insert fresh perspectives into the conversation as needed and to ask questions that will help young learners manage their own talk equitably.

We see book clubs as an elastic structure helpful for students with autism for a number of reasons. They can be formed around texts related to individual students' fascinations, allowing them to share these intense interests with others as a sanctioned part of the curriculum. They can also be formed around pre-existing social relationships, allowing students to be grouped with one or more peers with whom they feel comfortable, and overall group size can be adjusted to reflect an individual student's tolerance for working with more than one person at a time. For students who need it, additional support can be provided prior to a group's discussion of a given section of text by their listening to that portion on CD, reading and discussing it with a peer or resource teacher, or working on it at home with a family member. Finally, the response options that book club members often use to prepare for discussion—making a sketch, constructing a graphic organizer, or selecting vocabulary words to discuss—accommodate multiple literacies beyond traditional composition. All of these features increase the chances that students with autism or other learning differences will be able to participate meaningfully as readers and responders. See Table 3.2 for suggestions for adapting book clubs for diverse learners in the inclusive classroom.

Learning Stations

In their book *Teaching the Best Practice Way*, Harvey Daniels and Marilyn Bizar define learning stations, sometimes known as centers, as "special spots in the classroom where the teacher has set up curriculum-related activities that students can pursue autonomously" (2005, p. 147). During station time, students typically move from station to station in groups of four to six, with the teacher circulating around the room to monitor progress and trouble shoot problems. (Later in the year, once students are familiar with the procedures for stations, many teachers use part or all of this time to conduct small-group instruction or to confer with individual learners.)

According to Daniels and Bizar, successful centers or stations have the following characteristics in common:

1. They require students to discover or apply new learning. (Students are not merely assessed on something they have already mastered.)

Table 3.2.   Book club: Adaptations for diverse learners

Consider allowing a student with autism to choose a book based on a personal passion or interest. To create a true literature circle, at least one other student needs to read the book, so teachers might engineer "reciprocal obsession" circles in which students agree to read books related to one another's fascinations.

Use books written by people with autism. Such books are available and appropriate for learners of almost all ages. Some of these would be excellent choices for literature circles, and would give students with and without this label opportunities to learn about autism from an expert–someone with that label.

Encourage students to bring written or drawn notes to their circles. If a student is not able to create notes on his or her own, teacher-created notes might be provided or a student might work from the notes of a peer. Or the student might be allowed to write notes or highlight passages in his or her book (or on copies of the pages) so the text can include notes for discussion.

Create a new role for a student who could not participate in the group as it is typically structured. For instance, a nonverbal student with autism served as the topic changer for his group. This child brought a stack of illustrated cards to his group and at key points in the discussion, the facilitator asked him to suggest a new topic by choosing a card. In another classroom, a student served as the discussion recorder. This child was extremely anxious about participating in unstructured discussions, so for the first four times that he worked with his group, he did not share comments, but instead listened to the conversation, moved a microphone around the table, and occasionally reminded his peers to speak up or add something to the recording. After listening to the tapes for 4 weeks, he was able to join in the discussions.

Show a videotape of a book club before students participate in the structure. Some students will do better with an informal and open-ended activity when they have visual examples of how students interact, take turns, and question one another.

Be explicit about what types of comments, feedback, and interaction you expect from students. If you want students to ask "clarifying questions," provide a list of examples of such questions.

2. They include some kind of student interaction. (Students are encouraged to work together or to talk with each other quietly as they work independently.)

3. They lead to a tangible outcome. (Students may take a product such as a sketch away from them as they leave the station, or they may create a text like a poem or a log entry that will be read or used by subsequent visitors.)

Some of the most common literacy-focused centers in elementary and English language arts classrooms include the following:

*   *Writing centers,* including various kinds of paper, writing utensils, and art supplies that students can use to begin a new composition

*   *Editing/publishing centers,* including tools such as correction fluid, Post-its, and different kinds of stationery that students can use to prepare a piece of writing in the final stages of publication

*   *Alphabet centers,* including magnetic letters and games that students can play to explore letter–sound relationships

*   *Sequencing centers,* including cut-up sentence strips in pocket charts that students can rearrange and read

*   *Poetry centers,* including a range of poems in books and on charts that students can read before creating their own poems

*   *Listening centers,* including headphones and books on tape

*   *Computer centers,* including software programs such as KidPix or Microsoft

Word that students can use for composing, CD-ROMs and computer games that students can use to practice reading skills, and Internet access that kids can use for inquiry and communication.

It is important to note, however, that even when centers and stations are used to explore content associated with disciplines other than English language arts (e.g., when they're labeled as a "math center" or a "lab center"), they almost always involve students in using some important form of literacy: talking to a peer, listening to an audiotape, recording results on a clipboard, reading instructions, and so forth.

We see centers and stations as elastic structures that are potentially helpful for learners with autism or other disabilities because these structures, like workshops and book clubs, can accommodate student choice of activity, thus catering to individual interests and strengths. They also create smaller working groups within a classroom, which can be less intimidating than a whole-group setting for some students. This kind of pedagogy also allows educators to personalize content and instruction for students, perhaps even addressing a learner's IEP objectives, because all students do not need to complete the same tasks. Centers or stations are also ideal for use in the inclusive classroom because they allow teachers to work with individual students or small groups of learners without having to use a more restrictive pull-out model of instruction (especially if you are using a co-teaching model). For example, a general educator can be facilitating the entire class as they move through the rotations while a special educator can be checking in with those learners needing differentiated questions, materials, or instruction. Alternatively, a speech-language pathologist can be assigned to work on articulation at a poetry-focused station (open to any student needing help in that area) while a general educator observes and takes notes about students' participation in all the other stations.

In addition to highlighting these potential "pluses" of stations, we offer cautions for you to think about as you design them. For one, stations can be overwhelming for students on the autism spectrum (as well as those with other learning profiles) if the procedures for choosing and interacting within them are unclear or if students are not well-prepared to work independently within them. Think, for example, about how a student with sensory difficulties might have trouble tolerating the chaos and din of students scrambling to move from one center to another. For this reason, we recommend that you create a visual schedule for how students will rotate among the centers and provide some explicit instruction to your whole class about your expectations for their work within (and between!) them. (See Fountas & Pinnell, 1996, for what we consider the best description of how to teach students to work in centers independently.) You may want to follow up this instruction by assisting individual learners who need additional help to rehearse what their participation in centers might look, sound, and feel like, and to increase their comfort when the centers actually run.

We also recommend that you think carefully about how you convey your expectations for student completion of tasks. Although teachers who use centers most commonly direct all students to complete all of them (though perhaps not in the same order or even over the same time period), we have reservations about this practice. Requiring a struggling literacy learner to complete the same number of tasks as do peers with more experience or skill is still one-size-fits-all instruction, regardless of whether those tasks are completed in a whole-group setting or pursued in a succession of centers. Giving struggling learners more time to do the same number of tasks (for example, during recess or choice time) just means less opportunity for them to do something of their choosing. To avoid these pitfalls, you might use a Center Assignment Form like the one in Figure 3.3, which specifies differentiated center expectations for individuals while still ensuring that all students will participate in a small number of essential common tasks. See Table 3.3 for a list of ideas for adapting centers and stations more generally.

Use Flexible Grouping

As much as we support the structures in the preceding section for the way they connect the various language arts, promote peer interaction, and allow meaningful practice of reading and writing, we need to point out that most students— whether or not they are identified with disabilities—can't learn everything they need to know about literacy from participating in those structures alone. The vast majority of students will also need their teachers to use whole-class instructional methods that allow for more explicit explanations of particular reading and writing processes (Duffy, 2003) through think-alouds, demonstrations, and teacher-directed practice, none of which is featured prominently in the "elastic" structures discussed previously. Moreover, students with gaps in their knowledge base or skill repertoire will need additional literacy support—most likely provided in small-group or individual settings—to accelerate their progress. If a seventh grader hasn't learned to use the subheadings of his or her textbook to predict what will be important in the content that follows, it's unlikely he or she is going to construct that understanding for the first time in the context of buddy reading (it would be an unusual peer indeed who could identify the need for that lesson and

Center Assignment Form

Student	Center	Date completed
Georgia	1. Computer Center (exploring bookmarked web site on Japan tied to social studies unit) 2. Listening Center 3. One center of your choice from Probability Center, Poetry Center, and Writing Center	
Oliver	1. Computer Center (exploring bookmarked web site on Japan tied to social studies unit) 2. Two centers of your choice from Probability Center, Listening Center, Poetry Center, and Writing Center	
Javier	1. Computer Center (exploring bookmarked web site on Japan tied to social studies unit, with peer assistance from Dimitri) 2. Writing Center (can be completed during workshop time tomorrow with one-to-one aide if he needs it) 3. One center of his choice, if he has time	

Figure 3.3. Sample Center Assignment Form differentiated for individual students' needs in a fifth-grade class.

Table 3.3. Stations/centers: Adaptations for diverse learners

Allow the student with autism to rotate stations with a partner so he or she will have built-in support for reading directions and completing tasks.

Provide a rotation schedule. Some learners may only need a list to remind them what stations they should visit (e.g., computers, word work) while other students may need a picture schedule featuring images of the stations.

Be sure to provide clear directions at every station. For students with disabilities, as for very young learners, picture directions or directions on tape are helpful.

All stations do not need to be visited by all students. Create a center that allows the student with autism to practice a skill targeted on his individualized education program (IEP) (e.g., learning to program his communication device). Allow other students to access that station as well.

Bring your co-teaching partners into the classroom when you use stations. This is the perfect time for occupational therapists to support student writing or for a speech-language pathologist to assess a student's communication. Base this professional at a station so all students can profit from his or her expertise.

deliver it!). If a fourth-grade student doesn't know that most consonant-vowel-consonant syllables should be sounded out with a short vowel, the best place to acquire that knowledge isn't from a peer-led novel discussion during a book club meeting or a teacher's think aloud for the whole class (it's likely that most of the students in a heterogeneous fourth grade would not need or benefit from this kind of information).

In cases like these, we see flexible grouping—temporary groupings based on students' varying instructional needs—as the way for teachers to support individuals' continuous growth and development (Flood, Lapp, Flood, & Nagel, 1992; Opitz, 1999). In many classes where such grouping occurs, the teacher meets with the targeted students while the rest of the class works productively using one or another of the elastic structures above. Table 3.4 provides a useful overview from Flood and colleagues (1992) of ways in which teachers might organize these groups to supplement teacher-directed methods as well as the elastic structures from the previous discussion.

We want to be clear, however, that our call for flexible grouping should not be interpreted as support for a deeply flawed, traditional model of ability grouping that assigns students to a high, middle, or low cohort and keeps them together in that cohort for the bulk of their reading instruction. A great deal of research data gathered over time on ability groups in reading suggests the following problems with that model:

- Ability grouping does not enhance achievement.

- Once students are assigned to a low-ability group, they very seldom move to a higher ability group later in their educational career.

- Students in low-ability groups receive fewer opportunities to read and less instruction related to critical thinking than their peers in high-ability groups.

- Students' self-confidence and self-esteem are damaged by assignment to low-ability groups.

- Members of minority groups are more likely to be assigned to low-ability groups than peers from dominant groups. (Fountas & Pinnell, 1996, p. 97)

Table 3.4. Flexible grouping variables

Possible Basis for Grouping Learners

Skills development
Interest
Work habits
Prior knowledge of content
Prior knowledge of strategies
Task/activity
Social
Random
Students' choice

Possible Compositions for Groups

Individuals
Dyads
Small groups (3–4)
Larger groups (5–10)
Half class
Whole group

Possible Leadership Formats for Groups

Teacher-led
Student-led
Cooperative

Possible Materials for Groups

Same material for all groups
Different levels of material with similar theme
Different themes within a topic
Different topics

From Flood, J., Lapp, D., Flood, S., & Nagel, G. (1992, April). Am I allowed to group? Using flexible patterns for effective instruction. *The Reading Teacher, 45*(8), 608-616. Reprinted with permission of the International Reading Association.

From our perspective, ability grouping is one of the most significant contributing factors in what Stanovich (1986) has called "the Matthew effect," the widening of the achievement gap between good and poor readers as they progress through the grades, and our commitment to more just and equitable schooling requires us to speak out against it.

At the same time, we see evidence that some students with special education classifications never receive appropriate literacy instruction, even in inclusive classrooms, because their teachers' goals for them are limited to cultural literacy (e.g., knowing the facts of a particular novel) rather than their ability to read and interact with texts independently. These students often spend too much time with texts that are too difficult for them to navigate, and they receive little or no instruction that would allow them to handle those texts or others, either now or sometime in the future.

We want to make it clear that we see value in all students participating in literacy-focused instructional activities at their grade level, even if they can't read those grade-level texts on their own. But listening to a story isn't the same as reading one independently, and our own experiences combined with research with literacy learners labeled with low-incidence disabilities (for example, Chris Kliewer's [1998] work on reading for students with Down syndrome) has convinced us that the latter and more ambitious goal is attainable for many more learners than we have imagined.

Well-meaning colleagues sometimes say to us—when we raise these concerns—that they would prefer that students be in inclusive settings that don't squarely address their literacy skill deficiencies than be relegated to segregated classrooms that focus on discrete literacy skill acquisition. We don't disagree, but we don't see why such an either/or choice even needs to be made. Flexible grouping driven by ongoing assessment in the general classroom, combined with intervention from literacy specialists as needed, can allow learners to participate in a vibrant and diverse classroom community while still receiving instruction appropriate to their skill levels (see Table 3.5 for ideas on how to individualize instruction without pulling students out of their general education classrooms). As we see it, such a choice is the only one that truly fulfills the promise of inclusive classrooms as spaces where all children are positioned as literate.

Table 3.5. Ideas for meeting the needs of diverse learners without leaving the inclusive classroom

Co-teaching

When two teachers are available to deliver instruction, roles can be differentiated, the teacher-to-student ratio goes down, and instruction can be tailored to meet the needs of a wide range of students. During student work time, instructors can move through the classroom addressing the needs of individual learners and providing extra enrichment or help as needed.

Integrated therapy

When therapists, social workers, counselors, and other related services professionals enter general education classrooms, all learners benefit. When Nathan, a student with autism, began receiving his speech and language supports in his first-grade classroom, he was able to study the same stories as his peers while gaining much-needed competencies in the areas of articulation and language development. Nathan's speech-language pathologist also profited from this experience as she began to function as an instructor for a small group of 6-year-olds. She learned new ways to teach Nathan communication skills and, after observing the classroom teacher, she discovered new ways to teach using standards-based and curriculum-based strategies.

Independent instruction

In some instances, students are pulled from their classes to learn new skills; other times they are pulled to practice skills that have already been introduced. There are many ways learners can direct their own learning within the classroom: by selecting work from a teacher-created study folder, testing themselves using flashcards, playing individual games such as crossword puzzles, engaging with activity kits, or using computer programs.

Peer support

Before students are pulled out for instruction or skill practice, teachers should always consider the possibility of using peer support or tutoring to meet student needs. One school responded to the need for individual support by pairing all students with a partner for a part of the school day that was challenging and novel: working with a new software program. Both students were learning something new so neither one had more knowledge or skill than the other.

Study/work time

In almost every classroom (including those in secondary schools), teachers designate some part of the school day or week for individual work, project-based work, or partner learning. If teachers plan together up front, this can be a time where any learner in the classroom can meet with someone for extra support (e.g., special educator, speech-language pathologist, enhancement/gifted education teacher, reading specialist, parent volunteer, community mentor, cross-age tutor).

Differentiate Instruction

In their chronicle of an inclusive classroom, Mary Donnet Johnson and Sherry Henshaw Cordon shared a simple adaptation they used for Pace, a student with autism, during the kindergarten year:

> Each child has a Pictionary notebook in which he or she draws each week. For instance, over the course of a week, a child will draw several pictures of words beginning with a "b" for the "Bb" page. Since Pace was not drawing yet he was allowed to select "b" pictures from a set of precut pictures that featured "b" words as well as pictures of things that began with one or two other sounds. This would at least give him practice in sounding out the letter, identifying words that did or did not begin with the letter, and gluing pictures onto his pages. (2004, p. 164)

These teachers also adapted expectations (e.g., asking Pace to master one classroom rule at a time), the classroom environment (e.g., providing quiet work space when needed, taping lines on floor showing where to line up), and personal supports (e.g., using peer tutors and a classroom aide). This example illustrates how thoughtfully constructed adaptations do not need to be complicated or necessarily time-consuming. Of course, some supports do require more time and creativity, but we have found that this work becomes easier and less arduous with practice. And all students typically benefit when we differentiate to meet individual needs.

Unfortunately, this process of adapting and differentiating is often missing from the educational programs of students with disabilities. And the results can be devastating. Too often, students with autism are seen as unsuccessful in an inclusive classroom because they are expected to perform, learn, attend, and interact without appropriate adaptations. One mother we know has said that having your child in an inclusive classroom without differentiated instruction is like "being invited to a party without being given a fork." Even the student with autism who has the least significant communication, social, or learning differences will likely require some differentiation in the classroom. To that end, we offer examples of how teachers can provide that metaphorical fork by adapting, changing, or modifying classroom climate and environment, goals, teaching strategies, lesson formats, and materials (Udvari-Solner, 1996).

Classroom Climate and Environment

Guy, a young man with disabilities, constantly disrupted lessons because he arrived late to his classes, struggled to find a place to sit, and often did not have the necessary course materials. Although some of his team members generated a simple adaptation to encourage his success, seeing it implemented would not be so simple:

> After discussions between his mother and the Head of Special Needs it was suggested that he should be allowed to have a fixed desk at which to sit in every lesson—preferably at the back of the class where he would be less of a distraction to other pupils. In each classroom the desk would also contain the minimum equipment necessary for him to cope with the lesson (paper, pens, ruler, etc.). Some teachers were happy to implement these suggestions and in their classes Guy's behavior improved rapidly. Others refused to change long-established teaching practices and in these classes his behavior remained highly disruptive and erratic. (Howlin, 1998, p. 244)

Sometimes, as in Guy's situation, teachers will need to create changes to the environment itself, including creating different seating options (e.g., rocking chair, seat cushion), changing the lighting (e.g., shutting off a bank of lights, using upward projecting lamps), or minimizing sounds and distractions (e.g., offering a study carrel to those who need it, putting a rug in the reading corner to absorb sound). Adaptations might also be needed, however, in classroom demands, expectations, or climate. For instance, in a study of students with autism in inclusive classrooms conducted by Paula and one of her colleagues, a teacher created a classroom culture that allowed students to demonstrate individual differences without being seen as difficult or odd:

> As the students arranged their pattern blocks, practiced forming their letters, and read their stories, Anna was observed humming to herself. Occasionally this humming became quite loud; however, other students in the classroom did not seem distracted by the sound. In fact not one student appeared distracted by or even particularly aware of Anna's humming. [The teacher] commented on this and said, "It has

all become a normal part of the class now. You know Anna hums and sometimes she screams. When she screams too loud we can usually calm her down by talking to her about what we are doing but sometimes she takes a walk or goes for a swing and comes back in and finishes what we are doing." (Kasa-Hendrickson & Kluth, 2005, pp. 10–11)

The humming and singing that were common occurrences in this class were not seen as disruptions, but as a part of how some students interacted in the class. The students with autism in this classroom who were nonverbal (and some without autism) hummed, sang, flapped their hands, jumped, and rocked; and when this was not distracting to others, it was ignored, accepted, and—by some—appreciated. The choice to allow these movements to continue and to create classroom experiences where different responses, behaviors, and movements became normal was an important component of this inclusive classroom.

Teaching Strategies

Another example from the same study illustrates how one second-grade teacher, Jackie Holder, used teaching strategies to enhance the participation of Shantel, a child with autism who did not have reliable communication. During a small-group reading lesson on blends beginning with the /s/ sound (e.g., str-, spr-), Ms. Holder used a variety of strategies to engage and challenge Shantel, including creating flashcards for the lesson, using praise and feedback that was specific, and encouraging peer support. As students sat around a table, each one of them took a turn reading a section of the worksheet in front of them and then verbally chose a word (from a word bank) to fit the sentence and identified the blend the word started with:

> When it was Shantel's turn she pointed to the words while her neighbor read them out loud. Her sentence read, "The boy ___ the guitar." Because Shantel could not accurately circle the word on the worksheet or write it in the box provided, Jackie had written the possible choices out on index cards. Each word was written in a different color. She set them out before Shantel and said, "OK, Shantel, I want you to pick the right word and hand it to Lauren [a student sitting next to Shantel]." Shantel began to look at each of the words. Jackie continued to encourage her selection by saying, "That's right, Shantel. I see you looking, very good. I see you stopping on a word. It looks like you are looking at the right word. Pick up the right word. Pick it up." Shantel reached over and picked up the word *strummed*. She then handed it to Lauren. Jackie continued, "Shantel, what blend does strummed start with?" Jackie then placed three blends on the table and continued to encourage her young pupil even when Shantel did not move for several moments. Instead of assuming that Shantel did not know the answer because she did not give an immediate response, the teacher simply said, "That's right; you're looking those three blends over. Good looking. Pick up the correct blend." At that point, Shantel picked up the *str-* card and handed it to her partner. (Kasa-Hendrickson & Kluth, 2005, p. 8)

With these subtle yet critical supports in place, Shantel, a child described as having fairly significant disabilities, was able to answer correctly in each of the three opportunities she was given. Other teaching strategies a teacher might employ include providing multimodal instruction (e.g., talking and showing a visual), modeling, being clear and explicit with directions or requests, providing useful feedback, and adjusting lesson pacing to meet individual student needs.

Goals and Standards

Another differentiation technique we promote is the adaptation of goals and standards. This means simply that teachers in the inclusive classroom should feel comfortable creating literacy objectives based on those targeted for students without disabilities but appropriate for individual learning needs. For instance, in a fifth-grade classroom, students were all supposed to learn to write for multiple audiences by the end of the year. Ross, a student with autism, had the same goal, but he was required to demonstrate that he could write for just three audiences (instead of the six targeted for his classmates). Furthermore, his writing consisted of either creating a document using an Intellikeys® Overlay or arranging sentence strips created by peers. See Table 3.6 for more examples of personalizing standards and documenting student progress for Ross.

Materials

A wide range of materials should also be part of the inclusive classroom and can be the difference, for some students, between presence and participation. A student with autism, for instance, may not be able to participate in chanting a poem from a big book if she is nonverbal and does not have a communication device or other type of augmentative or alternative communication to assist her. Existing instructional materials can be altered to be more manipulative, concrete, tangible, or simplified. New materials can be introduced for a learner who needs something different from what is typically offered in the classroom. A third grader Paula worked with in her student-teaching experience preferred to learn her spelling words when they were printed out with a raised-letter label maker, for instance, because she could feel, hear, and see the text (see Table 3.7 for more ideas on differentiating materials).

One of the primary concerns teachers have, of course, in this category of materials is text. Texts of different genres, reading levels, and even formats (e.g., hard copies of newspapers versus online versions) should be made available to all stu-

Table 3.6.   Examples of ways to adapt literacy standards and assessments for a student, Ross

Standard	Adapted standard	Assessment
Students will be able to use appropriate mechanics, usage, and conventions of language.	When using his Alphasmart™ to copy sentences from the chalkboard, Ross will include all punctuation.	Keep two work samples per week.
Students will differentiate fact from opinion across texts.	When given a paragraph of an informational text to read, Ross will identify one fact from that paragraph.	Offer Ross an opportunity to practice this skill during science and social studies lessons. On a checklist, keep a record of how many times he answers correctly.
Students will identify literary elements in stories (e.g., characters, setting, plot).	Using Kidspiration® software, Ross will create a story map that includes at least three story events.	Print and collect the map from each story. Review with Ross and provide feedback.

Table 3.7. Differentiating instructional materials for the inclusive classroom

In addition to using . . .	Try
Books	Adapted books (laminating favorite pages for easy gripping, rewriting text to make vocabulary more or less complex, replacing illustrations with personal photos), other reading materials (magazines, pamphlets, technical manuals, comic books, advertisements, flipbooks), electronic books/computer, audio books, posters, movies
Pencils/pens	Computer (word processing programs), communication devices, typewriters, rubber stamps (pictures, letters, or words), magnetic letters or words, pencil grips, letter guide
Paint/crayons	Colored pencils, paint pens, drawing/painting software programs, "sensory" art supplies (shaving cream, pudding), markers, stickers, charcoal, tools for print-making (potatoes, blocks)
Papers/worksheets	Adapted worksheets (important information highlighted or written in bold letters), laminated sheets and grease pencil, mini chalkboard or wipe board, overhead projector, colored overlays

From Kluth, P. (2003). *You're going to love this kid!": Teaching students with autism in the inclusive classroom* (p. 191). Baltimore: Paul H. Brookes Publishing Co.; reprinted by permission.

dents and for a variety of purposes. Although this recommendation may seem commonsense to some, one of our colleagues did not appreciate how vast of a range of materials she needed to make available until she encountered a student who loved to read cereal boxes more than any other "text" she offered him during the year. In order to meet his needs, she collected dozens of boxes and designed learning experiences around them. Eventually she coaxed the student into designing his own cereal boxes inspired by popular literature. His products included Sounder's Sugar Pops, Charlie's Chocolate Factory Crisps, and Super Fudge Snaps, all generated in response to different award-winning novels for children.

Similarly, in a biography penned by his father, it was reported that Kim Peek, the man with autism who inspired the film *Rain Man,* enjoys reading, among other things, fiction and nonfiction books, record jackets, CD labels, information on cassette tape boxes, catalogs on both classical and contemporary music, almanacs, and encyclopedias (Peek, 1996). And Donna Williams has disclosed that she was fascinated with telephone books throughout her childhood and adolescence. Although these types of materials may not be the typical texts offered in K–12 classrooms, they may be keys to learning and growth for some students and should, therefore, be considered as literacy tools.

Classroom texts may also need to be modified to meet the specific needs of the targeted learners. Textbooks, basal readers, and even chapter books can be adapted for individuals. Common changes we make include enlarging text or making it less complex, adding icons, pictures, or even American Sign Language symbols throughout, laminating the book itself or putting the pages in sheet protectors, and adding glossaries or annotations. PowerPoint (Microsoft) books are also a very simple and effective way to give students who either cannot turn pages or decode all of the text in a book an opportunity to do so. Simply scan pages into the computer, save them, and then "paste" them into the different slides of a presentation. PowerPoint software also allows users to record narration, so the text can be accessed by the student "reading" the book. For the learner, moving from one page to the next is as easy as a click of the mouse or a push of a button. See Figure 3.4 for examples of how specific books have been adapted for learners of different ages.

Of Mice and Men (Steinbeck, 1937/2002)

A high school English teacher needed to adapt *Of Mice and Men* for a student that read on a second-grade level. Among other supports, she used the following:

- A dictionary of vocabulary related to the text (e.g., depression, acres)
- Illustrations of several concepts the class discussed including threshing machines, farms, mules and an orchard
- Graphic organizers related to the story (e.g., timeline, Venn diagram comparing Lenny and Curly)
- Periodic summaries of the story (page by page or chapter by chapter); and
- Book on CD and a DVD of the movie

The Light in the Forest (Richter, 1963)

A sixth-grade team created adapted books for much of the literature used across the classrooms. The following versions were created for use by any student:

- A copy using repetitive and less sophisticated vocabulary
- A copy with key words highlighted (Indians, boy, family, white, little, settlers)
- A copy with only illustrations to be used by any learner wanting to write their own version of the story
- A copy featuring only the repetitive text with room for students to illustrate or take notes

Polar Bear, Polar Bear, What Do You See? (Martin & Carle, 1997)

A first-grade teacher needing to adapt the book for a student who recognized a handful of words and had low vision made the following changes

- Enhanced illustrations with added texture (e.g., pipe cleaners used for flamingo legs, nylon stockings used for the elephant)
- Added raised text (traced words with glue and let it dry)
- Enlarged the text and highlighted key words (e.g. polar bear) with a bright color

Figure 3.4.   Examples of text adapted for students with autism labels.

Other materials that are critical to the success of many students with autism are visual aids. When students are studying a novel, the teacher might provide the student who has a disability (and perhaps the entire class) with a pictorial timeline of the events in the story. A Venn diagram might be used to show learners how to compare and contrast two time periods in history. Photographs or drawings might be used to illustrate the meaning of new vocabulary words (e.g., show a picture of an angry, red-faced person when introducing the word "furious"). Students might participate in creating these illustrations in order to boost understanding for everyone in the class and to give artistic and visual learners an opportunity to shine. Visuals that can be used across lessons include physical objects (e.g., globe, puppet, three-dimensional model of human ear), charts, graphs, diagrams, photos, teacher- or student-created drawings on chalkboard, graphic organizers, and slides or overhead transparencies of lectures. Three-dimensional materials such as models or manipulatives may be especially helpful for learners with more significant motor challenges who struggle with movement and do not interact with pencils, papers, and books easily.

Lesson Formats

Finally, teachers must differentiate lesson formats themselves if they are to reach this population of learners. Although all students need variety and even joy in their teaching and learning experiences to keep interest high and to practice and show their skills across different contexts, students with autism rely on this practice, perhaps, more than others. Since most of the learners we are concerned with in this book need movement and interaction to learn, and they struggle to read, write, speak, and listen in conventional ways, giving them as many different options for learning and honing these skills is critical. Whereas more traditional formats such as whole-class instruction, class discussion, and individual work can be useful, they cannot be the only structures used to teach literacy. We recommend that teachers use not only the elastic structures we describe earlier in this chapter but also other formats including drama, simulation, cooperative and active learning, project-based instruction, and even community-based instruction.

Classrooms with interesting and varied formats are featured in one of our favorite studies on inclusive schooling and literacy. Fisher and Frey (2001) reported on a fifth grader named Lillian who was successful in a literacy lesson that was active, engaging, social, and varied in its possible roles for students. The assignment was to study a period of U.S. history and design an amusement park ride around that period of time. In this problem-based learning activity, Lillian's group was assigned westward movement. The group read *Sarah, Plain and Tall* (MacLachlan, 1985) and information/factual books, watched related films, and explored the Internet. Adaptations and accommodations for Lillian included reading a number of picture books on the topic with a partner, "reading" *Sarah, Plain and Tall* at a listening station, and examining a picture communication symbol version of the textbook chapter. In addition, a special education teacher added wagon and other frontier images to the picture cards used in Lillian's speech output device so that the youngster could participate in class discussions. The authors describe how Lillian, who had communication difficulties, was able to share both her enthusiasm and her ideas with her peers when it came time to design products for their unit:

> When her group received the assignment to create an amusement park ride based on the information they had gathered thus far, Lillian ran to the classroom library and grabbed a book about wagons. She pointed to a specific wagon in the book, the Conestoga. Paulo, a member of the group, added that they could make bumper cars that looked like Conestoga wagons. When asked how this fit into U.S. history, Paulo said, "Everybody knows that you had to travel across the land in a wagon; it was too far to walk. And on the trail, you bumped into lots of things." (2001, p. 148)

Although the teachers who planned this lesson definitely differentiated the lesson in several ways, the active and collaborative nature of the format surely contributed to Lillian's success in this cross-curricular unit. By creating products, solving problems, and working with peers, Lillian not only was able to address goals in literacy and social studies but also, undoubtedly, in communication and social skills.

CONCLUDING THOUGHTS

When most of us think of our favorite teachers, we think about someone who knew us well, someone who thought that we were capable. Therefore, even though it is critical that our educators are knowledgeable and skilled, stories of favorite or most effective teachers are seldom about curricula. Although a good teacher certainly needs to know how to develop lesson plans and draw students into learning, we believe that the teacher's orientation toward the students is the most powerful predictor of success in the classroom. A teacher's beliefs matter. His or her language, relationships with students, and values matter. In fact, these things matter in very real and very practical ways. Clearly, the best lessons, curricular adaptations, and teaching strategies are useless if a teacher does not consistently question his or her own assumptions or consider his or her values and beliefs; a teacher's "ways of knowing" *must* be constantly reviewed and reflected on in the inclusive classroom.

Whereas such self-scrutiny in a teacher is important for all learners, it is especially essential for students with autism, given how often their literate potential has historically been underestimated or even dismissed. Jamie Burke, the student whose voice opens this chapter, again says it best:

> The idea of school inclusion can be a lousy or a lovely happiness. It's really all in the hands of the teachers along with the permission of the big boss, the superintendent. Teachers must be willing to not just give me a desk and then leave me to fill the chair. I need to be asked questions, and given time for my thoughtful answers. Teachers need to become as a conductor, and then guide me through the many places I may get lost. (2005, p. 253)

To help you think about what kinds of questions might elicit "thoughtful answers" from students like Jamie, as well as consider other methods for eliciting data about all students' learning, we turn to the topic of inclusive approaches to literacy assessment and evaluation in the next chapter.

Recommended Resources
Future Reading on "Elastic" Structures for Literacy Learning
Literacy Workshops
Allen, J., & Gonzalez, K. (1998) *There's room for me here: Literacy workshop in middle school*. Portland, ME: Stenhouse Publishers.
Hindley, J. (1996). *In the company of children*. Portland, ME: Stenhouse Publishers.
Roller, C. (1996). *Variability not disability: Struggling readers in a workshop classroom*. Newark, DE: International Reading Association.

(continued)

Recommended Resources *(continued)*

Partner Reading

Boyd, F., & Galda, L. (1997). Lessons taught and lessons learned: How cross-aged talk about books helped struggling adolescents develop their own identity. In J. Paratore & R. McCormack (Eds.), *Peer talk in the classroom: Learning from research* (pp. 66–87). Newark, DE: International Reading Association.

Opitz, M.F., & Rasinski, T. (1998). *Good-bye round robin: 25 effective oral reading strategies*. Portsmouth, NH: Heinemann.

Samway, K., Whang, G., & Pippitt, M. (1995). *Buddy reading: Cross-age tutoring in a multicultural school*. Portsmouth, NH: Heinemann.

Book Clubs

Copeland, S., & Keefe, E. (2006). *Effective literacy instruction for students with moderate or severe disabilities*. Baltimore: Paul H. Brookes Publishing Co.

Daniels, H. (2002). *Literature circles: Voice and choice in book clubs and reading groups* (2nd ed.). Portland, ME: Stenhouse Publishers.

O'Donnell-Allen, C. (2006). *The book club companion: Fostering strategic readers in the secondary classroom*. Portsmouth, NH: Heinemann.

Centers and Learning Stations

Diller, D. (2003). *Literacy work stations: Making centers work*. Portland, ME: Stenhouse Publishers.

Fountas, I., & Pinnell, G.S. (1996). *Guided reading: Good first teaching for all*. Portsmouth, NH: Heinemann.

Gould, P., & Sullivan, J. (2004). *The inclusive early childhood classroom: Easy ways to adapt learning centers for all*. Upper Saddle River, NJ: Prentice Hall.

Chapter 4

Assessing
Literacy Learning

In her autobiography, *Lucy's Story*, Lucy Blackman, an Australian woman with autism who had little reliable communication as a child, shares her belief that she learned to read at an early age: "I must have been very young because I think I could understand some of the words in [my sister's] very first reader, and she started school when I was two and a half" (1999, p. 46). According to Blackman, she developed important literacy skills by perusing the books her mother left in the family bathroom, watching *Sesame Street*, and listening to her four older sisters do their homework:

> They had sat at the kitchen table making heavy weather of the reading books sent home from school, while I flapped and cooed with delight that I could do what they were trying to learn. For indirect learning, there had been stacks of magazines and newsletters all over our chaotic home. (1999, p. 61)

Sadly, Blackman's precocious ways were mostly unrecognized by those in her life. When loved ones and teachers tried to determine Lucy's abilities, she was usually unable to demonstrate her knowledge and skill through the measures and techniques used. As Lucy's mother, Jay, recalls, one teacher did feel confident that her pupil could read some words, partly based on how she moved her eyes. The same teacher, however, was frustrated that she could not get Lucy to "provide any proof" of her abilities (1999, p. 60).

According to Blackman, the problem was not one related to intention. Rather, she struggled with movement and communication and could not provide desired responses when and how they were requested:

> I never developed the urge to follow a written or symbolic instruction and I never became automatic in speaking a written word. So no one knew I could read. At that stage I would

not have seen any point in showing that I could. I still have problems making an instinctive move toward something I am supposed to identify by picture or word. It is not only a matter of reading because although I obviously know I am a girl, I have to be reminded to go into the public toilet identified by the little skirted icon, rather than by the one representing a man, and be watched until I actually push the door open, in case I get confused on the way. (1999, p. 46)

In other words, Blackman failed many assessments because the tasks required her to speak, match, draw, or otherwise perform in ways that were difficult, albeit not cognitively, for her. Perhaps the most intriguing piece of Lucy's quote is her reference to "making an instinctive move" and her explanation of the difficulties involved. We can glean from her account that most assessments would have been incredibly challenging for her, including those designed for nonverbal students that involved choosing or pointing to cards, items, pictures, or words. Because many students with autism *can* point to or manipulate objects, it is often assumed that their movements are intentional and accurate. Blackman suggests, however, that this assumption can be far from the truth.

As a result of her difficulties, most people in Lucy's life assumed that she was not literate, and Lucy herself doubted what she knew: "Because I had learnt by observation with no feedback, I was [not sure] I was really literate in the sense of continuous reading of texts" (1999, p. 87). All of this changed for Blackman when she met a teacher, Rosie Crossley, whose assessments acknowledged her problems with movement and expression:

The preliminaries were similar to the language-based activities that I had been given over the years as far as the materials used were concerned. However, there was an important difference. Such tests usually depend for their outcome on the child carrying out the nominated activity or speaking the word which represents the answer that most people would give, or on the onlooker observing the child pointing to or picking up the symbol or object required. This woman had developed another approach. She watched my hand very closely to see if I were initiating the correct movement, or she touched my hand or wrist to feel from the action of my finger whether I was attempting to touch the correct symbol. (1999, p. 80)

Using this approach, the teacher was able to see that Lucy was attempting to demonstrate understanding despite the hazards of her uncooperative body.

In this same session, another effective technique was used. The assessment tasks required Lucy to work not from word or letter cards but from whole paragraphs:

The reading tests I had previously been given had relied on speaking words or small groups of words, or on card matching. Now I had the opportunity to glance quickly at the paragraph. Then, still tracking my hand against the light grip of my teacher, I would point at one of several sentences randomly listed below to indicate which of them most accurately reflected what I understood to be the gist of the whole passage. Whereas slowly working word-by-word confused me and robbed me of the meaning, in this method I could not only show the other people in the room that I could read, but I could also prove it to myself for the first time. (1999, p. 46)

Blackman's account illustrates the many reasons why teachers should be cautious—to say the least—when assessing learners with autism spectrum labels. In

Blackman's case, successful assessment required careful observation, patience, and creativity on the part of her evaluator. In addition, we are intrigued by her mention of text-based materials (versus the use of single letter or word cards). In our experience, instruction and assessment for students with autism (especially those who cannot easily demonstrate what they know) often involves work on isolated letters, sounds, or words as a precursor to working with continuous text. Blackman's comments, however, provide a reason to question this practice.

Many students like Blackman perform poorly on assessments, especially formal ones, and some even appear incapable of demonstrating any skill or ability at all. Unsure of what these learners know and can do, teachers may assume that where there is no evidence of ability, there is *no* ability. This orientation often leads teachers to make inappropriate or flawed instructional decisions.

After much discussion of cases like Lucy Blackman's, we decided to devote a separate chapter to assessment in this book. We had mixed feelings about this decision because we believe that assessment and instruction are closely tied to each other, and we feared that separating the two might undercut that message. We hope you will see, however, that many of the approaches we describe in subsequent chapters can serve instructional and assessment goals simultaneously. For example, Reader's Theater, discussed in Chapter 5, is a structure that helps teachers promote students' oral reading fluency, but a rehearsed performance documented with a simple scoring rubric can also serve as an effective assessment of growth in that area.

Ultimately, we decided to discuss literacy assessment for students with autism spectrum labels in its own chapter for these reasons:

1. We wanted to acknowledge that some students with autism are very difficult to assess. They will need plenty of support and adaptation to demonstrate what they know and can do.

2. We wanted to state our unequivocal opposition to using assessments as gatekeepers to literacy. We too often see students unable to pass particular assessments who are then locked out of inclusive classrooms, age-appropriate curriculum, or meaningful and varied instruction.

3. We wanted to emphasize the idea that careful, sensitive assessment should both precede and accompany instruction, rather than occur only after instruction has concluded—a stance that we know others have taken but that we still see enacted in schools too infrequently. By sequencing this chapter before those on teaching specific aspects of literacy, we hoped to underscore that responsive literacy pedagogy has assessment at its foundation, not as an afterthought.

We find it helpful to talk about approaches to literacy assessment on a continuum of formality, with one end of the spectrum anchored by highly structured assessments that are consistently administered, often in decontextualized settings, and the other by assessments that are flexibly adapted for individual learners' needs and deeply embedded in daily classroom life. For the sake of convenience, we divided the material that follows into three main sections—formal literacy assessments, literacy assessments with both formal and informal dimensions, and informal classroom assessments—but it's worth noting here that some of the approaches we discuss could be placed under one subheading as easily as the other, depending on where the continuum is (arbitrarily) divided.

FORMAL LITERACY ASSESSMENTS

The term *formal literacy assessment* is used to describe approaches to assessing literacy that involve standardized administration (everyone who administers them does so in exactly the same way) and standardized norms for interpreting results (students' performance can be scored in such a way that indicates whether they have learned particular material and/or how they compare with other students who have taken the same test). These assessments may take several forms, including *diagnostic tests* that are intended to identify students' strengths and weaknesses in particular sub-areas of literacy; and *achievement tests,* including those administered by various states, which are intended to indicate students' mastery of specific literacy skills or content. Most diagnostic literacy tests are designed for individual administration, and they are typically given only to students about whom there is some concern. In addition to the detailed data about student performance yielded by the numerous subtest scores typical of these tests, those who administer them have an opportunity to observe a student closely during what can often be a lengthy examination period. Achievement tests, in contrast, are usually given to large groups of students over a shorter time period, and their results tend to be more useful in evaluating instructional programs than in pinpointing areas of difficulty for individuals (Gillet & Temple, 2000). A few achievement tests are designed to be administered individually, though the exclusively quantitative nature of their results limits their diagnostic value.

Achievement tests may be either *criterion-referenced*, meaning that they compare students' performances to a predetermined outcome or benchmark; or *norm-referenced*, meaning that they compare students' results with those from a population that is assumed to be similar to the students (the latter are the kinds of tests that yield percentiles and grade-level labels in students' official records). Most state tests tend to be criterion-referenced because one of their purposes is to track student progress regarding an agreed-on set of content standards and performance indicators. Commercially available standardized tests tend to be norm-referenced because they are intended for use in many different settings, where literacy standards and programs vary tremendously, and administrators often select them to help ascertain how a given school or district compares with others, both locally and nationally.

Challenges of Formal Literacy Assessment

Wendy Lawson, a woman with Asperger syndrome, explains in her autobiography, *Life Behind Glass* (1998), that testing can be a very confusing and stressful experience when the proper supports are not offered and when the work space is less than comfortable. In the following passage she recounts the frustration she felt when directed to take a placement exam for secondary school:

> I was accompanied into a small room not far from Sister's office. It had only one desk and one chair in it, plus a loud ticking clock on the wall directly opposite where I sat. I was given a pencil and several sheets of paper and told it was important to my education that I concentrate and work to the best of my ability. Whatever "important to my education" meant, being in that office with those bits of paper did not feel very important to me. I drew on paper, played "noughts and crosses" and felt very anxious—I had told one of the nurses earlier that I would roll some bandages for her and I felt that really *was* important. (p. 42)

Not surprisingly, Lawson did not pass the exam. In reflecting on this negative experience, she offered suggestions for how the situation might have been more supportive:

> Maybe if the exam had been explained to me and I had been told to read the information sheet accompanying the writing paper, I might have attempted to answer the questions. It would have been very helpful if the exam had been broken down into smaller chunks of information so that I could have worked without being overwhelmed by so many words all lumped together. This did not happen and neither did the "eleven plus" exam for me! (1998, pp. 42–43)

It's important to keep in mind that students like Lawson may have sensory problems or anxiety that keeps them from performing, teachers must also remember that those with autism may have had their motor skills, social skills, communication and language abilities, adaptive behaviors, general "intelligence," and even their sight and hearing tested or evaluated more than once before they reach school age. One student Paula taught had been evaluated by 12 different experts by the time she was 6 years old. Given these constant requests to engage in tasks and activities that may be confusing, challenging, and even uncomfortable or painful, it is not surprising that many students with autism resist formal testing experiences (Marcus & Shevin, 1997). Other challenges include assessment conditions and environments, test anxiety, and measures that lack sensitivity to difference, each of which is discussed below.

Assessment Conditions and Environments

Many formal assessments (especially diagnostic ones) require students to work in rooms that they have rarely (if ever) been in before and use tools with which they have had little practice. Some assessments ask students to engage in unfamiliar tasks or play games they have to learn on the spot. Many tests, especially those of reading, require students to respond to language structures that they encounter infrequently in everyday life—for instance, cloze passages omitting a word from a sentence (e.g., "The girl ____ up the staircase") or analogies ("cat–meow, dog–____"). Although some students relish the novelty of such situations, many on the autism spectrum find these departures from the norm disruptive and confusing.

Students may also find the testing conditions hard on their sensory systems. As we shared in Chapter 1, classrooms pose sensory challenges in general for some students. "Test days" often exacerbate these issues because they cause teachers to create the most formal classroom climate (e.g., fewer opportunities for movement and breaks) and environment (e.g., bright lights, all students in desks sitting in rows). It may also be difficult for students with autism spectrum labels to sit still and quietly for long periods of time as is often dictated for testing.

Test Anxiety

Many students with autism (and a number of students without that label, too) experience anxiety about formal assessments. Some feel inadequate or unprepared to deal with the content or task being assessed. Others fear how the results may be used, particularly in situations in which a student's performance may result in a change in placement or teacher. In still other cases, the individual may not trust the process of assessment or the person administering the assessment, especially if that individual is a stranger. Dawn Prince-Hughes, a woman with Asperger syndrome, shared this last sentiment, arguing that many with autism do not want to reveal themselves to those who may not be trustworthy:

> A significant number of autistic people who care deeply about all manner of things, and are profoundly emotional about them, share these capabilities in the privacy of their journals, diaries, and poetry. They do not show them to the world, which is too intense and often too destructive, or worse, dismissive. They do not show them to professionals, whose beliefs about the abilities of autistic people and the power they wield over their clients sometimes make them too frightening to challenge. They do not even show them to one another. And so a vast resource of knowledge about the diversity and beauty of autism rests on countless pages, like layers of archaeology, covered with the dust of fear. (2004, p. 31)

Lack of Instrument Sensitivity

Results from many formal assessments do not adequately reflect individual learners' progress with literacy, especially when the growth still leaves that student at the bottom of the class in what MacIver called "comparative terms" (1991, p. 4). Some of the learners we are concerned with make gains that are too subtle to be reflected on traditional assessment tools normed on populations with dramatically different profiles than theirs.

Also problematic is the fact that many formal literacy assessments require students to have a single correct answer, allowing for little flexibility in interpretation by the student of the test item or the student's response by the examiner. We have both worked with teachers who have expressed their frustration at testing learners whose response indicated understanding but could not be counted as correct, given the precise scoring instructions in the testing manual. Frustration from the learner's perspective is shared, again, by Dawn Prince-Hughes, who wrote about providing incorrect answers on an intelligence test because of her unusual interpretation of the material:

> I remember telling [the tester] that noodles were "happy" because they went in circular motions in the pan when the water was boiling, that willow trees were "sad" because they couldn't straighten out their branches. I couldn't come up with a concept for "scared." To me this was just a general state of being. I did take a chance and reveal to her that I felt "special" when I rode the Round-Up ride at the fair. When she asked me for clarification, I told her, "It makes me sleepy." I didn't have the sensation-discrete vocabulary to tell her it made me feel content and relaxed as well as joyful. (2004, p. 45)

Prince-Hughes recalled that although she never did get the scores from her test, she was allowed to spend more time with language-based projects (something she preferred) as a result of the experience. We don't know how the assessor interpreted her unusual remarks, but it is clear that Prince-Hughes had a learning profile that was considerably more complex than formal instruments would have indicated.

For all of these reasons, students' performance on formal assessments may be inconsistent with data from other, more personalized sources. A young man with Down syndrome we know, for instance, failed an item on a diagnostic test of adaptive behavior because his language and speech problems prevented him from telling the evaluator what he should do if he was playing outdoors and it began to rain. His mother was exasperated because "he knows very well to come in, get an umbrella, or duck into the garage even if he can't explain it on the test!" Furthermore, in a study Paula and her colleagues conducted on families who move to find inclusive schools (Kluth, Biklen, English-Sand, & Smukler, 2007), one mother, Darcy, reported that conflicting assessments of her daughter, Cindy, contributed to her decision to leave her district. According to Cindy's first-grade teacher, the child was reading at grade level. When Darcy participated in a formal assessment meeting, however, she was informed by other team members that Cindy had only "preschool skills" with reference to reading. In both cases, intimate local knowledge (Geertz, 2000; Kliewer, 1998) about students' literate competence was dismissed in favor of information generated by formal assessments, creating parental mistrust and making it more difficult for families to partner with members of their children's school teams.

Benefits of Formal Assessments

Clearly, we have significant concerns about the use of formal literacy assessments with learners on the autism spectrum. We believe that these sorts of measures do more harm than good for most learners with these labels. This is not to say, however, that formal literacy assessments are completely without benefit for this population. Before we move on to discuss other kinds of assessments on our continuum that we think should be emphasized more, we share three of these benefits here.

First, the inclusion of achievement testing data from students with disabilities in a given school or district's profile (something that is mandated by NCLB) can sometimes, though certainly not often enough from our perspective, focus needed attention and resources on literacy instruction for these learners. In some settings, the need to account for labeled students' achievement on these traditional measures has led educators to reflect in difficult but important ways about their level of commitment to the oft-repeated but less-often-enacted mantra that all children can learn. (We should note, however, that in other settings, the focus on accountability has driven teachers to limit curricular opportunities for all learners and to spend an inordinate amount of time on test preparation and drill, hindering academic opportunities for students with disabilities as well as their peers without labels.) When teachers and administrators take joint responsibility for poor literacy achievement by students with disabilities, viewing it as a challenge to be addressed collaboratively, then the increased visibility of having those students included in the overall data pool can have positive effects.

Second, well-designed formal literacy assessments, particularly those for diagnostic purposes, can sometimes illuminate student strengths in sub-areas that might otherwise be overlooked. People with autism labels can have quirky learning profiles, demonstrating unusual facility with one skill while failing miserably on another. It is possible that holistically oriented classroom assessments may not pick up these strengths, but that diagnostic instruments that disaggregate performance on a number of dimensions might do so, as long as the student is not stymied by the barriers we outlined in the previous section.

A third potential benefit from formal literacy assessments is tied to their authoritative status in our culture, both in and beyond educational settings. Although we oppose denying students opportunities for high-quality, meaningful literacy instruction on the basis of poor performance on these measures for all of the reasons described above, a *strong* performance by a student with an autism label can strengthen a case for increasing expectations for that student, countering potential resistance from others opposed to that move. If, for example, a student who is nonverbal scores highly on a standardized measure of reading comprehension, then that particular piece of data may challenge assumptions about his literacy levels tied to his lack of facility with oral language. For this reason, we advocate that data from formal literacy assessments be interpreted in ways that have the power to increase opportunities for students, not limit those opportunities. Table 4.1 includes a list of suggested selection criteria for formal literacy assessments that may be helpful if you have some influence over that selection process.

Creating Supports for Formal Literacy Assessments

For those occasions when formal literacy assessments are desirable (or, as is more likely the case, unavoidable), some strategies do exist to help literacy learners with autism reduce anxiety and perform more effectively. In our experience, social narratives (Gray, 2000; Smith Myles & Southwick, 2005) can be a useful tool in coping with the stress associated with taking tests. A social narrative is a story written by a teacher or other adult that describes "what most of us dismiss as obvious" (Gray & White, 2002, p. 17). The authors of these narratives attempt to take the perspective of a person with autism. The stories are written to give the person with autism information about what to expect and how to respond in a given situation. For instance, if a teacher was writing a story about going to the school play, she would want to include information about intermission and the clapping that is sure to occur. The story would most likely cue the student to join in with the clapping when he hears it or, in the case of a student who is sensitive to loud noises, to plug and protect his ears as soon as the curtain goes down. Such a story can instruct and reassure those who struggle with novel or unpredictable situations.

Table 4.1.   Suggested selection criteria for formal literacy assessments for students with autism

If you have a choice about which formal literacy assessments to administer to students, consider the following guidelines:

- Avoid tests that require students to read words in isolation but do not require them to comprehend connected text. Be wary of tests that purport to identify a reading level for students without asking them to read words in meaningful sentences and passages. Similarly, be wary of tests that claim to assess students' writing ability but require them to locate and correct grammatical errors, rather than to generate text themselves.

- Avoid tests that emphasize the reading of nonsense words to assess students' decoding skills without the "confounding" variable of prior knowledge. Scholars such as Richard Allington have questioned whether this practice yields much useful data about literacy learners in general; it is likely to be particularly distracting and disorienting for learners with autism.

- Select tests that do not depend solely on oral performance to assess reading because the communication difficulties experienced by some students with autism may interfere with their ability to pronounce words on demand. In many cases, silent reading will serve those students better.

- Select tests that include multiple-choice items with answers requiring high levels of inference and critical thinking. For students with certain kinds of communication and/or movement difficulties, these items may allow them to indicate higher levels of reading comprehension than they could easily demonstrate with tasks requiring them to produce sustained expressive language on their own.

These stories can be created in a number of ways. Students can co-construct them with the teacher, or the teacher can ask the student to lead the activity by sharing, in any way possible, information she may have about a given situation. For instance, if a student needs to write a social story about going to a pep rally, she may draw or act out anything she already knows about school assemblies or athletic events. Social stories can be written with words alone or with photographs, drawings, or magazine clippings. They can also be put on audiotapes or videotapes, with the teacher, a family member, or the student herself reading the story. (See Figure 4.1 for a social narrative related to assessment that was written by a teacher and her student.)

Once the narratives are constructed, teachers can read them to or with students, or they can be sent home for the family to share and practice. The stories can be kept in a desk, locker, or personal notebook so the student can read the stories often and keep them handy for quick review (these repeated readings may not only help to calm a student but they may also help to develop reading fluency—a topic we'll discuss more in the next chapter). In some instances, the student may only need to read the story once or twice to feel comfortable with a situation. In other cases, it may need to be revisited daily for weeks at a time. Once the student feels comfortable in the social situation depicted, use of the story can be faded.

Another way to help students perform better on formal literacy assessments is to teach relaxation strategies to apply in testing situations. Some strategies that might be helpful include taking deep breaths, tensing and relaxing muscles, and engaging in positive self-talk (remember that many students with limited oral language proficiency can use the latter technique, even if you can't teach them to do it aloud). These strategies can be used to reduce anxiety before the test (as well as during it, if students learn to initiate them on their own). Check with your school psychologist, social worker, or guidance counselor for help with this recommendation, as well as with caregivers to see if families have devised other methods for helping their children deal with stress and anxiety.

I will be taking a test on Monday. Mr. Oryall, a man I met at my old school, will be coming to give me the test.

I will sit in a quiet room at the end of the "B" hallway. If I want a cushion for the chair, Mr. Oryall will give me one. If I want a cup of water, Mr. Oryall will give me one. Mr. Oryall wants to help me and he wants me to be successful.

During the test, Mr. Oryall will ask me many questions. I will do my best to answer them. If I don't know the answer, it is okay to make a guess or to answer "I don't know." I don't need to get upset if I don't know an answer.

I will finish the test and answer all of the questions.
My teacher just wants me to try my best.
My mother just wants me to try my best.
I just want to try my best.

Figure 4.1. An example of a social narrative used to help a student prepare for a test.

Table 4.2. Sample testing environment adaptations

Adaptations for minimizing sounds	Adaptations to lighting	Adaptations to seating
Use earplugs or headphones.	Use lower levels of light.	Provide beanbag chairs, rocking chairs, lawn chairs, or old car seats.
Reduce classroom noise and echoes by installing carpeting (remnants may be obtained from a carpet store at low cost).	In classrooms with several windows, try using natural lighting.	Offer a seat cushion (the type that can be tied on to the chair can be found at discount stores).
Cut tennis balls open and place them on the bottoms of chair or desk legs; this adaptation muffles the sounds created when furniture is shuffled.	Use upward rather than downward projecting lighting. Replace fluorescents with incandescent bulbs.	Give a choice of sitting on the floor, if the student prefers it (with a reading pillow if needed).
Allow students to listen to soft music using headsets in noisy or chaotic environments or play soft music (e.g., classical) for all students at times.	Use sunglasses or baseball caps to avoid direct exposure to light. Move a student's seat; sometimes the problem is not the lights themselves, but the reflection of light on a wall or other surface.	Use couches, loveseats, armchairs, or large footstools if they are available in the school.

From Kluth, P. *"You're going to love this kid!": Teaching students with autism in the inclusive classroom* (2003). Baltimore: Paul H. Brookes Publishing; adapted by permission.

Finally, you can support students by making the testing environment as comfortable as possible. Making changes to a room can help a student without interfering with the standardization of formal tools. Common adaptations that might help the student include changing seating options, keeping lighting natural or low, and providing a space away from external noise and visual distractions (see Table 4.2 for more ideas on adapting the testing environment).

LITERACY ASSESSMENTS WITH BOTH FORMAL AND INFORMAL DIMENSIONS

A number of literacy assessments share some characteristics with formal measures like the ones we discussed in the previous section as well as with informal approaches that teachers employ in their classroom on a day-to-day basis. Although there are many literacy assessment tools that could be classified with this "hybrid" status, we discuss three here—the Dynamic Indicators of Basic Early Literacy, informal reading inventories, and unit and chapter tests—to illustrate the range of issues represented by the middle of our continuum of formality.

Dynamic Indicators of Basic Early Literacy

In recent years, many literacy teachers in the primary grades, especially those in schools supported by Reading First funding, have used an assessment tool called Dynamic Indicators of Basic Early Literacy, more widely known by its acronym, DIBELS (Good & Kaminski, 2002). This tool is intended to measure students' phonological awareness, knowledge about the alphabetic principle, and oral reading fluency—three key areas of focus from the National Reading Panel report (NICHD, 2000a). Most of the individual measures included in the tool (see http://dibels.uoregon.edu/measures.php for a brief description of each) were designed to be administered in 2 minutes or less, with assessments taking place at the beginning, middle, and end of the school year so that student progress can be tracked over time. Although the DIBELS are not norm-referenced in the traditional sense of the term (the comparison group reflects the students in the DIBELS database rather than a nationally normed sample), teachers can consider their students' scores in light of grade-level benchmarks, yielding information similar to that from an achievement test. Like other formal assessments, the DIBELS have also undergone a good deal of testing to increase their reliability.

At the same time, the DIBELS have a good deal in common with less formal literacy assessments because they were designed for use by teachers, not school psychologists or other specialists, and they can be given in a corner of a familiar classroom, rather than in a segregated testing environment (the test developers even mention parents as potential administrators of the tool if they are provided with some minimal training). Because results are available so quickly, the DIBELS can be used by teachers to guide instructional moves for individual learners in ways that results generated by most standardized tests cannot. Moreover, the tool can be adapted for individual learner needs. Although fidelity to the recommended procedures is encouraged by the test developers in most cases, even they acknowledge in an online position paper that teachers of students with what they call "fluency-based speech disabilities" (a category that could well include students with autism) may find it "necessary to adjust goals and timelines" as well as to "use out-of-grade-level materials for progress monitoring" (Dynamic Measurement Group, 2006, p. 1).

We are cheered by this explicit recognition of teachers' capacity for decision-making related to their own students' needs, and we encourage you to experiment with one or more components of the DIBELS if you need data about these aspects of early reading and have access to the tools. If a given measure is inappropriate for a student with autism in your care (e.g., if he or she balks at reading nonsense words aloud or struggles with phoneme segmentation because of communication difficulties), this should become apparent almost immediately. You can then abandon the measure in favor of something more suitable without wasting time or subjecting your student to unnecessary stress. If your student does respond well, however, you'll have another approach in your repertoire for understanding his or her literacy development (and you'll have data to share with others using a measure that has a good deal of currency in nationwide conversations about early literacy).

Informal Reading Inventories

Another useful "hybrid" assessment is the informal reading inventory (IRI), a tool composed of graded word lists, text passages, and accompanying sets of questions "intended to test readers' comprehension and recall after reading" (Gillet & Temple, 2000, p. 88). Like the DIBELS, informal reading inventories can be used by general classroom teachers, although they might also be part of the diagnostic repertoire of a specialist called in to evaluate a student having difficulty with literacy. IRIs are used for a variety of purposes, including determining students' independent, instructional, and frustrational reading levels; assessing students' listening comprehension; and pinpointing areas where further assessment is necessary (Walpole & McKenna, 2006). Depending on how comprehensive they are, IRIs take from 20 to 90 minutes to administer. Commercially available IRIs (e.g., Ekwall & Shanker, 2000; Roe & Burns, 2006) have some formal elements because their manuals offer standardized scripts for administration, their passages are graded using specific guidelines, and their scoring procedures are spelled out explicitly—none of which is likely to be the case with informal literacy assessments.

At the same time, teachers have plenty of choices, even when administering these established instruments, about where to begin with a student in the sequence of tasks, what passages to read even at a given grade level, and what to ask students to do following their reading. IRIs may generate less performance anxiety than more formal measures because most of the tasks associated with them (e.g., reading short passages, answering comprehension-focused questions) are similar to those associated with reading instruction in school. Another positive aspect of an IRI for students with autism is that many of the inventories include both oral and silent reading components. Teachers of students with significant communication difficulties can skip the former portions and concentrate their energy on the latter. With a number of IRIs, teachers also have the option of asking students to retell their reading or to answer questions, depending on which approach they think is most likely to suit students' needs.

In addition to commercially available tools, teachers can and do make up their own IRIs using reading material from their reading series as well as other available sources. When this occurs, the IRI approach should be moved closer to the informal end of our continuum, and users should be aware that what they gain in their ability to tailor passages and/or questions to students' interests and prior knowledge is likely to be accompanied by losses in precision associated with text leveling and so forth. It can be time-consuming to construct an IRI, so most teachers we know prefer to make adaptations to preexisting ones, sometimes supplementing them with grade-level passages from a textbook or anthology, rather than assembling their own from scratch. And if you work with a student who lacks reliable speech but whom you think can read and understand connected text, you may prefer to use your time devising ways for him or her to indicate comprehension (e.g., by generating multiple-choice answers for him or her to choose from or creating text-related overlays for a communication device) than on locating and checking the grade-level texts in the first place.

Unit and/or Chapter Tests

Unit or chapter tests administered by the classroom teacher are a third literacy assessment approach blending formal and informal aspects. Where these measures should be located on our continuum—and how the students who take them experience them—depends on who constructs them and how they are administered. Tests authored by commercial publishers tend to be more formal than those teachers make up themselves. For instance, fourth-grade teachers using *Reading Street*, a popular elementary series published by Scott Foresman (Afflerbach et al., 2005), have six unit tests at their disposal, each of which includes 40 multiple-choice questions, two short-answer tasks, and one open-ended written response task tied to the skills covered in the last two chapters of the textbook (Gatti, 2005). A test composed of such traditional—and for the most part, rigid—tasks has the potential to generate the same kind of performance anxiety for students with autism (and at least some of the same interpretation challenges around their responses for their teachers) as a diagnostic or achievement test, even though the stakes and purposes for the standardized measures may be different than they are for a unit-specific, classroom-based assessment.

When unit or chapter tests are teacher-made, they, like teacher-constructed IRIs, tend to occupy a place closer to the informal end of our assessment continuum than their published counterparts. The formatting for teacher-made tests may look less intimidating to students, and they may be better aligned with the literacy skills and strategies taught daily in the classroom. That a test is teacher-made does not always mean it's better for learners, however. Some teachers lack experience and/or skill with designing assessment items that accurately reflect the range of what students have learned; if this is the case, literacy learners may be better able to demonstrate their knowledge and skills with items that have been field-tested—and often revised on the basis of how pilot students responded—than with poorly constructed items written by their teacher. Table 4.3 provides suggestions for creating good test questions for heterogeneous learning populations.

Regardless of who authors a chapter or unit test, a teacher's administration procedures also have a significant influence on the degree to which it will reflect learning for students with autism. Teachers make choices about seating arrangements, noise level, use of resources such as word processors or dictionaries, and norms around peer collaboration that sometimes influence assessment results as much as the quality of the items. What's more, teachers' views on whether a given assessment should be seen as the last word on learning for a unit can have a profound impact on whether those assessments reveal the nuances and complexities of individual students' performance. Teachers of diverse populations need to be as willing to provide differentiated assessment options as they are to provide differentiated instruction.

Here's an example of how these sorts of adaptations might play out. In a sixth-grade classroom, students were studying the book, *Roll of Thunder, Hear My Cry* (Taylor, 1976). The teacher, as usual, drafted a quiz to assess student learning midway through the novel. She included open-ended questions such as "What role does family tradition play in the novel?" and multiple-choice questions like "Who is the narrator of the book?" Three students, including one young man with autism, failed the quiz, but their teacher felt strongly that they knew more about the book than their performance indicated. As she had done in the past when stu-

Table 4.3. Suggestions for creating good test questions for inclusive classrooms

Use a variety of questions and prompts, including both forced-choice items (e.g., true/false, matching, multiple choice) and constructed-response items (e.g., drawings, short answers, flow charts).

Make the items efficient for students (e.g., keep matching items on the same page, write out *Ts* and *Fs* for students to circle to avoid confusion about their handwriting).

Avoid confusing negatives (e.g., "Which of these does NOT describe. . . .").

Keep the test short (e.g., by asking students to answer two or three questions to show mastery of the same concept rather than eight or ten).

Avoid timed tests as much as possible.

Incorporate students' names and interests into the items where you can.

Tier questions (e.g., put questions of varying difficulty in different sections of the text and specify which levels individuals should answer, or design one test for everyone and circle the items that you want a particular student to do).

From *Fair Isn't Always Equal: Assessing and Grading in the Differentiated Classroom*, by Rick Wormeli, © 2006, with permission of Stenhouse Publishers.

dents did not perform well on assessments, she asked the three students to create another quiz as a group, to study for it, and to set a time to take it. The three boys, eager to be charged with such an important task, worked on the quiz after school for two days. All three passed the new quiz and were able to give the teacher feedback about what kind of preparation they needed and what types of items they could best answer. Some of their suggestions included changing the essay questions into interview questions so the students could respond verbally and allowing them to show their knowledge by rewriting the text in comic book form using their own words.

Having students help with the creation of tests and quizzes is just one way to make classroom-based tests less stressful and difficult for learners in a diverse classroom. Table 4.4 includes a list of other testing adaptations with which teachers might experiment throughout the year, seeking feedback from students about the effectiveness of each. These adaptations need not be reserved for the learner with autism or other disabilities, however, because all students may benefit from expressing knowledge and skills in different ways. (Some of these same adaptations may be appropriate for more formal literacy assessments, depending on the assessment tool, the purpose for using it, and the individual student's accommodations provided by his or her IEP.)

For us, these three assessments with both formal and informal dimensions point out some key principles around assessment for learners with autism spectrum labels that transcend the individual tools themselves. First of all, they suggest the importance of careful experimentation with assessment methods in the same way that savvy, experienced teachers routinely experiment with instruc-

Table 4.4. Sample testing adaptations before, during, and after testing

Preparation for the test	Support during the test	Evaluation of test performance
Share information with students about the content, format, setting, and time of the test.	Read the test directions and/or items aloud to students.	Allow students to retake tests.
Give a practice test.	Have students repeat directions to a peer to be sure they understand them.	Let students take two similar tests and count their best score.
Provide study guides in advance of the test.	Give students opportunities to ask questions during the test.	Create a test with 75 points and allow students to choose items that total 50 points.
Allow students to bring a "cheat sheet" to the test to help them remember key ideas.	Give students opportunities to answer one question with a partner.	Weight some items on the test more heavily for some students, depending on their strengths.
Let students write some or all of the test items themselves.	Allow students to use strategies from the "Who Wants to be a Millionaire?" television show (e.g., the 50/50 or "ask the class" options) for one question.	
Give an open-book test and allow students to use highlighters and post-it notes to mark important passages.	Allow students to skip any one item.	
	Eliminate selected test items for some students.	
	Allow students to answer some questions in a variety of ways (e.g., drawing diagrams instead of writing).	

tional approaches for this same population. We urge you not to assume that a measure won't yield useful data for a labeled student without attempting its use and documenting how that student responds. Consideration of these three tools also reminds us that it's sometimes easier and faster for teachers to adapt and adopt existing tools, devising only what they need, than it is to invent an entire set of assessment tools from scratch. Measures like these are much easier for teachers to adjust for individual learners' needs than formal ones. At the same time, they can make data-gathering more efficient and precise than is often the case with the context-specific but often time-consuming methods we profile in the next section.

INFORMAL LITERACY ASSESSMENTS

There are many things we cannot learn about students, especially those with autism, from formal or even "semiformal" measures, no matter how well designed, thoughtfully chosen, or sensitively administered they are. In order to support and challenge all literacy learners in inclusive settings, teachers need the richest and most current information about what students know and can do. The best way to gather this diversity of data is to use a wide range of informal assessment approaches that are, in Darling-Hammond's words, so "closely entwined as to be often inseparable" from teaching and curriculum (1997, p. 115). We think that these classroom-based assessments are most powerful when they are student-centered—that is, when learners make choices in how to be evaluated, participate in designing assessment tools and criteria, and document their own progress from their own perspectives—and we believe that teachers should spend the bulk of the time and energy they devote to assessment on approaches such as those we profile here: observation, conferences and interviews, analysis of student work samples, presentations and performances, IEP checklists, and portfolios.

Observation

Although observation is more commonly used in elementary grades than in middle or high schools, teachers of all age groups report its usefulness in gathering data about how their students read, write, listen, and speak in meaningful contexts (Atwell, 1998; Henry, 1995; Hindley, 1996). Often called *kidwatching*—a term coined by literacy researcher Yetta Goodman in 1978—observation can be structured in a variety of ways, ranging from a few minutes of spontaneous note-taking on a sticky note to the systematic completion of a checklist addressing a range of previously taught literacy skills and strategies. Possible contexts for observation include the following:

- Students' interactions with literacy materials (e.g., books, writing supplies)

- Students' interactions with peers during literacy activities (e.g., literature circles)

- Students' interactions with assistive technology including computers and software programs

- Students' responses to whole-group literacy activities (e.g., teacher read aloud)

- Students' literacy-related choices, behaviors, and interactions during free time or down time

One of the strengths of observation as an assessment approach is that it often suggests directions for future instruction that can be implemented immediately. For example, we know a third grader with Asperger syndrome whose teacher and principal repeatedly observed making intricate, detailed sketches of superheroes during transitional times in the classroom. His focus on his drawings appeared to increase during stressful times at home, such as when his mother was ill. This observational data about his engagement in his drawing was useful in two ways: 1) it cued the adults in the school community to provide extra emotional support for him at these times, and 2) it suggested that his reluctance to write might be addressed by encouraging him to sequence a series of drawings about one superhero, caption them with written text, and provide speech bubbles for dialogue. Without carefully attending to how he was using noninstructional time, however, these insights would have been lost.

The previous example illustrates the value of open-ended observations, but there is also much to be learned from observations targeted at specific literacy strategies or skills. Running records and miscue analysis are specialized methods of literacy observation that focus on recording the dimensions of students' oral reading. Although there are some differences in how each is performed (e.g., running records typically document students' in-the-moment reading of a text on a separate sheet of paper, whereas miscue analysis is often undertaken with an audiotaped reading), both approaches rest on a common set of assumptions about reading and assessment, most specifically that students' errors are windows on their processing and that identification of patterns in their errors and self-corrections can suggest next steps for instruction. Both provide information that can be used to determine students' reading levels, strategy use, and degree of reading fluency.

It is beyond the scope of this text to provide you with detailed procedures for carrying out these kinds of observations, but the Recommended Resources at the end of this chapter will guide you in where to acquaint yourself with these details quickly. Kelly, who (unfortunately) did not assess oral reading very often while teaching secondary English, taught herself in graduate school to do a serviceable running record during 2 weeks spent as a visitor in a first-grade classroom. We can only imagine how much more easily you might do so in your own teaching context.

Because students with autism may experience struggles with communication, sensory, learning, and movement differences that manifest themselves in ways not apparent to the eye, it is important for teachers to be cautious about how they construe literacy-focused observational data. Whenever possible, we suggest the use of videotapes as a way to share information about a student with autism with several members of a team. When video is used collaboratively, with teachers sharing multiple perspectives about the same data, it is less likely that a student's behavior will be misinterpreted. One teacher observing a child, for instance, might assume that when he pages through a book very quickly, it means he is "fidgeting" or "stimming" with it, rather than reading. Another teacher or family member who knows him better might be able to point out that this student always pages quickly through books the first dozen or so times he "reads" them and that after he feels acquainted with the layout of the pages, he feels ready to examine the book in a more systematic way.

Beth Kephart, the mother of a child with the label of pervasive developmental disorder (PDD), shares another example of how an uninformed observation can be as misleading as any other type of assessment. When Kephart took her son, Jeremy, for a visit to the preschool where she hoped to enroll him, the principal followed him around the school with a clipboard, making marks each time Jeremy struggled. Meanwhile, Kephart could only look on anxiously, as she documented in this excerpt from a memoir:

> Jeremy tries—valiantly—to go along with the morning routine. He sits at the computer beside another boy, then attempts to take on the software himself. It's new to him. He fails, gets frustrated. The principal, watching from the corner of the room, strikes a check across her clipboard, and we're asked to move on and join the children in another room who are convening for a snack. There's only one slight problem with the principal's worthy plan—all but Jeremy have special, placarded chairs. When the principal asks Jeremy if he wants something to drink, he circles the room looking for space at the table, offers no answer, returns to me, hurt and teary-eyed. Another check and we move on. (1998, p. 164)

Kephart noted that her anxiety was heightened when Jeremy was asked to engage in the common preschool activity, "circle time." The only problem, of course, was that Jeremy was the only one who did not know the rituals; he was unfamiliar with the songs, the accompanying motions, the chants, and the games the other children—who participated in these activities daily—engaged in with ease:

> In the circles Jeremy sits and stares. He watches with magnificent patience and I am immensely proud, until the principal asks him if he wants to be the farmer in the dell, and pulls him to the center of the room. *What's a dell?* his eyes seem to be imploring, and what can he possibly do if he doesn't know the answer and the principal's not saying and the other children giggle until Jeremy finally sits down? Another mark on the despicable clipboard, and I throw a spear of hatred across the room. (1998, p. 165)

Although few teachers will be able to develop the intimate knowledge of an individual learner that a parent has, Kephart's story reminds us of the importance of contextualizing one's kidwatching within an ongoing relationship with the student. Consequently, teachers who use observation as a method of assessing literacy learning for students with autism should keep the following guidelines in mind:

- Make judgments based on patterns in the data over time because notes from a single incident may not accurately reflect what learners with autism know and can do.

- Triangulate your observational data with other sources of information such as interviews and student work samples.

- Alternate observing with a checklist to guide you with open-ended observations where you simply take running notes. The former allows you to target desired learning objectives, whereas the latter will allow you to notice new behaviors that you might otherwise overlook.

- Invite others who know the learner (e.g., a parent, another teacher, an occupational therapist) to make observations during a literacy activity and share their data with you, especially during activities such as a whole-class discussion or demonstration when you are otherwise engaged.

Conferences and Interviews

Conferences and interviews are a natural complement to observations as an informal assessment approach, and they, too, are frequently used by teachers with a constructivist, student-centered philosophy of literacy instruction (Anderson, 2000; Atwell, 1998; Hindley, 1996). In Chapter 3, we discussed the importance of eliciting students' perspectives on their reading, writing, and learning as a way of inviting them into the classroom community and getting to know them as people. Here, we consider how to use those same methods to determine what kinds of student learning have taken place, as well as to determine the next steps for instruction.

The Burke reading inventory (Goodman, Watson, & Burke, 1987) is one of the best-known interview protocols for getting a sense of how students conceptualize reading. It includes questions such as the following:

- When you are reading and come to something that you don't know, what do you do?

- Who's a good reader that you know?

- What makes him or her a good reader?

- How did you learn to read?

- If you knew that someone was having difficulty in reading, how would you help them?

Wilde (1992) adapted some of the questions for spelling (e.g., "How did you learn to spell?"), and the same framework could be used for writing, though we are not familiar with a published study that has done so. In asking these kinds of questions with a wide range of learners (including once, in Kelly's case, to all students in a K–5 elementary school), we found that the most illuminating items are often not those that ask students to talk about their own processes but rather those that ask them to identify someone else who is proficient at some aspect of literacy, and to explain their choice. When we hear that a first grader thinks her mom is a good speller because she "never makes a mistake" or that her dad is a good reader because he "says the words really, really fast," we know what work we have to do in deepening students' perceptions of what it means to be proficient in literacy. In such instances, a one-to-one interview or conference allows us access to students' ideas as well as a natural opportunity to extend and clarify those ideas together.

In addition to structured protocols like the Burke, teachers often use questioning within individual conferences to assess students' comprehension of a text they are reading or have read. Sometimes teachers ask their own questions; other times, they ask those that come from published materials such as a commercial reading series or worksheets from the Internet. Whereas some learners with autism may relish answering comprehension-focused questions due to their predictability and familiarity, others struggle with them. For instance, some students wonder why they are being asked questions to which their teachers already know the answers, and they balk at participating in what appears to be an inauthentic activity. Some students with this profile may be more willing to answer comprehension-focused questions in a conference setting if they are simply given a detailed explanation about why you have chosen to engage in such an activity (Mont, 2001). Others may not be as easily redirected and therefore might prefer to be asked genuine questions about what they've read by someone like a parent, peer, or principal who does not already know the answers.

Some students with autism spectrum labels are tripped up not by the nature of the questions but rather by the intimacy of the one-to-one conference or interview approach. For them, it may be helpful to find ways of interacting that look and feel more indirect. For instance, one student we know found it more comfortable to answer questions about her favorite book when the teacher interviewed her as a famous talk-show host and gave her a microphone to use during the "show." Another young student used an alligator puppet when he needed to answer teacher questions becaues he could participate in his lessons more easily when "Felix" was responsible for the answers. Other students respond favorably when their teachers ask questions in a funny voice or foreign accent or even sing them (Newport, 2001; Robinson, 1999; Williams, 1996). Group conferences including trusted peers or e-mail conversations (even when you're sitting at computers side by side) are other ways that you can make these exchanges a bit less direct. We urge you to vary your approach and gather systematic data about how each option works if you sense that students are not completely comfortable with common methods of classroom interaction.

Although we encourage you to use interviews and conferences with students themselves whenever possible, you should be aware that interviews of other team members may also be necessary to gather the most reliable and extensive information possible, especially when a student cannot share information for himself (Downing, 2005). Most individuals with significant disabilities have unusual ways of demonstrating their interest and abilities in literacy. Sometimes it is only in talking with those who know the learner best that teachers can get information about what a student understands and can do. For instance, Darren, a student Paula observed as part of a research project, had little formal communication and was seen by some as a young man with behavior challenges. One behavior Darren's team had to address was his constant self-abuse, which included biting his own wrists and hands whenever he rode the city bus on the way to his job at a fast food restaurant. Darren's team quickly realized that this behavior only appeared on the bus when Darren was not with his teacher, Ms. Curran. As an attempt to solve the problem or at least gather more information, Ms. Curran volunteered to ride the bus to observe Darren with Ms. Weaver, a classroom paraprofessional who also sometimes rode the bus with Darren. Ms. Curran noticed that the biting behaviors seemed to begin right after the two took seats on the bus and continued until they arrived at the restaurant, despite Ms. Weaver's attempts to distract Darren or discourage the behavior. When Ms. Weaver asked for recommendations at the end of the ride, Ms. Curran shared that she always used the time on the bus to share *USA Today* with Darren. They read it cover to cover, and occasionally Ms. Curran shared her views on the articles. While neither woman knew if this was the missing piece to the puzzle, Ms. Weaver thought it was worth a try and bought a paper for the next trip. During this ride, Darren sat quietly with his eyes on the paper and appeared more relaxed than Ms. Weaver had ever seen him. Both educators were amazed. Ms. Curran was struck by how a simple ritual created for socializing could be so powerful, and Ms. Weaver was stunned by how a fairly severe behavior could subside with a literacy intervention! When the story was shared with Darren's mother, she exclaimed, "Well, of course! Darren has to have his morning news."

Following this incident, the team decided to interview everyone working with Darren, including his family members, his therapists, his social worker, and his brother, to get information about what types of interests, strengths, knowledge, needs, and struggles he might have so that the team could help him best. Through this process they learned what types of materials he was drawn to (magazines, newspapers, and telephone books) and a handful of different ways he demonstrated his literacy-related abilities including pacing back and forth in front of the magazine rack at his grandmother's house until she picked up a copy of *Time* and read it to him.

Analysis of Student Work Samples

Analysis of student work samples has been a primary method of informal assessment of literacy development for many years, particularly in the area of writing. Teachers often review student work using *rubrics*, a term used to describe scoring guides that "elaborate the characteristics of written responses at various levels of competency" (Salinger, 2002, p. 690), to help students focus on particular aspects of the task. As definitions of literacy have expanded (see Chapter 2), teachers' analysis of student work has extended from traditional academic genres such as the essay to multimedia forms such as PowerPoint presentations (Perry, 2003) and three-dimensional visual art (Kist, 2002). In all of these cases, the opportunity to look closely at artifacts of student learning helps teachers see individual students' progress toward mastery of key literacy skills and strategies as well as identify learning trends across groups and classes that can be used to guide subsequent instruction.

In addition, analysis of student work has emerged in recent years as a popular professional development approach, with groups of teachers collaborating to examine their beliefs about teaching and learning; develop community standards for excellence; and explore the links among teaching, learning, and assessment in today's classrooms (Fisher & Johnson, 2006; Krebs, 2005; Langer, Colton, & Goff, 2003). Where students with autism spectrum labels are concerned, such analysis can be helpful for two reasons. First, when the analysis is collaborative, including insights from more than just a single teacher, it increases the chances of students' performance being interpreted in the most complex ways possible. Second, teachers who participate in analysis of work by students with autism but who don't currently have a student with autism in their classes can be sensitized to the challenges associated with assessment for these learners and be better prepared for the day when they *do* have students with that profile in their care.

One common framework for analyzing student work is 6 Plus 1 Traits, an approach to assessing writing popularized by the Northwest Educational Regional Laboratory (http://www.thetraits.org). The catalyst for the framework was the grassroots effort of a group of teachers from Oregon who scored and discussed hundreds of papers by third- through twelfth-grade students in the early 1980s (Spandel, 2001). Today, 6 Plus 1 includes the following criteria that most composition experts see as central to good writing:

- *Ideas* (the content of the writing, including the degree to which the writer develops his or her main ideas with relevant supporting details)

- *Organization* (the degree to which the paper is structured and sequenced appropriately)

- *Voice* (the degree to which the writer has put his or her personal "stamp" on the page)

- *Word Choice* (the precision and appropriateness of the writer's language selections)

- *Sentence Fluency* (the clarity, variety, and flow of individual sentences)

- *Conventions* (the degree to which the writer controls such aspects of language as punctuation, spelling, grammar and usage, etc.)

- *Presentation* (the appropriateness and appeal of the format given the writer's purpose and audience).

Teachers who use the framework to evaluate writing typically give students a score between 1 and 5, with *1* representing the least effective and *5* the most, for each of the categories just mentioned (see a sample rubric at http://www.nwrel .org/assessment/pdfRubrics/6plus1traits.PDF). Some teachers apply the categories generically to different types of texts, whereas others add language to their rubrics to make each more specific to the genre or task being assessed. One of the reasons we believe that this framework has been so popular in K–12 schools is that the categories have a good deal in common with the criteria used by many state education departments to assess on-demand writing in the kind of grade-level examinations we discussed in the previous section on formal literacy assessments. Considerable evidence, including some gathered by the Department of Education in Maine, where Kelly taught, suggests that students who regularly evaluate their own writing with criteria such as these tend to do better on state examinations than students who do not. Although we see writing assessment as concerned with numerous agendas, not just preparing students for tests, we find these data compelling, especially because they point to the importance of students' involvement in the evaluation process.

Whereas analysis of student work with a rubric can be beneficial, it is also helpful to examine student samples in other ways. For example, during a study of spelling instruction conducted with the members of a schoolwide inquiry group (Chandler & The Mapleton Teacher-Research Group, 1999), Kelly discovered the power of combining the conference and interview approach detailed in the previous section with analysis of students' written or artistic products. Interested in the growth she saw in spelling accuracy between one fifth grader's first draft of a letter to a classroom guest and an edited draft in which all seven misspellings had been self-corrected, Kelly asked Christina, the writer, to discuss her spelling strategies in a brief interview. Kelly documented the explanations Christina gave for each of her self-corrections right on Christina's piece of writing, making the document a rich source of information about Christina's thought process about spelling, not just what she wrote on the page. Any of the following categories of information might be helpful to note in the margins of student work or on Post-its attached to those samples:

- Observations of what the student said or did while producing the piece of work

- Observations of any resources the student consulted to create the piece of work

- Impressions of how this piece of work compares or contrasts with an earlier draft of the same piece or a similar task

- Notes about the degree of assistance received from peers, teachers, or paraprofessionals (this can be especially helpful information with students who struggle to write independently)

- Notes to yourself about instructional support the student might benefit from next, either in revising the piece of work or in tackling similar tasks in the future

We think that a similar approach to documentation could be used profitably when assessing work samples by students with autism because these students may not always be able to show us what they know, how they know it, or why they do what they do when we assess in only one way. A perfect example of this complexity is shared by Stephen Shore, a man with autism who felt dismissed as a child by a teacher who did not take the time to learn about his written work before judging it to be inappropriate:

> In second grade, for a class assignment, I wrote a story about some kittens that alternated between existing as little cats and puppies. In fact they were so much in demand that they fetched 47,000 each; or the price of a house at the time. The ideas for this story were spun out of my current life events. Cats were a special interest at that time. One of my family's many cats had recently given birth to five kittens, we had acquired a puppy, and our house was on the market for the same price as these mythical felines sold for. My teacher discounted the assignment as being babyish. However, if she had asked me where my ideas for the paper had come from, perhaps she would have been more understanding and helpful in getting me through the writing assignment. (2003, pp. 74–75)

Presentations and Performances

Presentations and performances are among the best ways for students to demonstrate their ability to apply and synthesize information they have learned from reading, viewing, and listening to a diverse range of texts. They can be supported by student writing of various types, including notes, outlines, and scripts. Most important, perhaps, they can directly assess students' communication skills, including their facility with oral language as well as their ability to use nonverbal forms of representation such as gesture, costume, and visuals to support a message. Presentations and performances can range in duration, degree of preparation, and scale from a spontaneous skit illustrating a scene from a novel to a classwide set of oral presentations for an audience that includes family and community members.

Exhibitions are a specialized kind of performance common in schools associated with the Coalition of Essential Schools (CES), a reform network of American secondary schools that includes the following among the ten Common Principles to which its member schools adhere:

The school should demonstrate non-discriminatory and inclusive policies, practices, and pedagogies. It should model democratic practices that involve all who are directly affected by the school. The school should honor diversity and build on the strengths of its communities, deliberately and explicitly challenging all forms of inequity. (CES, 2007, n.p.)

Ted Sizer, the Coalition's founder, chose the term *exhibition* to describe integrative, culminating assessments that reflect the complexity of student learning over a given period because he wanted to hearken back to public demonstrations that students in both college and K–12 settings made in front of their communities in the 18th and 19th centuries (McDonald, 1991; Sizer, 1992). Although exhibitions do not have to be exclusively oral (some of the best examples in Sizer's book and related CES publications include the creation of written or visual texts), they often do have a presentational component. In her book on inclusive approaches to secondary schooling, Jorgensen (1998) provides numerous examples of exhibitions like the following that accommodate and capitalize on learners' heterogeneity:

- A group presentation to a hypothetical advisory board about the creation of a transportation network to link African countries and spur their economic development

- An oral reading of a story about a student-created hero, using characteristics of an epic learned while studying Homer's *Odyssey*

- The creation of a one-act play or videotape about the life processes of single-cell organisms using metaphors and analogies

- A presentation on a career requiring math and science applications, based on an interview with a professional in that field

Each of these examples requires students to learn new content and communicate in important academic genres that would be important for literacy educators to assess.

We, like Jorgensen, believe that teachers can find ways for all learners, including those with unreliable verbal communication, to participate meaningfully in complex, authentic learning activities like these. It's important to note, however, that not all learners will feel at ease in front of a group. Jerry Newport, a man with Asperger syndrome, shared that the first time he had to walk in front of his class to make an oral presentation, he felt sick. His knees were shaking so severely that he felt he would collapse, and his voice instantly turned high and squeaky. As he remembered it,

> When I sat down I was humiliated and embarrassed. I knew I'd made a terrible mistake to take this class, but I refused to give in to my fear. The second speech was no better. When it was over, the teacher told me that I had to stop clutching my arms when I spoke, that I had to relax. I looked at my arms and saw that they were covered with deep scratches. (2001, p. 226)

Other people with autism report greater confidence in their literacy abilities when given opportunities to perform, especially when they can use a different persona than their own. We know one student named Kyle, for instance, who was never more fluent in his reading than when he was handed a script. He delighted in being in the spotlight, if only for a few moments in front of 20 classmates. He shared that performing as someone else was much easier than speaking from his own perspective because the characters he played were more predictable and, therefore, more comforting than scenes from real life.

Sometimes students who initially balk at oral presentations and other performances discover new strengths in themselves, as was the case for Dan, a young man with autism who was a student in one of Kelly's inclusive 10th-grade English classes. An interdisciplinary project co-planned with Kelly's social studies and resource teammates required students to select and research a historical figure from the period prior to the American Civil War and then to team up with a classmate to script an imaginary dialogue between their characters on the issues of the time. Although Dan was nervous about the project, Kelly and her colleague who taught special education were able to coax him into playing Henry David Thoreau, whom he admired and whose cabin on Walden Pond he had visited during a team field trip. The conversation he had in character with a classmate playing abolitionist John Brown was ultimately successful, as is shown by the narrative assessment that appears in Figure 4.2.

Given the differences in comfort level with public presentation, as well as communication difficulties that learners with autism spectrum labels may exhibit, you will want to think carefully about how you use presentations and exhibitions as literacy assessment tools. Some students will need more rehearsal than others; some will need adjustments in group size for both their collaborators and their audience; and some will need extra help in developing tools such as note cards, picture cues, posters, or other memory aids to help them stay focused.

Another strategy that might be used to encourage successful exhibitions is to allow students to use material that is familiar to them or even topics that are connected to their areas of passion or special interest. For instance, Smith, a young man with Asperger syndrome who was usually anxious about talking in front of other students, was very excited about sharing his learning when he was able to present on gorillas, his area of expertise. Although Smith already knew a lot about gorillas before the exhibition, his teachers were able to use the experience to increase his literacy skills in the areas of composition, organization, and oral presentation.

You will also want to consider ways to capture the data from performances and presentations so that you can document individual student learning over time

---

Assignment from Section 3: Henry David Thoreau Meets John Brown

Dear Dan and Billy:

Your conversation was wonderfully scripted—funny and often exactly what I imagine the two might have said to each other. I liked your scenario and thought it set the scene well. You were fairly calm and cool in front of the class—an experience I know you weren't looking forward to—and your classmates seemed very engaged in your presentation. Several of them mentioned in their peer feedback that they liked the humor. You might have touched a bit more on historical events—you were pretty focused on the two characters' own experiences—and used the primary sources a bit more. Nonetheless, a good job, and you two made a fine team.

Grade: B+

Figure 4.2.   Sample teacher narrative assessing a student presentation.

as well as consider patterns across a group or class of students. The best way from our perspective to do this is to videotape or audiotape the performances because these methods allow you to observe the performance more than once as well as to invite others to help you interpret it. It can also be helpful to keep a running tally or create a simple rubric of behaviors or skills that you see as important to track, such as the use of notes to guide one's talk, the ability to answer questions from audience members, and the avoidance of interruptions when others are speaking. (Figure 4.3 summarizes one teacher's coding system for tracking participation during a whole-class role-playing exercise.) Other data about presentations and performances can come from peer evaluations (we often ask our students to provide anonymous written comments about peers' performance that we quote or summarize in our own feedback) and self-evaluations (when students are asked to comment on the quality of their presentations, they often come to new insights about their own work that are useful to them as well as to their teachers). And videotape can have another benefit in that students with autism may find the experience not only a fun assessment but also helpful for new learning (Delano, 2007). *Video modeling,* or the viewing of oneself or of competent others engaged in target behaviors or activities, can be effective for teaching students with autism a range of skills; therefore, taped presentations might be shown to the learner not only as a review of content but also as a way to give that individual confidence for future exhibitions.

Name	Contributions	Tally
Oliver	? V+ ? ? ? ? ? ? ! D V V+ V+	13
Eileen	? ? ? V V ? V	7
Julia	D V D V(cut off)!	5
Dimitri	D V V ? ? V V !	8
Georgia	? D	2
Mari	D V V V	4
Philip	D ! V	3
Elena	D V+ V D V D V	7
Sam	? D ? V	4
Colin	? D V ! ? ? ? V V ? V	11
Garrett	D V V	3
Lexi	D V D V V V+ V ! V ?	10
Jack	? V+ ?	3
Liam	! ! ! V V ?	6
Ella	V V D ? ?	5

Figure 4.3. Sample tracking system for student participation in whole-class role play. (*Key:* ? = questions another participant; V+ = complete, thoughtful contribution; V = basic contribution; ! = quick interjection)

Individualized Education Program Checklists

Occasionally, you may want to assess a skill or ability that is unique to an individual learner and collect systematic, ongoing data regarding this skill. In these instances, it is sometimes most efficient and effective to gather information by creating a data form or checklist that addresses the personal goals targeted for the learner with autism (see Figure 4.4 for an example).

Although checklists can be developed around any set of goals, objectives, or standards, these tools are particularly useful when assessing progress on a learner's IEP. Forms can be tailor-made for each student and for different parts of the instructional day, and they can give teachers ongoing information pertaining to student progress and accomplishments.

Because some students with autism will have goals and objectives that are different from those identified for peers, IEP checklists can be helpful to remind both special and general educators of the skills and competencies that must be integrated into daily lessons. Often, general educators feel frustrated when they cannot see the progress of a learner with a disability. This is most likely to occur when that student's growth is very gradual. For instance, Ms. Kader, a second grade teacher, questioned the success of Amir, a nonverbal student with autism, in her classroom. He did not use materials in the way other students did, he did not demonstrate attention in the way other people did, and he did not interact in class discussions in typical ways. After viewing an IEP checklist complete with 2 weeks of data, however, she could clearly see that Amir was making gains in print access, use of augmentative communication, and identification of key vocabulary words.

Checklists allow teachers to maintain awareness of a learner's goals and be mindful of addressing them often, if not daily. When planning instruction, educators can review goals and progress and make adjustments in teaching, supports, or materials based on the data. This assessment, therefore, can be used both as an evaluation and as a planning tool for next steps and future objectives.

Portfolios

Portfolios are "a purposeful selection by a student of work that represent the student's pursuits, explorations, and projects as a way of evidencing the student's progress, effort, achievements, and growth" (Tierney & Clark, 2002, p. 443). We present portfolios as the final approach of this section because they are typically designed as culminating assessments that can include samples and artifacts from all of the other informal tools we've already reviewed. In our view, portfolios are a promising assessment approach for students with autism spectrum labels. According to Clagett, portfolios

> Allow for and reward the diversity that we find in our classrooms. Portfolios, with their breadth of presentation methods, permit us as teachers to validate all kinds of learning.... They encourage varying modes of expression—the written, the oral, the graphic, the three-dimensional model, the video, the audio. They allow students with differing learning styles to show what they've learned and how they've learned it. They also allow students to validate their own primary way of knowing, and to gain expanded awareness and understanding of other ways of knowing. (1996, p. 110)

Student _____Rhada_____

Assessed by: _____Mr. Fogerty_____

Mark a (+) if Rhada performs without support. If Rhada does not perform the skills, give her a tactile cue (e.g., tap the book) and wait to see if she will perform the skill. If she performs the skill after she is given the cue, mark (+C).

IEP objective	Dates					Cues offered (if any)
	4/14	4/15	4/16	4/17	4/18	
Given a choice of three books, Rhada will 1) choose a book and 2) hand it to a peer partner to read aloud.	1) 2)	1) 2)	1) 2)	1) 2)	1) 2)	
Upon opening a book to the first page, Rhada will hit her switch to "read" the page independently.						
When listening to a book on tape, Rhada will independently turn the pages after the tone sounds.						

Comments:

_____

_____

_____

Figure 4.4.   Sample individualized education program (IEP) checklist.

More than any other assessment tool we've profiled so far, they can be used in ways that are consistent with the multiple literacies perspective described in Chapter 2.

How portfolios are organized, however, makes a big difference in what they can accomplish, both for student learners and for teacher evaluators. According to Clagett (1996), with portfolios "purpose governs product" (p. 111). Her work suggests that there are three main kinds of portfolios:

- The *showcase* portfolio, which includes only a student's best work

- The process or *formative* portfolio, which includes artifacts showing a student's growth and change as a learner over time

- The *standards-based* portfolio, which includes artifacts meant to show a student's progress in meeting pre-specified learning objectives.

We see a place for all three kinds of portfolios in the literacy classroom, as well as for portfolios that blend elements of more than one kind. What's important from our perspective is that 1) the purpose or purposes be explicit to both teachers and students, so that they can make choices accordingly, and 2) student portfolio-keepers be actively involved in all three of the key verbs of the portfolio development process: *collecting* a wide range of artifacts; *selecting* key artifacts from that range to include in the portfolio given those purposes; and *reflecting* on those choices with oral, written, and/or graphic representations (Tierney, Carter, & Desai, 1991).

Depending on their purposes, literacy portfolios can have different components. Most include the following, at minimum: a preface or introduction by the student explaining his or her process in compiling the portfolio, a table of contents, selections of work, reflection or entry slips accompanying and explaining those selections, and a final self-evaluation or concluding note to the audience observing the collection (Clagett, 1996). Selections of work, what many consider to be the heart of the portfolio, might include but are not limited to items such as the following:

- A list of books and other texts the student can read/has read/shows interest in

- A list of videos he or she has viewed/shown interest in

- Photographs, images, or pictures the individual responds to

- Photographs, drawings, or graphics he or she has created herself

- Photographs of the student engaged in literacy-related activities, especially if his or her participation looks different than that of neurotypical learners

- Descriptions authored by a parent or someone else who knows the student well about how he or she interacts with text or other literacy materials (e.g., "She likes to page through books related to travel and often picks up tourism brochures when we are at restaurants")

- Samples of writing produced independently and/or with support

- Multimedia files such as PowerPoint presentations, web sites, or video created by the individual, either independently or with support

- Audiotapes of the individual reading, speaking, or singing

- Videotapes of the individual engaged in literacy experiences (e.g., listening to a story, watching a play, using a communication device)

Although we support portfolio assessment for students with autism (as we do for all learners), it's important to note that there can be some pitfalls associated with this assessment approach for students on the spectrum, especially if they lack reliable communication. Even though portfolios can (and in our view, should) be multimodal, much of the professional literature about them for teachers privileges print literacy, assuming that students will be able to produce a good deal of written language to generate a large range of artifacts from which to choose. For a student like Michael, the young man with autism we profiled at the beginning of Chapter 2, writing, although important, was slow and laborious. The volume of writing he could produce in, say, a 9-week marking period would of necessity be significantly less than that of peers who could type more quickly, with or without assistance. For this reason, we urge you to think carefully about how many artifacts you will require, as well as what modes you will encourage, for students' portfolio artifacts. In fact, we advise differentiating portfolio requirements for individual students explicitly in much the same way we advocated for differentiating literacy center expectations in Chapter 3.

CONCLUDING THOUGHTS

The assessment choices we make as literacy educators are not neutral. Assessments can obscure as much as they illuminate and shape a learner's profile as much as they reveal it. This is perhaps more obvious with standardized assessments than it is with less formal measures, but even the latter can, in the words of assessment expert Dennie Palmer Wolf, "offer students lessons that are destructive to their capacity to thoughtfully judge their own work" (1989, p. 36). One of our primary goals in assessing and evaluating students' literacy learning should be to make ourselves obsolete at some point: to give learners the necessary tools and habits of mind for ongoing assessment of their own literacy so that they can become more sophisticated thinkers and communicators in their lives beyond school.

Although we certainly believe that this goal might be more easily reached if students with autism were formally tested less often and in less intrusive ways than they currently are, this does not mean that formal assessments have no place in an overall assessment schema. Our colleague Marilyn Chadwick, a frequent consultant to families of children with autism, reminded us as we were writing this chapter that crucial decisions regarding assessment are often not about which measure to choose, but when and how to use it and how to combine that new information with what is already known. She advocates using informal literacy assessments to get to know students well enough to make informed choices about adopting and adapting more formal measures. We see this as incredibly helpful advice.

One of our favorite assessment-related stories illustrates how this process might work. A few months ago, Paula met a mother, Shanette, who shared that her son Brian, who has a label of PDD, did not respond to learning the letters in typical ways, did not play with the alphabet-inspired toys that littered the recreation room at his house, and did not seem interested in his brother's many attempts to sing him the ABC song. He did, however, love the colorful rug at his kindergarten that was embellished with numbers and the alphabet. His mother noted that he often jumped around the rug before he left for the day, which she thought was peculiar. One day when she was paying closer attention, she noticed that his lively feet held a message; as she watched him leap from letter to letter, she saw his friendly and nearly perfectly spelled message: "g-o-o-d-b-i-e-k-i-d-s."

The story of what we have come to call "the bouncing speller" is a perfect example of a literacy demonstration that would probably not be caught by any other type of assessment other than careful observation by someone who knows the learner well. It's the kind of literacy-related event that we would ask a parent like

Shanette to document through photographs and/or a short note for inclusion in a student's literacy portfolio. If Brian's kindergarten teacher were savvy and proactive, she would likely observe him in class for other behavior suggesting knowledge about letters, sounds, and spelling patterns. She might eventually decide to administer a more formal assessment of his skills in these areas, keeping in mind that a lack of performance on such a measure might not mean a lack of knowledge on Brian's part but could instead indicate the need for a different tool. In this case, the more formal measure would not be intended as the kind of unequivocal "proof" of competence that Lucy Blackman's teacher appears to have sought but rather as another lens through which to view Brian's literacy learning, in hopes of planning the most responsive and appropriate instructional program for him. We turn to that topic—instructional approaches for teaching reading, as well as teaching writing and other forms of representation—in the next two chapters.

Recommended Resources

Miscue Analysis and Running Records

Clay, M.M. (2000). *Running records for classroom teachers.* Portsmouth, NH: Heinemann.

Davenport, R. (2002). *Miscues not mistakes: Reading assessment in the classroom.* Portsmouth, NH: Heinemann.

Goodman, Y., Watson, D., & Burke, C. (1987). *Reading miscue inventory.* Katonah, NY: Richard C. Owen.

Johnston, P. (2000). *Running records: A self-tutoring guide.* Portland, ME: Stenhouse Publishers.

Shea, M. (2006). *Where's the glitch? Running records with older readers, grades 5–8.* Portsmouth, NH: Heinemann.

Focus on Reading

In his memoir, Luke Jackson, an adolescent boy with Asperger syndrome, described books as his "doorways into other worlds." He explained, "They cheer me when I am upset; they make me laugh, cry, and quake with fright. A good book should keep someone entranced right till the end" (2002, p. 118). By his own admission, however, Luke wasn't always so entranced with reading. During his first few years of school, he struggled mightily with this area of the curriculum. Then, unexpectedly, he began to read as if "someone had switched a light on" in his head:

> [When I was younger] the school gave me all sorts of extra help with reading and I couldn't even remember one letter from the other. However much anyone taught me, it just would not sink in. I had an assessment by an educational psychologist when I was seven years and eight months old and my reading age was not assessable because I just couldn't read anything. The next day Mum got a phone call from the school asking her to come in and see them. She told me that she was very worried as that usually meant that I was having a massive tantrum, but when she got there the teacher had something that they just couldn't wait to tell. I had picked up a copy of *A Midsummer Night's Dream*, which the teacher was using to show how plays are written. It seems that I opened the book and began to read it fluently. How weird is that? (2002, p. 117)

Shortly afterward, Jackson's reading score, determined to be "not assessable" before this incident, was found to be 14 years and 10 months. He has been an avid reader ever since that time.

We've seen some of the same themes from Luke's story in accounts and observations of other learners with autism, including difficulties with phonics-based instruction, poor performance on standardized reading tests, and an unusual spike of progress not clearly attributable to specific teaching methods. We share more about each of these ideas later in the chapter. It's important to remember as you move through this chapter, though, that individuals with autism differ widely in their skills, experience, and interest in reading. In contrast to Luke Jackson, some flourish with intensive phonics instruction. Some can decode text well orally but struggle with comprehension and engagement. Others' communication differences make it difficult for their teachers to know if they can read at all, and if so, how well. Because of this diversity, it is necessary to assess readers with autism carefully, using multiple sources of data over time, and to develop sensitive instructional plans tailored to their needs.

This chapter is organized around what we perceive as the key components of reading—phonemic awareness, phonics, word recognition, fluency, comprehension, and vocabulary—that readers need to integrate in order to be successful. Each section that follows defines one of these components with reference to its research base, explains how each might be experienced by learners with autism, and recommends some teaching practices designed to promote greater competence and confidence in that area for these students. We hope that implementation of instructional approaches matched to these learners' profiles will increase the chances that they will experience the success and satisfaction with reading that Luke Jackson reports.

PHONEMIC AWARENESS, PHONICS, AND WORD RECOGNITION

In this section, we review material on elements of the reading process that attend to the smallest components of language: words and the letters and sounds that compose them. Further on in the chapter, we explore subprocesses of reading that are broader in scope, such as fluency and comprehension. But before we do, we think it is important to address the aspects that many people, especially members of the public, see as the building blocks of reading. In putting this section first, we do not mean to suggest that these elements of reading are the most important—or even that they need to be taught before the others can be addressed—but we do recognize that they are likely to be areas of emphasis in literacy instruction for new or inexperienced readers, so it makes sense to talk about them early on.

Members of the National Reading Panel (NRP; NICHD, 2000a), whom we cited in Chapter 2, devoted two sections of their final report to what they called *alphabetics*, a term used to cover two different aspects of literacy, phonemic awareness and phonics. The NRP defines *phonemic awareness* as the ability to focus on and manipulate the smallest units of spoken language—for instance, the ability to recognize that the word *chat* is made up of three phonemes (/ch/, /a/, and /t/) that can be isolated from each other, blended together, or replaced to make new words (e.g., by changing the word's initial sound to make "chat" into "cat"). *Phonics* refers to knowledge of the correspondence between letters such as *c, h, a,* and *t* and the sounds they make, both on their own and in combination with each other (e.g., the letters *c* and *h* make a different sound when they appear together than they do when they appear with other letters). Phonemic awareness and phonics are not synonyms for each other—the first refers to an oral competence and the second deals with skills applied to print—but they are related to each other in that research suggests that children who develop good phonemic awareness often have an easier time cracking the code of print text than those children who do not have good phonemic awareness (Blachman, 2000; NICHD, 2000a).

Knowledge of phonics, in turn, is one of the resources that learners use for *word recognition*, defined by Fox as "the immediate, accurate, and effortless ability to read words in context or in isolation" (2003, p. 678). When readers encounter an unfamiliar word in print, they may sound it out letter by letter—the strategy most often associated with phonics instruction in school—or they may use picture cues or logos to make informed guesses or structural analysis to identify "chunks" of the word that they know (e.g., suffixes such as *-tion* in the word *reaction* or parts of a compound word such as *ball-* in *ballplayer*). However readers choose to attack a word, their goal should be efficiency, because quick and easy word recognition allows them to concentrate on other aspects of reading.

Considering Students with Autism

The NRP (NICHD, 2000a) reviewed research suggesting that training in phonemic awareness helps children learn to read and spell better and that those who received systematic phonics instruction in the early grades comprehended what they read better than those who did not. Although there has been vigorous debate in the literacy community about the implications of these findings for organizing—or worse, mandating—particular kinds of instruction, few within the field question the NRP's basic claim that phonemic awareness and phonics play an important role in reading acquisition for most children. We find the evidence about the value of focused and explicit instruction in these areas to be quite compelling, especially for learners who show early signs of reading problems, and we encourage all teachers with direct or indirect responsibility for literacy to be familiar with this body of research.

At the same time, we're mindful that the vast majority of the research cited by the NRP was conducted with neurotypical learners, not people with disabilities, and nowhere does this gap appear more important than in the areas of phonics and phonemic awareness. Considerable evidence from people with autism spectrum labels (Blackman, 1999; Jackson, 2002; Shore, 2003) and their teachers (Broun, 2004; Mirenda, 2003) suggests that these learners can have difficulties isolating sounds in verbal speech and associating those sounds with symbols. For example, Lucy Blackman reported in her memoir that she liked her phonics lessons because of the candy she received as a reward for successful responses (!) but that the learning didn't stick with her for long: "Somehow my speech memory could not contain the decoding messages for more than six or eight written words. If I learned more, some of the ones I had learnt previously went into limbo" (1999, p. 52). Pat Mirenda, a scholar in special education, shared something similar about problems that learners with autism often have with phonics, although she framed her ideas with language that was more technical than Blackman's. Specifically, she critiqued a "readiness" model of literacy—one requiring students to demonstrate certain "gatekeeper" skills before being introduced to others—that she argued continues to be employed in special education:

> [T]he decontextualized nature of traditional phonics instruction makes it almost impossible for many [students with autism] to demonstrate mastery of the subskills in this area. Students without functional speech who require augmentative and alternative communication (AAC) are at especially high risk for failure in readiness-based literacy programs because of the supposition that reading is impossible in the absence of the ability to sound out words phonetically. For them, the readiness ap-

proach to literacy instruction "only serves to highlight [their] disabilities and emphasize differences in each student's performance from that of the mainstream population" (Ryndak, Morrison, & Sommerstein, 1999, p. 5). Those who prove themselves
unable to master the "necessary" prerequisite skills are thus considered ineligible for
further literacy instruction. (2003, p. 272)

In highlighting the potential issues with alphabetics-focused instruction that
Blackman and Mirenda raised, we do not mean to suggest that all learners with
autism will fail to benefit from thoughtfully planned instruction in phonics and
phonemic awareness. This is simply not true. A good example of success in this
area comes from Temple Grandin, who reported that her mother taught her to
read with 30-minute daily lessons over several months:

> I was still a poor reader at age eight, when my mother tried a new approach. Every after-
> noon after school, I sat with her in the kitchen and she had me sound out the words in a
> book. After I learned the phonetic rules and the sounds, she read a paragraph out loud to
> me. Then I sounded out one or two words. Gradually, she had me read longer and longer
> passages. We read from a real book that was interesting instead of a little kid's beginning
> book. I learned well with phonics, because I understood spoken language. It took me a
> long time to learn to read silently, though. (1995, p. 98)

From our perspective, several aspects of the approach used by Grandin's mother
are worth highlighting. As Temple specifically notes, the two worked from age-
appropriate texts, not from "a little kid's beginning book." This detail is crucial because it illustrates the importance of respecting students' life experiences (versus,
for instance, their chronological age on a standardized test) and their need to learn
in ways that are rich and motivating. Temple's mother also planned the instruction carefully and purposefully; their lessons took place for the same amount of
time each day over a period of months, and she introduced Temple to the rules
and sounds systematically, rather than haphazardly. Grandin, who has shared information about her love of logic and order in other autobiographical writing,
likely thrived on the structure provided both by the new content, which gave her
some strategies to make sense of print, and by the lesson's predictable structure.
Her mother apparently took care to embed the rule-governed phonics work in a
broader context that included modeling and practice of fluent reading of meaningful, continuous texts. All of these factors likely contributed to the success of
these interactions.

Despite having shared Grandin's success story, we remind teachers to pro-
ceed with caution regarding the "when" and "how" of teaching phonics to students with autism. Like Mirenda (2003), we feel strongly that lack of demonstrated facility with phonemic awareness and phonics should not prevent
students with autism from participating in instruction focused on fluency, comprehension, and vocabulary while they master or move beyond the smaller
subprocesses of reading. Instead, attention to alphabetics and word recognition
should be part of a balanced literacy program for these students, with their teachers keeping in mind that some of these approaches may work well for some students while having little or no impact on others. The section that follows includes
our best recommendations for instructional approaches focused on these subprocesses of reading, given what we know about learners with autism.

Instructional Approaches

Given the communication differences profiled in Chapter 1, it is probably no surprise that it can be difficult for some learners with autism to develop and/or demonstrate phonemic awareness. Because many of these students neither produce nor hear speech in the same way that typical learners do, the oral activities meant to promote this competence often make little or no sense to them, especially at first. (This can be true of even those learners with autism whose speech is fairly reliable.) Consequently, the more phonemic awareness training can be incorporated into fun, relaxed classroom routines, preferably with peers without disabilities around to serve as literacy models and collaborative partners in instruction, the greater the chances that students with autism will experience success with such skills as recognizing and producing rhymes, hearing syllables, blending sounds together to create words, and segmenting words into their corresponding sounds.

Rhythm and Movement

Including some physical movement with sound work may be useful for all students, including those with autism. If you are working with young children, you might ask them to clap out the syllables in their own names and in the names of their classmates—first in unison as a class to model the process, and then perhaps with a partner to help reinforce the learning. Later, as the students become more experienced at identifying syllables and coordinating their clapping, they can practice this skill on their own, using words that are less familiar than names.

Similarly, we think that many students with autism will benefit from the multisensory approach of the Say-It-and-Move-It activity included in the Road to the Code program developed by Benita Blachman and her colleagues (Blachman, Ball, Black, & Tangel, 2000). This activity involves having children move a disk or other high-interest object such as a tile or block (or, in the case of Peter, a student with autism who loves padlocks, a key) for each sound they hear in a word. Once all of the sounds have been isolated, the children blend them together to produce the whole word. Although the lessons were designed for students with functional speech, those who communicate in other ways can still participate by moving objects to indicate their understanding of the various sounds said by others or of sounds generated by augmentative communication devices or by observing as peers do so. Often, in these types of exercises, we exclude learners who cannot physically participate. But students who have fine motor problems can certainly observe, hold tokens, and hand tokens to peers in order to participate in Say-It-and-Move-It.

Poems, chants, and songs are also recommended to help learners develop phonemic awareness (Adams, Foorman, Lundberg, & Beeler, 1997; Strickland & Schickendanz, 2004). We think that these musical texts can be particularly good for helping students with autism learn, given that a number of authors on the spectrum, including those with significant communication impairments (Blackman, 1999; Shore, 2003), report that they can sing more easily than they can speak and that learning, in general, is easier when it is paired with music or a rhythm of some kind (Shore, 2003; Waites & Swinbourne, 2001). Musical texts are also meant to be performed multiple times, providing authentic repetition with the rhymes for students who need it, with less risk of boredom or embarrassment than would be associated with the rereading of conventional print texts. For these reasons, we recommend that teachers build songs and chants regularly into their instruction, and, once students are familiar with them, call their attention to particular aspects of the lyrics, including alliteration and syllabication as well as rhyme patterns.

This strategy is appropriate and effective not only for students in the early grades but also for those in secondary classrooms. A geometry teacher whom Paula observed often asked students to stand and chant new vocabulary words (e.g., *parallelogram*, *Pythagorean*) as a way to aid them in learning the words and to increase their ability to recall those words in future lessons. A middle school general music teacher we know asked her students to read Dr. Seuss books to one another to learn what a rhythmic, rhyming text sounds like. She then had them work in groups to create similar books, which they eventually set to music. This lesson was fun and interesting to all students but was especially helpful to Sara, a young woman with autism, who was learning to read and needed help learning rhyming words and word families.

It's possible that your students may take a little while to show progress in the area of phonemic awareness, even if the activities you've planned are appropriate for them. Although many students develop this competence with ease, others will need repeated experience with particular activities before they begin to pay off. You may need to be patient and to celebrate small signs of growth. At the same time, we do not advocate overemphasizing phonemic awareness training for students with autism given the difficulties with oral language we've discussed. We're also aware that some literacy scholars (e.g., Moustafa, 2006) believe that phonemic awareness is best sharpened *in the midst* of print-based experiences, not prior to them. Consequently, we suggest that teachers provide small, focused doses of this kind of training to their students—evaluating its effects continually and remaining open-minded enough to provide more or less of it, depending on how students are responding—while simultaneously providing other kinds of literacy experiences.

Tactile Letter Recognition

Students' ability to use phonics—the relationships between letters and sounds—as a cueing system for reading depends, in no small part, on their ability to recognize those letters. In helping students with autism develop these skills, it is important to remember that these learners may experience print differently from their peers who do not have disabilities. The challenge for most young children without disabilities is to help them pay enough attention to the shapes of the letters so that they can be distinguished from each other; the typical developmental sequence has them paying attention to the "big picture" of reading first (e.g., the meaning carried by illustrations, a predictable rhyme) and then attending to letters on the page later, as they become more experienced as readers (Weaver, 1994). In contrast, students with autism often pay *too much* attention to features of print, including some that may be overlooked or dismissed as irrelevant by people less attuned to sensory input. One of Paula's former students reported that she routinely spent more time formatting her school papers than writing them and that, on more than one occasion, she had spent 2 hours or more just moving the margins and changing accompanying graphics. The challenge in working with a student sharing this profile is to help him or her zero in on features of the print likely intended to convey meaning—in this case, to tell one letter from another—rather than those that few others will see as significant.

A number of people, including parents (e.g., Eastham, 1992), report that tactile approaches can be very useful in helping those with autism labels learn their letters. Teachers might allow students to feel letters cut from sandpaper or drawn with shaving cream or, depending on their fine motor skills, to form the letters themselves from clay or dough. (Of course, different substances will be appealing to different students, given the sensory differences described in Chapter 1.) Alphabet stencils and stickers, especially those with pronounced textures, may also help some students attend to the differences in letters and words.

Alphabet Books

We also recommend providing students with a variety of alphabet books to browse, especially those tied to subjects or areas of specialty or fascinations such as trains, animals, or computers, because the combination of the letters and familiar objects they represent can aid with letter recognition as well as beginning phonics connections (see Recommended Reading at the end of this chapter for a list of alphabet books appropriate for both younger and older readers). If books don't exist on topics of interest, they can be created by a teacher or parent, using words and images of significance to—and perhaps even selected by—the learner. As with phonemic awareness, a combination of experiences requiring the use of more than one sense will help many students develop skills with letter identification.

Again, this is a strategy that can be used in the secondary classroom to support the language learning of all students. One chemistry teacher whom Paula knows has used this technique to acquaint all students with unfamiliar language and concepts. In a unit on acids, the students were charged with creating alphabet books on new concepts introduced in the classroom (e.g., *A* is for acids, *B* is for bases). The products they created were subsequently used as a review for upcoming tests. Although, in this case, the books served as a way to examine content more closely, they also helped students needing help with language—ESL students or students with disabilities, for instance—to learn about letter–sound relationships.

Word and Letter Sorts

Word and letter sorts are another way to promote students' letter identification skills, as well as knowledge of letter–sound correspondences crucial to both reading and spelling. These activities involve students in creating categories, recognizing patterns, and making decisions about certain features of letters or words. Sorting may appeal to learners with autism for a variety of reasons. Some will like the active, physical work of creating piles or categories. Others will enjoy the cognitive challenge of creating groups with something in common. Gunilla Gerland, a woman with autism, reported that she often sorted letters as a child, not as an academic chore but as a chosen play activity:

> I often used to sit on the floor somewhere in our house arranging the alphabet cards I kept in a white plastic bucket. Father had made the cards for Kerstin, cutting them out of cardboard and drawing the letters on them. He was good at this kind of thing, and now I had taken them over from my sister. I used to lay out the cards in patterns or arrange them in various ways, perhaps putting all the Es in one pile and the As in another. I loved those alphabet cards. They were so clean and clear, on white cardboard with red edges. But it

disturbed me that there weren't equal numbers of each kind. I thought there ought to be as many Xs as Ss, so that all the heaps became equally large. And just as many Ys as Es. I didn't know why the letters were in such unequal numbers. (1996, p. 47)

One of the best-known sorting activities is Pat and Jim Cunningham's (1992) Making Words, the phonics-focused component of their popular *Four Blocks* literacy program. During a Making Words session, students are given a number of cards with letters on them. They are then instructed to use the cards to create as many words of two letters, three letters, four letters, and so forth as they can, recording the words on the chalkboard if the activity is done as a whole class or on a sheet of paper if it is done individually or in small groups. The "challenge word" is one that can be created by using all of the designated letters (see Figure 5.1 for a sample set of words with the challenge word *hibernate*). Challenge words are selected on the basis of the opportunities for learning that they will offer particular groups or classes of students. Young or inexperienced readers are thus asked to

---

Challenge word: HIBERNATE

Vowels: *A, E, E, I*

Consonants: *B, H, N, T, R*

2-letter words	**3-letter words**	**4-letter words**
AT	ATE	RATE
AN	EAT	BEET
IN	BET	NEAT
IT	BAT	HEAT
	BIT	BEAT
	HAT	BEAR
	RAT	TEAR
	TAR	HEAR
	HIT	NEAR
	EAR	BRAT
	TIE	BATH
	THE	THAN
		THEN
		THIN
		RAIN
		TREE
		TIER
		BITE

5-letter words	**6-letter words**	**7-letter words**
HEART	HEATER	NEITHER
BATHE	BEATER	BREATHE
TRAIN	BATHER	
TREAT		

Figure 5.1. A sampling of sorted words from Making Words activity. (*Source:* Cunningham & Cunningham [1992].)

work with shorter words (e.g., those with one or two vowels only) or words that yield more familiar patterns and word families (e.g., *-an, -ell, -it*). More proficient readers might work with words yielding blends (e.g., *bl-, fr-, str-*) or vowel teams (e.g., *ay, ea, ou*) when rearranged. In either case, choosing content-area vocabulary such as *hibernate* can give students the chance to review previously learned material or to explore a word from a current area of study.

After students have created all of the possible words from their cards, either on their own or with guidance from the teacher, they are then instructed to sort those words into categories using criteria focused on particular features—for example, "Words that begin with *b* and words that do not begin with *b*," "Words with a short *a* sound and words that do not have a short *a* sound," or "Words with one, two, and three syllables." This kind of sorting gives them valuable experience in thinking through how written language works and provides many practice opportunities for developing phonemic awareness and phonics skills.

Rasinski (1999) pointed out that sorting small letter cards can be difficult for some students, either because they lack dexterity or because the cards can be easily lost, making it impossible to form certain words (we can see this last issue as a potential frustration for students with autism). To address these drawbacks, he proposed a variation of the activity requiring students to write the words they make on a worksheet designed for that purpose—an adaptation that also provides them extra practice with the words. The worksheet is then cut up, either by students themselves or by the teacher, for the word-sorting portion of the activity. Your decision about whether to use cards or a worksheet for students with autism will depend on your assessment of those students' dexterity, need for writing practice, and frustration level. Either way, we think you'll see many students on the spectrum make gains with this approach.

Sight Word Recognition Plus

In Chapter 2, we critiqued the historical overemphasis on sight words in literacy instruction for students with autism, and we remain concerned about this trend. We do recognize, however, that judicious attention to sight words can have big payoffs for readers, including those students with autism who report special strengths in visual learning (Grandin, 1995; Hall, 2001; Mukhopadhyay, 2000). Special education teacher Leslie Todd Broun (2004) reported that her students with autism experience a good deal of success with a visual approach to word recognition and phonics adapted from a model developed by Oelwein (1995) for students with Down syndrome. Although Broun doesn't use this term in her article, we've chosen to call this approach "sight word recognition plus" because she goes beyond the traditional approach to sight words, using them as a launching pad for students' further learning about phonics, sentence structure, and vocabulary.

With this approach, students are introduced to personalized sets of flash cards with words tied to their families, interests, and experiences. Students work with these cards in three stages: Level 1 (matching a word card to the same word on a word grid), Level 2 (selecting a word on request by picking it up or pointing to it), and Level 3 (saying or signing the word, either in response to a teacher's question about what the word is or in a self-initiated fashion). Broun (2004) recommended that the matching and selecting process be repeated at least three times for each word.

After the students have used the match-select-name sequence of activities to become comfortable with between 25 and 50 words, Broun (2004) advocated using these words to begin instruction in sound–symbol correspondence—for instance, to explore the idea that the familiar and recognizable word *Mom* begins with the letter M. In this way, the phonics instruction is put into context for learners, increasing the chances that the learners will be able to use and generalize the information. She also suggests that teachers introduce students to a few high-utility "sentence builders," including words such as *I, see, here,* and *is,* which learners can then combine with their personal words to create phrases and sentences.

We like this approach very much because it ties different pieces of the reading process together including sight word recognition, phonics, and beginning comprehension. It also includes explicit ideas about how to support the participation in reading instruction of students who don't speak—for instance, by teaching them simple signs for the key words that they're learning to read. Like many of the other approaches we've profiled in this section, it is multisensory, combining visual, auditory, kinesthetic, and expressive (digital or spoken) modes of learning. We also like Broun's emphasis on building letter and word skills for the purpose of getting students interested in book reading.

FLUENCY

According to the NRP, fluency is the ability to read "with speed, accuracy, and proper expression" (NICHD, 2000a, p. 31). Although fluency can refer to either silent or oral reading, it tends to be associated with—and assessed most often in the context of—oral reading. Research suggests that fluency is related to comprehension in that readers who don't have to use so much cognitive energy in figuring out how to pronounce individual words can devote more to monitoring the meaning of what they've read (Pinnell, Pikulski, Wixson, Campbell, Gough, & Beatty, 1995; Rasinski, 2003). It's important to note, however, that this relationship is a complex one: It is possible to read fluently without understanding what is read, as many students with and without autism have demonstrated, especially when reading their secondary textbooks. It is also possible, though less common, for learners to understand the meaning of a passage even if it is read in a halting fashion with many errors.

 ### Considering Students with Autism

For students with autism, achieving fluency as a reader can be complicated by a variety of factors. Like all learners, students with autism need to develop automaticity with word recognition and decoding. Where oral reading is concerned, many people on the spectrum also need to overcome problems related to prosody (i.e., the patterns of stress and intonation in a language), which learners who are typically developing do not face. As we discussed previously, the speech of students with autism may be flat, stilted, or unusual in its pacing, and these peculiarities can manifest themselves in the context of oral reading, as this excerpt from an autobiography by Donna Williams, a woman with autism, demonstrated:

> My reading was very good, but I had merely found a more socially acceptable way of listening to the sound of my own voice. Though I could read a story without difficulty, it was

always the pictures from which I understood the content. Reading aloud, I would confi-
dently continue, despite mispronouncing or inverting some of the letters or words. I
would use different types of intonation to make the story sound interesting, though I was
merely experimenting with my own voice, and my tone probably did not match [the] content of the story half the time. (1992, p. 25)

Dysfluency by people with autism may suggest that they are having difficulty
with recognizing particular words, but it can also indicate something completely
different. For example, Liane Holliday Willey's memoir includes this description
of her early experiences with reading:

I loved the way most words played on my tongue. I loved the way they caused different
parts of my mouth to move. But if I did come across a word that hurt my ears, typically
words with too many hyper-nasal sounds, I would not say them aloud. Similarly, I would
refuse words that looked ugly by virtue of being too lopsided or too cumbersome or too
unusual in their phonetics. (1999, p. 25)

A teacher with a conception of reading fluency focused primarily on its cognitive
rather than its affective components might easily have misinterpreted Holliday
Willey's refusal to pronounce certain words as an indication of a lack of knowledge about certain letter–sound correspondences. Such an inference might have
led that teacher to plan repeated experiences with words containing the same
kinds of features—an instructional decision that might have unintentionally created stress for a child like Holliday Willey. If examined using a different lens, however, her reluctance to pronounce these words can indicate proficiency rather than
a weakness related to decoding. Her hyper-awareness of the sounds that letters
produce in particular combinations was uncomfortable for her because of how she
experienced them bodily, and this discomfort prevented her from reading aloud
fluently when she encountered those sounds encoded in print. Without probing
these data from Holliday Willey's perspective, however, it would be difficult for
any teacher to reach this conclusion.

These examples illustrate why teachers must be very cautious in how they interpret a learner's skills, abilities, and behaviors. These individuals who have
shared their stories with us help us, as teachers, understand that we must consider
the perspective of the learner as we assess our students and, furthermore, we must
take into consideration the sensory, communication, and movement differences
that might create fluency and other reading performance problems for students
with autism labels.

No story perhaps better emphasizes this point than one about Stan, a young
man with Asperger syndrome, who was trying to read Shakespeare's *Romeo and
Juliet* while others in his classroom were building props for the end-of-the-week
performance. Stan, who could read fluently and appropriately when the room
was calm and relatively quiet, lost this ability when his sensory system became
overloaded. Because he could not hear others over background noises, he often
spoke very loudly when there was any additional noise at all in the classroom. In
these instances, he also read less fluidly. Therefore, when his teacher asked him to
read in a less stilted and softer voice and "with feeling" when his turn came in the
script, he replied, "I AM reading with feeling. . . . I am FEELING loud and
choppy!"

Instructional Approaches

A number of instructional approaches can be used to promote students' fluency development. Among our favorites are the following: read alouds, collaborative oral reading, repeated reading, and Reader's Theater.

Read Alouds

Almost every teacher, elementary or secondary, shares a book or some passage from a text with students during the school week. Including students with autism in this simple activity with both fiction and nonfiction texts can be powerful for individuals with disabilities because it exposes them to a model of fluent reading they might otherwise not have (Koppenhaver, Coleman, Kalman, & Yoder, 1991). Because many learners with autism struggle to read body language and emotions (Blackman, 1999; Lawson, 1998; Shore, 2003), listening to the teacher read with expression may help them to understand postures and facial expressions and provides them with a model for uses of volume, tone, and inflections in speech. When the teacher reads about a child fighting with his brother, the student has an opportunity to review the language that is associated with anger and, if the teacher reads with feeling, the facial expressions and body language that an angry person might use.

Of course, more than a few students with autism find the passive nature of the read aloud a challenge. For these learners, see Table 5.1 for a variety of ways that the read aloud can be adapted to meet learners' diverse needs. These suggestions may work for students who need to fidget or move during whole-class instruction, those who need materials to keep focused, those who profit from having an active role in lessons, those who benefit from collaborative learning, and those who require alternative ways of demonstrating attention, engagement, and interest. Some of these suggestions work best for younger children (e.g., having them use props or a puppet) but most of them would be appropriate for students in Grades K–12.

Recorded books such as book on tape or CDs or audiotapes of familiar rituals, interactions, or ceremonies might also help students become more fluent. Stephen Shore, a man with Asperger syndrome, recalled that he could not master the unfamiliar words of the "Bereshit" for his Bar Mitzvah, so his parents audiotaped a cantor singing the prayer:

> I had no idea what I was saying but I did a good imitation of the cantor right down to the dry gravelly voice, melodies and davening, which involves rocking back and forth from the waist up in a rhythmic manner as the Hebrew words are sung. (2003, p. 81)

Although we hope that students understand what they read and say in most situations better than Stephen did with this prayer, his experience suggests that media representations of fluent reading can be helpful, on some level, to learners, especially those students with autism who are skillful mimics.

Recorded books may be useful for those working with young people who cannot stay in one space during a traditional read aloud. One mother who struggled to read aloud to her son because he was very active and nonverbal used recorded books exclusively to share favorite stories. To ensure that he would hear

Table 5.1.   Read aloud: Adaptations for the diverse classroom

Give students the same book so they can follow the story as the teacher reads.

Give students an adapted version of the book (e.g., a book with extra pictures, large type, or laminated pages) so they can follow along as the teacher reads.

Let students explore a "story kit" filled with objects related to the story (e.g., a bag for *A River Ran Wild* [Cherry, 1992] could be filled with a map of the Nashua River, a little vial of water, a pressed wildflower, and a small plastic frog).

Give students a puppet to hold during the story and let them perform parts of the book on their own or for the class.

Give students a copy of the text to highlight words or phrases of interest as the teacher reads.

Give students a copy of the text to doodle on or code with symbols as the teacher reads.

Give students cards to hold up during key passages (e.g., every time the bad wolf is mentioned, a student holds up a picture of the wolf; every time the teacher says "respiratory system," the student holds up a photo of the lungs).

Give students something text-related to hold as the story is read (e.g., the student fidgets with a train car as the teacher reads a newspaper article about transportation).

Give students a job during the read aloud (e.g., a smaller child can help turn the pages of a big book, an older child can click a PowerPoint slide with the pages of the text displayed on it).

Have students read the book (if possible) to the class alone or with a partner, instead of listening to the teacher read it.

Have students co-teach the book by asking key questions prepared on cards or programmed into a communication device throughout the read aloud (e.g., "What do you think will happen next?")

Have students participate by reading the first sentence (verbally or via a communication device), the last sentence, and/or repeating or important passages.

Give students a notebook to draw images that come to mind as they listen to the story or passage. (This may also help to boost comprehension.)

Give students a notebook to write key words or ideas that they hear as they listen to the story or passage. (This may also help to boost comprehension.)

Give students a notebook to write down questions about the text that they might ask the teacher later.

Give students a special "book listening space" to use during the read aloud (e.g., sitting in a special chair, standing at a lectern).

the tales from beginning to end, she played them during long car trips, when her son would be staying in one place for a substantial period of time. Over time, he began handing her CD boxes to indicate which stories he wanted to hear. Likewise, a sixth-grade teacher assigned her student with autism to listen to short classroom books using WriteOut: Loud®, a talking word processor program that allows students to hear the computer read their texts aloud. The program held the student's attention better than a simple CD of the story because he was able to constantly change the computer voice reading the text, an aspect of the activity that never failed to delight him. The teacher typically asked this student to listen at least two times to the books before the corresponding lesson because this exercise appeared to improve the fluency of the boy's in-class reading as well as his comprehension.

Collaborative Oral Reading

During read alouds, the teacher is usually the only one to view the printed text. Shared reading, choral reading, and echo reading are all variations on what we call *collaborative oral reading*—activities meant to increase fluency because they engage more skilled readers in navigating a shared text—one that everyone can see—in some way with less skilled ones.

Shared reading (Allen, 2002) involves the teacher or another fluent reader in voicing the text while the learner tracks the print at the same time. In the elementary grades, this activity often takes place with a Big Book (a commercially produced version of a picture book that is enlarged so that a group of children can see it from their seats) or a chart on an easel. Teachers of older learners are more likely to project the shared text for the class on an overhead transparency or computer screen. Either way, the benefits are the same: Students get to see the print as it is voiced by another person, a process that helps them learn how to pronounce unfamiliar words, how to work with conventions of print such as punctuation, and how to pace their reading differently for different purposes or while reading texts in different genres.

Choral reading is an approach that includes some of the same features as shared reading, such as a proficient reader's modeling and a common text, but that introduces a new variable: supported oral reading by the learner. One of the best examples we know of choral reading comes from an autobiography by Tito Rajarshi Mukhopadhyay, a young man with autism whose teacher required him to follow along in a text as she read to him, with the voice–print connection helping him to stay focused:

> When she read, I had to naturally follow the words in order to keep pace with her speed. Slowly my concentration improved and I could keep my eyes fixed on a page without getting distracted. Mother practiced it at home and within a month I read a two hundred page book, reading about seven pages a day, reading in chorus with my mother. (2000, p. 75)

In the classroom, choral reading is more likely to take place in a whole-group setting, with the teacher and all students reading the text in unison. Such a strategy not only promotes fluency but also encourages participation by all students because individuals may feel less self-conscious about their reading performance when acting as a group. Figure 5.2 includes a helpful checklist developed by Elfi Berndl, a fourth-grade teacher from Ontario, Canada, that students can use to self-evaluate their choral reading performance.

Did you (circle one). . .		
Read aloud all the words you knew how to pronounce?	YES	NO
Try to say words you did not know when you heard others say them?	YES	NO
Speak loud enough to be heard but not too loud?	YES	NO
Put life in your voice and pause at the punctuation?	YES	NO
Follow the pace set by your teacher?	YES	NO
Point at the words as they were being spoken?	YES	NO
Make an effort to improve your performance?	YES	NO
Reading partner's initials _____	Score ____ /7	

Figure 5.2.   Miss Berndl's self-evaluation for choral reading. (Available at http://www.rocksforkids.com/FabFours/choral_reading.html; reprinted by permission.)

The strategy of echo reading positions learners a bit more independently than shared reading or choral reading, and consequently, it is often employed after students have developed familiarity with those other methods first. With echo reading, the teacher or another expert reader reads a portion of the text fluently while the learner follows along, tracking the print and paying attention to how it is voiced by the model. After completing a meaningful chunk of text—a few sentences for a beginning reader or a paragraph or section for a more experienced one—the expert turns the reading over to the learner, who rereads the same material while trying to use similar pacing and inflection. As students become more proficient, they might alternate passages with the more proficient reader rather than repeating what has previously been read by the expert.

We feel it is important to emphasize that many students—those with and without disabilities—profit from choral reading experiences. This is true not only in elementary school classrooms but also in middle and high school classrooms. Keep in mind that choral reading in the upper grades can serve both as a tool for helping students with fluency *and* as a demonstration of how reading together with expression can express the beauty and meaning of a piece of literature. For expository text in science or social studies, choral reading can make a lesson more playful or humorous and often makes the content easier to remember.

Repeated Reading

According to the NRP (NICHD, 2000a), the method of promoting fluency with the most unambiguous research support is repeated reading, associated most closely with work by S. Jay Samuels (1979). The approach works like this: A learner first reads a designated passage of text along with a teacher, a parent, a more competent peer, or even a tape recording, to ensure that the student comprehends the text. Next, the learner is challenged to read the passage in the same length of time it would take a fluent reader to do so at a moderate pace (generally estimated at between 200 and 350 words per minute). The student then reads the passage as many times as is necessary to achieve that goal, timing him- or herself with a stopwatch and recording how much time elapses for each reading. Some versions of the activity also require students to keep track of their errors and to reread the passage until they can do so with accuracy as well as at an appropriate pace.

Repeated reading activities will appeal to some students with autism because these activities set clear, unambiguous targets for performance, such as "The student will read a 100-word passage in 40 seconds." These activities also involve students in charting data about their progress in an organized fashion, which some students on the spectrum will likely enjoy. (A Google search with *repeated reading* and *chart* as search terms should yield a number of options students might use for this purpose.)

Although the strategy of repeated reading is beneficial in some ways, we have a few cautions to share about this approach. First of all, many students with autism balk at participating in instructional activities that they perceive as "pointless," to borrow a word from Kenneth Hall (2001), a young author with Asperger syndrome. Unless their teachers are clear about the purpose for and benefits of repeated reading (e.g., focused practice with fluency, increased comprehension), it's likely that some students might greet a request to reread with a response like this: "Why do you want me to do that? I already read it once." Students with autism may also become too "stuck" on their immediate goals for a passage rather than the bigger picture of developing fluency. To keep individuals from worrying or focusing on reaching 100% accuracy in their reading (a focus that might lead them, for example, to unnecessary correction of small substitutions that don't interfere with the meaning of the passage and actually reflect their comprehension of the text), some learners may need their teachers to set a limit on the number of repeated readings they do. (Rashotte and Torgesen [1985], for example, recommend that students with learning disabilities read a given text no more than four times.)

Students with autism who are reluctant to engage in repeated readings might be coaxed into participating if their teachers can find authentic opportunities for them to do so. For instance, a reading specialist we know encouraged several fifth-grade students to plan and develop a "poetry slam." This activity required the students to write their own poems and to practice them several times before performing them in the school library. In another school, students were asked to create books on tape for a local child care. This activity required students to read the book a few times with peers to make sure they knew the words and thus could create a professional-sounding tape during the "recording session."

Reader's Theater

We are especially fond of Reader's Theater (RT) because it involves students in a powerful literary performance without committing time and resources to creating costumes, blocking scenes, or memorizing lines. The very simplicity of RT ensures that a class can engage in the activity multiple times, refining their approach as they explore different pieces of literature.

Prescott breaks the process of RT into the following five steps:

1. *Choose a script.* Choose a prepared script, or have students choose a book from which to develop an RT script.

2. *Adapt the script.* Kids identify speaking parts (including narrators) and break down the story into dialogue.

3. *Assign parts.* Kids might try out different parts to get a feel for them, then choose their roles themselves.

4. *Highlight parts and rehearse.* Kids highlight their dialogue, then practice their lines at home and in groups during school.

5. *Perform.* The cast reads the play aloud for an audience, often made up of parents or younger students. (2003, n.p.)

The bulk of students' fluency practice takes place during step 4, the rehearsal phase. Once students have selected or been assigned a part, they reread it until they can voice it with ease and expression. Teachers, peers, or family members may assist students in preparing for their roles using one or more of the collaborative oral reading methods (e.g., echo or choral reading) profiled earlier in this chapter. These suggestions can be helpful at the beginning of the rehearsal period when students are becoming familiar with their lines.

From our perspective, RT can be motivating for and supportive of the needs of learners with autism for a variety of reasons. First, performance anxiety about oral reading is decreased for all learners by the use of a script, as opposed to memorized lines. Second, the size and difficulty of an individual student's role can be adjusted based on skill and comfort levels. If a student struggles to read orally, he or she can be assigned a small part and then receive extra practice time and coaching to master it; if he or she reads comfortably, the student can be given a larger part, creating an opportunity to shine in front of his or her peers. Third, the social nature of the activity provides built-in scaffolding; others' lines will help to cue an individual student about how to perform, and students can be encouraged to rehearse together in small groups. Finally, cast size and audiences can be selected with the needs of students with autism in mind. Students who are uncomfortable in large-group settings can work on a script with three or four characters rather than the whole class, and they can stage their performance for a class of younger children or a hand-picked group of friends or familiar adults.

Another way the activity can be designed to reach a wider range of learners is to integrate assistive technology into the performances. The fun and low-risk nature of RT makes it a perfect opportunity for trying out a new communication device or assistive technology support. For instance, Jon, a student practicing using a new Step-by-Step Communicator (AbleNet, http://www.ablenetinc.com), a voice output device with up to three pre-recorded messages stored in it, was very motivated to use the technology during an RT performance of *Polar Bear, Polar Bear What Do You Hear?* (Martin & Carle, 1991). His group was responsible for chanting, "Lion, lion, what do you hear?"; "Flamingo, flamingo, what do you hear?"; and "Zebra, zebra, what do you hear?" Jon had to wait for his group's turn and hit his communicator to read each of his three lines. During this exercise he gained valuable practice with the communication device while "reading" and rehearsing with the group.

Although many excellent scripts are available for RT, either from commercial vendors or online at web sites such as Aaron Shepherd's RT Page (http://aaronshep.com/rt/) or Reader's Theater Scripts and Plays (http://www.teachingheart.net/readerstheater.htm), we encourage you to involve students in constructing their own scripts from literature they have read or even have them write them on their own. The process of determining what to include and writing dialogue as needed is part of what makes RT so powerful, and it gives students valuable practice with comprehending the text—the subject of the next section.

COMPREHENSION

In the executive summary of their report, the NRP defined comprehension as "an active process that requires an intentional and thoughtful interaction between the reader and the text" (NICHD, 2000b, n.p.). The emphasis in their definition on process, not product, is in stark contrast to how comprehension used to be framed, which was the apprehension of a stable, singular meaning for the text that could be measured definitively, usually by questioning after the reading was done. Instead, current thinking on comprehension underscores it as ongoing (one's comprehension often changes over the course of a reading) and purpose-driven (a book such as Frances Mayes' memoir *Under the Tuscan Sun* [1996], for example, will be read differently if one is interested in her story of personal growth than it will be if one is looking for the polenta recipe that she includes). As the NRP and others (see Sweet & Snow, 2003) indicate, comprehension is influenced by characteristics of the text (e.g., structure, topic, vocabulary load), of the reader (e.g., skill

Table 5.2.   Comprehension strategies used by proficient readers

Proficient readers

- Make connections between what they're reading and their own lives, other texts, and the world around them.
- Ask themselves questions as they read.
- Visualize, or create mental images, as they read.
- Make inferences, or informed guesses, that go beyond the information stated explicitly in the text.
- Determine what information is most important in a text, given a particular purpose for reading.
- Synthesize information, or combine new material with existing knowledge, to come to a new understanding of the text.
- Monitor when their understanding breaks down and take steps to repair it.

Note: From *Strategies That Work: Teaching Comprehension to Enhance Understanding*, by Stephanie Harvey and Anne Goudvis, © 2000, with permission of Stenhouse Publishers.

level, interests, experience), and of the sociocultural context (e.g., instructional methods used in a classroom, values about literacy in a community).

Since the 1970s, a number of components in the comprehension process (e.g., comprehension strategies), have been identified, and it is generally understood that proficient readers use these flexibly, in concert with each other, as needed to understand a particular text for a particular reason. Although different lists of these component strategies exist, the terms included in Table 5.2 are recognized in the field as some of the most crucial for learners to master (Dole, Duffy, Roehler, & Pearson, 1991; Harvey & Goudvis, 2000); these strategies are the ones we share with the teachers with whom we work. Regardless of the terminology they use, nearly all comprehension strategy researchers share the assumption that these aspects of comprehension can and should be taught to students using a combination of modeling, guided practice, independent practice, and application (Dole, 2002).

Relationships between comprehension and other facets of reading have also been identified, with researchers demonstrating increases in comprehension when readers 1) use well-developed word-level skills to read the text fluently, 2) draw appropriately on prior knowledge relevant to the text, and 3) manage vocabulary challenges in the text (Pressley, 2000). In addition, *metacognition*, a reader's ability to reflect on, evaluate, and adjust his or her own strategic processes, has been shown as a crucial component in proficient reading (Baker, 2002), making approaches that help a student monitor his or her own thinking as a reader particularly valuable.

Considering Students with Autism

Many people with autism spectrum labels report that reading comprehension is a problem for them, sometimes because of the content of the text and other times because of its structure, syntax, or vocabulary. It is not uncommon for learners with autism to decode at or above grade-level expectations while performing substantially less well on tests of comprehension (O'Connor & Klein, 2004). A good example of this phenomenon comes from Donna Williams's autobiography:

> I eventually realized that I wasn't getting anything out of the novels I was being made to read at school. I could read them all fluently, but I was unable to pick up what the book

was about. It was as though the meaning got lost in the jumble of trivial words. Like a person learns to speed-read, I would read only the main words in any sentence, and tried to let the feel of the book somehow wash over me. It worked to an extent. Instead of reading a book thoroughly and gaining nothing in terms of content, I was now able to scan one and be aware of the names of some of the characters and some of the things that happened to them. (1992, p. 43)

Donna's scanning approach helped her get a sense of the gist of her reading, and it was likely adequate for many of the school-based literature tasks she was asked to complete, many of which didn't require deep comprehension. At the same time, her method is clearly neither the most efficient nor satisfying way to interact with text.

This difficulty in separating main ideas from details is not uncommon for people with autism spectrum labels, as one mother learned while assisting her child with a homework assignment:

In fifth grade my son was assigned to write a paper on Benedict Arnold. When I looked at his rough draft, I noticed that he had included all of the important facts about Arnold's life except for one—the fact that he had betrayed the Revolutionary Army to the British for 10,000 pounds and a commission in the Royal Navy! I asked him whether he hadn't left out something important, to which he replied, "But all of it is important!" (Rosinski, 2002, p. 1)

Other learners with autism labels find it difficult to make inferences—to read "between the lines," as some people say—because they tend to interpret language very literally. This can be difficult with texts such as novels, poetry, or folklore whose power depends on literary devices such as metaphor. Stephen Shore, a man with Asperger syndrome, shared his frustrations in this regard in his book, *Beyond the Wall*:

I remember being infuriated at one of those assignments in fifth grade because it was entitled, "How the Earth Was Formed." I knew how the earth was formed. Astronomy was my current special interest and I spent many hours reading astronomy books and copying the pictures and diagrams onto pieces of paper. The explanation in the reading assignment about the earth being part of the back of a large turtle seemed so stupid that it infuriated me. Why should I spend time on such stupidity? Now that I am older, I can appreciate the story for what it is—an American Indian legend. (2003, p. 57)

Similarly, Luke Jackson (2002) included an illustrated dictionary of idioms in his "user guide to adolescence" for people with Asperger syndrome. He shared that figurative uses of language were initially difficult for him to understand and encouraged those who interact with people on the autism spectrum to make themselves as explicit as possible. Others (Broun, 2004) have reported that understanding character motivation can be difficult for students with autism, especially if the dimensions of the characters are revealed through subtle details of gesture, tone, or behavior rather than spelled out clearly in the narration.

Although these examples demonstrate that many learners with autism face challenges with comprehension related to dimensions of their disability, we want to make it clear that many learners who are neurotypical find it difficult to comprehend at high levels as well, especially when faced with discipline-specific reading such as textbooks, reports, and journal articles. In fact, one of the strongest recommendations arising from comprehension-focused research in the past two decades is the importance of explicit strategy-focused instruction for all learners across the curriculum and across the grade-level span (Biancarosa & Snow, 2004). For this reason, the instructional approaches to promote comprehension that we profile in the next section will be useful for most, if not all, learners in a classroom, not just those with autism labels.

Instructional Approaches

Although students' reading comprehension can be supported with some of the instructional ideas we have already described—read alouds, for example—the following approaches have comprehension instruction as their primary goal: boosting background knowledge, think alouds, reciprocal teaching, and retellings.

Boosting Background Knowledge

Research has shown that good comprehenders draw on relevant prior knowledge to make sense of texts they are reading (Pressley, 2000). Students' comprehension can be increased when their teachers help them to activate—and sometimes even build—background knowledge about the topic in question. Many students with disabilities need this type of support because they are more likely than learners who do not have disabilities to be excluded from in-school and out-of-school activities that lead to the development of extensive background knowledge.

A range of approaches can be used to assist students in calling up what they know about a topic and/or learning new information that can enhance their comprehension. For example, you might tell students a story from your own experience on a topic related to the text (students are almost always intrigued by narratives from their teachers' lives) or ask them questions about relevant experiences they might have had or media texts they may know (often, students don't realize that prior knowledge from television, film, computer games, and the Internet can be valuable in understanding school-based topics). To help students create mental images as they read, you might show them a movie clip or share slides of artwork or illustrations related to the topic. You might also help students create connections between their experiences and the topic by using a graphic organizer such as a KWL chart used by learners to record what they know about a topic and want to learn before reading, as well as what they learned after navigating the text (see Figure 5.3 for an example). Other ways to boost students' background knowledge include the following:

- Brainstorm all of the associations learners make with the topic and record them on chart paper, or use planning software and a projector and have students shout ideas as you type them into the program and display them for the class.

- Share other books related to the topic, including easy picture books that can be reread by students to make explicit connections between the topic and students' special interests.

- Ask the students' parents to share experiences and to connect past family experiences to the new text or unit.

- Have students turn and talk to each other about their experiences, memories, or knowledge in a given area.

K: What I Know	W: What I Want to Know	L: What I Learned
Lacrosse was invented by the six nations in the Iroquois Confederacy.

It used to be played by whole villages at one time.

Lacrosse has some elements in common with soccer.

Some Onondagas have received scholarships to play lacrosse at Syracuse University. | How has the game changed over time?

How long does it take to make a wooden lacrosse stick?

When did European-Americans begin playing the sport?

Are girls allowed to play lacrosse in the Nation territory? | Most players use metal and plastic sticks now, but during traditional games, handmade wooden sticks are always used.

It takes at least 8 months to make a wooden stick.

People started playing box lacrosse in the 1930s. In the Nation, the Onondagas play in a box now, rather than on a field.

The name *lacrosse* was given to the game by French settlers.

Lacrosse was made the national game of Canada in 1867, so white people must have been playing it by the mid-19th century.

The Iroquois National team was not accepted into the International Federation until 1987. |

Figure 5.3. Sample KWL chart. The chart was completed before and after the students read *Lacrosse: The National Game of the Iroquois* (Hoyt-Goldsmith, 1998).

Perhaps the most significant support that can be offered in this area is to include all students in the typical routines and activities of school life. Students will build background knowledge daily when they are included in the social (e.g., recess, art class, locker routines) and academic (e.g., math class, orchestra, academic clubs) life of the school. Often, teachers make the erroneous assumption that reading skills are honed only during the literacy block when, in fact, students learn these skills and acquire these competencies all day long. If the class is reading a story about mummies, for example, and the learner with autism was not in his general education classroom when Egypt was studied, he will most likely have a harder time comprehending the story than his peers.

Think Aloud

The think aloud (Baumann, Jones, & Seifert-Kessell, 1993; Harvey & Goudvis, 2000; Tovani, 2000) is one of the best ways for teachers to help students control reading strategies such as the ones listed for retelling in Table 5.3 as well as monitor their overall comprehension. This approach requires readers "to stop periodically, reflect on how a text is being processed and understood, and relate orally

Table 5.3.   Retelling: Adaptations for the diverse classroom

Have peers demonstrate the strategy in order to provide multiple models of the process that are sometimes more accessible than an adult's model.

Encourage students to type or write part or all of the retelling rather than saying it orally.

Allow students to read their retelling aloud after they have written it (Biklen, 2005), if they prefer this approach.

Give students illustrations or photographs or sequencing cards to use in the retelling.

Identify key information that should be included in the retelling (e.g., "Make sure that you talk about all three challenges faced by the protagonist").

Have students retell the story by completing a graphic organizer that will cue them about some of the key elements (e.g., includes a box to discuss the story's setting and another to discuss its conflict).

Let students engage in the retelling in a dramatic way by acting it out.

Allow small groups of students to retell a story together.

what reading strategies are being employed" (Baumann et al., 1993, p. 192). Teachers who model the process offer students a helpful look at how a proficient reader deals with challenges associated with a particular text. For instance, they might model the strategy of prediction—a crucial one when beginning a novel—by saying, "The title of the book is *Tales of a Fourth Grade Nothing* [Blume, 1972], so I think it will be about a kid in the fourth grade. When I look at the picture on the cover, I think maybe the main characters will be a boy and a girl. The cover has a picture of a classroom, so I think a lot of this book will take place in a school."

According to Tovani, a professional development specialist who works with secondary teachers from all disciplines, preparing for and performing a think-aloud has four steps:

1. Select a short piece of text that will allow you to model the desired comprehension strategy.

2. Foresee difficulty, anticipating what aspects of the text might serve as obstacles to student comprehension. (You may want to make notes for yourself about what these obstacles are and how you solve them as a competent adult reader.)

3. Read the text out loud in front of students (using an overhead projector or computer or distributing copies to students), and stop often to share your thinking.

4. Point out the words in the text that trigger your thinking. (2000, pp. 27–28)

Most teachers who use this approach write their thoughts on chart paper or on a transparency as they share them with the class, so that students can see *and* hear the process. Tovani also recommended using body language to cue students when she is thinking aloud: "Looking at the transparency when I read and looking at the students when I share thinking helps them distinguish the difference between reading and thinking aloud" (2000, p. 28). This last idea should be helpful for students with autism because it makes the procedures that much more explicit for them.

Once students are familiar with the think aloud from teacher modeling, they, too, can use it to monitor and share their own strategic thinking, either with a single partner or as a member of a larger cooperative group. Students can either take turns performing their think alouds in front of each other, stopping as needed to ask questions of each other, or they can record strategy-focused notes outside of class on sticky notes or in journal entries that can then be shared with their peers. Students who don't speak can be given cards with symbols to indicate to their teachers and peers that they are using particular strategies at different points in a text (e.g., an eye to represent a place where they created a visual image, a bridge to show where they used the gap-filling process of a mental inference). If students have communication devices, they can be programmed ahead of time with strategy names from which they can select. Several teacher researchers (Cunningham & Shagoury, 2005; Miller, 2002) have found that students as young as first graders can share their think alouds successfully if they are encouraged to use drawings and symbols as well as to invent spellings for unfamiliar words. These accounts suggest that students who struggle with the physical act of writing might have similar success in using visual approaches to capture and share their strategy use with others. Adaptations that might be used for these learners include giving plenty of time to watch and learn from others collaboratively engaging in a think aloud with the student so he or she can build off of a teacher's examples, or providing examples of prompts that can be used (e.g., "I think _____ will happen next because ____") as part of a think aloud.

Reciprocal Teaching

Reciprocal teaching (Palinscar & Brown, 1984) has recently experienced a renaissance of sorts in schools because it was cited in the NRP report as a method for promoting comprehension that was backed by a good deal of research support. Combining the explicitness of a teacher think aloud with the power of cooperative learning, reciprocal teaching is essentially a dialogue between teachers and students. The dialogue is structured by the use of four high-utility comprehension strategies: summarizing, question generating, clarifying, and predicting.

Once students are comfortable with the four strategies and the reciprocal teaching procedures, they are invited to become "the teacher" and conduct reciprocal teaching dialogues with new material. At this point the teacher's role shifts from providing direct instruction to facilitating student interaction, monitoring progress, and providing feedback. As students become more skilled with the strategy, they can work in pairs or small groups to coach one another's strategy use in the context of many different reading tasks, from textbook chapters to poems.

Reciprocal teaching can be useful for learners with autism because its specific procedures create a clear set of expectations about students' roles and because it permits teachers to make decisions about group sizes and partnerships that will maximize student comfort. It also positions learners, during the time they play the "teacher," as an expert rather than a novice, which may give them confidence as well as the opportunity to shine in front of their peers. Whalon (2004), in fact, found that when she taught three students with autism reciprocal questioning techniques to use in the context of their inclusive classroom, all of the students increased their frequency of question generation and responding. In addition, two of the three participants increased their performance on standardized comprehension measures, and the parents of all of the participants reported improvement in their child's language, reading fluency, and reading comprehension skills. Undoubtedly, one of the reasons these learners achieved the level of success they did was due to the inclusion of several visual supports in the intervention. For instance, students had a checklist complete with icons illustrating key words/ phrases to monitor their own reading and their interactions with peers (e.g., "Before reading: Ask each other, 'Why is it important to ask questions when we read?'"). They also had a series of illustrated question cards (e.g., WHEN, WHO, WHERE) to help keep their discussions on track as well as to map their stories while and after they read (see Figure 5.4 for an example of cards that might be created).

Retelling

As we explained already, some learners may "fail" comprehension assessments because they are uncomfortable with the direct nature of question/answer interactions. For this reason, some students may respond well to being asked instead to retell their reading. Retelling (Hoyt, 1999) is an instructional approach that is also used as a tool for assessment. A retelling is done by the reader after he has read or heard a text. The student is asked to "tell everything" he can about what has been read after having the approach modeled by the teacher. (Do not assume that this behavior comes naturally; students need to be taught explicitly how to sequence their retellings as well as how to include essential information in them.) As students talk, you can record the key features of their retellings using a form like the one in Figure 5.5, reproduced from Chandler-Olcott and Hinchman (2005). With fictional texts, retelling reinforces story structure and the language and imagery used by the author; with informational texts, it helps students determine what material is most important. Putting the text into their own words helps students organize new information, connect it to what they already know about the topic, and remember it.

For those who communicate better visually (or for those who have unreliable speech) a graphic retelling might work better. Students who learn best in a multisensory style might do a retelling with a feltboard or with objects. Students can also be taught a story mapping strategy (Boulineau, Fore, Hagan-Burke, & Burke,

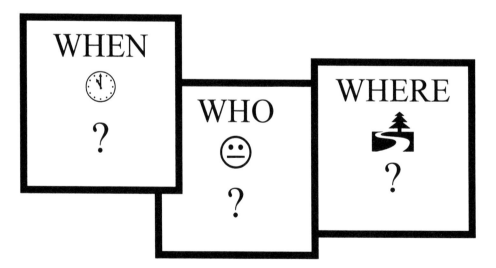

Figure 5.4. Reciprocal teaching visual supports. (From Whalon, K. [2004]. *The effects of a reciprocal questioning intervention on the reading comprehension of children with autism.* Unpublished manuscript. Tallahassee, FL: Florida State University; adapted by permission.)

Expository Retelling

Student Name: _____   Date: _____

Text Title: _____   Text Author: _____

Text Structure Elements	Unprompted	Prompted
Main Ideas		
Details		
Structure (e.g., main idea/ detail, cause/effect, compare/contrast)		

Comments: _____

_____

_____

Narrative Retelling

Student Name: _____   Date: _____

Text Title: _____   Text Author: _____

Story Elements	Unprompted	Prompted
Setting (time, place)		
Characters		
Problem		
Events Leading to Solution		
Solution		

Comments: _____

_____

_____

Figure 5.5.   Retelling checklists. (From K. Chandler-Olcott & K. Hinchman [2005]. *Tutoring adolescent literacy learners: A guide for volunteers* [p. 47]. New York: Guilford Press; reprinted by permission.)

2004; Sorrell, 1990) to help them capture information as they read or immediately after they finish a piece of text. Students can be taught to map out the events in an artistic and symbolic way by literally drawing a path or trail and inserting images as they move through the story. Or they can map by taking visual notes in chronological order in a notebook or in consecutive boxes on a page. For example, a third-grade teacher had her students map out *Mystery in the Night Woods* (Peterson, 1969) using an exercise we call 4-Corners Comprehension. This involves having students read sections of text (in this case, chapters) and then pause on their own or with a peer to draw or map what they read at the end of each section. Cora, a young woman with autism, could not draw pictures or use a pencil easily so she worked on her 4-Corners map with a peer. Cora's classmate drew the pictures and then, together, the two found pieces of dialogue to fit each quadrant (e.g., "Where is FS?"). Cora was responsible for creating a sticker of each piece of dialogue, using a hand-held label maker, and positioning the sticker on the correct quadrant. Figure 5.6 illustrates an example of this 4-Corners Comprehension exercise.

VOCABULARY

Vocabulary knowledge is related to both reading proficiency and overall school achievement (Beck, McKeown, & Kucan, 2002). The executive summary of the NRP report tied vocabulary development to reading comprehension, arguing that it was impossible to understand the latter without considering the role of the former, and calling for both direct and indirect teaching of vocabulary using a "com-

Figure 5.6. Collaborative 4 Corners Comprehension for one student, Cora, on the book *Mystery In the Night Woods* (Peterson, 1969).

bination of methods" rather than a single one (NICHD, 2000b, n.p.). Because of these strong links, we decided to include the section on vocabulary learning here, in the chapter on teaching reading. At the same time, we want to point out that vocabulary development is also related to other aspects of literacy, including writing and oral language.

Wide reading of a rich range of texts is one of the best ways to increase word knowledge (Nagy, Herman, & Anderson, 1985); indeed, we learn many of the words we know from reading without consciously realizing that we've learned them. But wide reading on its own is generally insufficient for developing a strong vocabulary (Beck, McKeown, & Kucan, 2002). For most learners, it must be supplemented by 1) the teaching of specific words, especially those of particular utility in the various academic disciplines; 2) the teaching of specific word-learning strategies, such as the use of context clues; and 3) the deliberate promotion of word consciousness, defined by Ryder and Graves as the "disposition to notice words, to value them, and use them in precise and effective ways" (1998, p. 32). Attention to all three of these aspects of vocabulary learning can and should be incorporated into literacy instruction for students with disabilities. This means that if students cannot read on their own, teachers will need to read to them a rich range of texts because they will need this background not only to make their lives more interesting but also to help them acquire literacy skill.

There is little evidence to suggest that traditional approaches to teaching vocabulary—for example, looking up and memorizing definitions in anticipation of a quiz—have much, if any, long-term impact on student learning. Instead, vocabulary experts recommend that instruction be guided by the following four principles we share here:

1. Students should be active in developing their understanding of words and ways to learn them (they might pursue semantic mapping activities, where they visually represent the relationships in meaning between words from a particular unit of study).

2. Students should personalize word learning (they should have some choice about the words they learn as well as be encouraged to develop individualized ways to remember them).

3. Students should be immersed in words (they should explore vocabulary in numerous contexts, not just language arts class once a week).

4. Students should build on multiple sources of information to learn words through repeated exposures (they should see, hear, and use words in a variety of contexts to cement understanding). (Blachowicz & Fisher, 2000, p. 504).

We'll discuss more specific approaches to vocabulary instruction that meet these criteria in a subsequent section of this chapter; first, however, let us share some information about how vocabulary learning might play out for students with autism spectrum labels.

Considering Students with Autism

As a number of authors have shared (Barron & Barron, 1992; Gerland, 1996; Prince-Hughes, 2004), words can be a source of comfort and fascination for people with autism. See, for example, this excerpt from an autobiography by Gunilla Gerland:

I liked words, and needed new challenges for it to be fun. I wanted to learn more and more complicated words. When I heard a new one, I always grabbed at it. . . . I could leaf back and forth through books and would start reading only when some word caught my interest. I was looking for new and untasted ones. My need for new words that could be discovered and investigated, that would then slip softly into place in my mind, was greater than my need for people. Words aroused my curiosity and a kind of hunger. I always had any amount of space for new ones. "Vendetta," "dilettante"—I reveled in them. (1996, pp. 124–125)

In some of the earliest autobiographical writing by a person with autism, Sean Barron shared his own quest to learn new words by reading the dictionary in sequence:

That day, after school, I started reading with the first definition. Every day I read as much as I could, concentrating as hard as possible. Nearly eight weeks later I finished the dictionary. I felt a sense of power, and I was eager to have people hear me use those words! I didn't know how to use them in context, I realized later. But when I was fifteen I thought I could substitute a big word for a small one and everyone would say, "Boy is he smart!" (Barron & Barron, 1992, p. 198)

Not every student on the autism spectrum will revel in the opportunity to learn new vocabulary words as Gunilla and Sean did. But even for students who like to discover new words, the teacher may struggle to turn this fascination into a lesson. We suggest that educators look for ways to bring new vocabulary into daily work so that students with autism (and any others needing extra support) do not see the learning of new words as an auxiliary activity but as a part of the work readers, writers, and communicators do every day.

Instructional Approaches

Students develop vocabulary knowledge from many sources, including incidentally from their membership in a print-rich community. We like the following instructional approaches, however, with vocabulary development as an explicit goal: fascination-focused books, word walls, vocabulary squares, and semantic mapping.

Fascination-Focused Books

From our perspective, one promising way to engage students with autism in improving their vocabularies is the use of what we have dubbed "fascination books." Many individuals with autism have a deep interest in one or more topics. Some interests are commonly seen across individuals with autism (e.g., trains, animals, weather), while others seem more unique to an individual. Good examples of the latter can be found in autobiographical writing by Sean Barron (Barron & Barron, 1992), in which he shares that he has been fascinated at different points in his life by the number 24 and by dead-end streets.

Any of the interests students bring to the classroom might be used to develop materials that will help them learn new vocabulary and develop what Ryder and Graves (1998) call "word consciousness." One student with autism, Joe, initially struggled with vocabulary-focused lessons, often retreating from them by paging through picture-book adaptations of the *Harry Potter* series by J.K. Rowling. In response to his interest, his teachers developed a learning tool—a Harry Potter dictionary—intended to push Joe to learn new words while honoring his main area of expertise and interest. New concepts and words were connected to material he had already mastered from watching Harry Potter movies and enjoying the books. For instance, the entry for the word *aloft* included a drawing of Harry Potter playing Quidditch and flying through the air on his stick. The entry for *terrified* showed Harry encountering ghouls in the hallways of Hogwarts.

Another teacher we know created a series of instructional materials related to an abiding interest in horses that Trey, a student with autism, demonstrated in her class. She cut out pictures of horses pulling carts and people riding on horses for a social studies text on transportation, a required topic in the curriculum. She also made reading materials by incorporating target vocabulary into a short story about horses. Trey's interest in the adapted materials enabled him to stay with the class during lessons because he could flip through his books if he needed to fidget. He was also able to learn new vocabulary and concepts by reading and rereading the horse books with teachers and classmates.

For us, the instructional decisions made by Joe's and Trey's teachers reflect several of the key principles proposed by Blachowicz and Fisher (2000) in their review of research on vocabulary, most notably, that word learning can be personalized—tailored to address particular students' needs and interests—as well as maximized through multiple exposures to the target words. Both boys were highly motivated to read and reread their teacher-made materials, and the informal talk and viewing of images that accompanied those readings served to reinforce the words' meanings even further. We recommend this kind of multisensory approach for vocabulary learning just as we did earlier for instruction focused on phonics and phonemic awareness.

Word Walls

A classroom word wall is "an interactive, ongoing display . . . of words and/or parts of words" pulled from meaningful contexts such as class discussions, group viewing of films, and independent reading (Wagstaff, 1999, p. 32). They may be related to a subject such as science or tied to a discrete unit of study such as colonial America. Some teachers even choose to have more than one word wall so that each can address specific needs or purposes—for instance, to accompany a word study of adjectives or to highlight all of the vocabulary associated with a new math concept such as statistics. Words walls can be used to support vocabulary development in various ways. Students can invent cheers and chants for words, suggest new additions to the wall as they read and write, group words for a new purpose, and use the words as a resource when spelling.

A word wall can also be used to inspire learning games appropriate for a wide range of learners' needs. For instance, one teacher used her word wall as an inspiration for bingo. Each student had a bingo card with nine blank spaces. The students wrote one word of their choice from the wall in each space. Then the words were removed from the wall, put into a hat, and called out one by one by the teacher while students listened for the words they chose. One student with autism in this classroom told the teacher that he "lived" for the weekly bingo review because he had a passion for game shows, and the teacher always let him be the caller so he could practice his "Bob Barker" voice (and get extra practice with the words on the wall at the same time). Activities like these ensure that students are constantly interacting with the words on the wall, rather than allowing them to fade into the background.

Some students with autism will need a bit more assistance than others to use a word wall. Some, for instance, may learn a new vocabulary word and even understand the definition but are unable to use that word in context or understand its exact meaning. We know a young man who loved using the word *jolly* but felt he could only use it in the context of Christmas because it was a word used to describe Santa Claus in one of his picture books. For a student like this one, we suggest a strategy we call extended word wall, which provides synonyms for the word, examples of the word in a sentence, and possibly even photos or illustrations related to the word (see Figure 5.7 for an example of this tool).

Another way to make the word wall more accessible to students with disabilities is to create a portable version of the wall that learners can study and manipulate at their own desks and take home at the end of the day. Karen Erickson and David Koppenhaver described such an adaptation in their book, *Children with Disabilities: Reading and Writing the Four-Blocks® Way* (2007). They create these supports primarily for learners with visual impairments or for those who have a hard time looking back and forth from the wall to their papers. The wall is simply recreated inside a manila folder and the student or a teacher adds new words to the portable "wall" when the classroom version is updated. A benefit of the portable wall is that it can be personalized for the learner with disabilities. If there are words on the classroom wall not seen as high priority for the student with disabilities, these can be omitted. Similarly, if there are words the class is not learning (e.g., vocabulary for the learner's augmentative communication device) but the student with a disability is, these can be added.

Word	Synonym	Sentence	Pictures
jolly	happy, in high spirits	Everyone was dancing and singing. The crowd was in a jolly mood.	
severe	very strong, extremely bad	The storm was severe. Trees fell down and buildings collapsed.	

Figure 5.7.   Example of an extended word wall.

Vocabulary Square

Although fascination-focused books and word walls help foster word consciousness and general vocabulary development in students, teachers also need some instructional approaches in their repertoire to assist students in learning-specific words or word families in deep ways. The verbal–visual vocabulary square developed by Hopkins and Bean (1998/1999) is a method that we see as promising for this second goal for students on the autism spectrum. One variation of this activity involves students in using a four-square graphic organizer to work with a prefix such as *tri-*, *pre-*, or *fore-*. After teacher modeling and class discussion about one or more of these word parts, students are given a new prefix and asked to browse the dictionary to define the prefix, choose a word using that prefix that will be meaningful to them, and create a personalized image of the word to help them remember it. See Figure 5.8 for an example of how each of these items is recorded on the vocabulary square organizer.

We like this approach to vocabulary development because of its potential to build on strengths with visual information reported by numerous authors on the autism spectrum (Grandin, 1999; Williams, 1992). It ties the ability to remember images, including some that might seem idiosyncratic to a teacher but be highly meaningful to an individual learner, to new academic learning. As such, it can be an important tool to support independent reading because students can be taught to monitor when they encounter a word part in a new context that they previously included in a word square. We also think that this activity's clear procedures and predictable graphic organizer ought to appeal to those students on the autism spectrum who like teacher expectations to be explicit and structured.

Semantic Mapping

One of the methods for teaching vocabulary that garnered the most research support in the NRP report was semantic mapping, the categorization of "new vocabulary words into familiar topics with other known words" (NICHD, 2000b, p. 4–33).

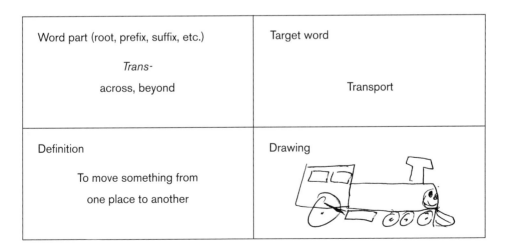

Word part (root, prefix, suffix, etc.) *Trans-* across, beyond	Target word Transport
Definition To move something from one place to another	Drawing

Figure 5.8.   Sample vocabulary square.

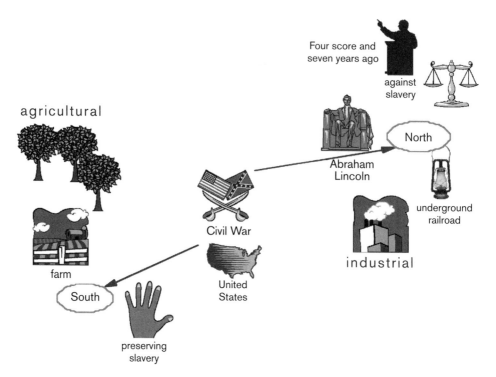

Figure 5.9. Sample semantic map on the American Civil War using Kidspiration® software (Diagram created in Kidspiration® by Inspiration Software®, Inc.; used by permission.)

This approach involves students in creating a graphic organizer such as a web that allows the relationships between the main concept and related words to be depicted spatially. See Figure 5.9 for a sample organizer of the American Civil War generated in a social-studies classroom with Kidspiration® software (available from Inspiration Software®, Inc. at http://www.inspiration.com/productinfo/kidspiration/index .cfm), a program that is useful for students with disabilities who have difficulty creating text or drawing on their own. Many teachers like using this program when they are demonstrating the creation of organizers for the class because Kidspiration® can create an organizer as quickly as the user can type in the content. Teachers can project an image on a large screen and students can watch and learn how to use the software and how to create and manage organizers at the same time.

Vacca and Vacca suggested the following sequence for creating semantic maps in the classroom:

1. The teacher or the students decide on a key concept to be explored.

2. Students suggest related terms or phrases from their experience and the teacher records them on the chalkboard.

3. Pairs or small groups of students are formed to create maps.

4. Students share their maps with each other and discuss similarities and differences in their groupings for words. (2005, p. 279)

As Vacca and Vacca pointed out, this process works much better when teachers model it once or twice before students engage in it on their own.

Similar to the vocabulary square discussed above, semantic mapping can capitalize on the visual strengths that some learners with autism report because the graphic representation of linked words and categories reinforces linkages of meaning between and among the words. At the same time, the approach explicitly addresses a struggle that some learners with autism report in separating main ideas from smaller details because it requires students to begin with a central concept and then to identify subcategories.

CONCLUDING THOUGHTS

Although our list of research-based instructional approaches in each of the components of reading discussed here is far from exhaustive, we hope that we've given you some useful tools for developing students' phonemic awareness, phonics skills, fluency, comprehension, and vocabulary learning. Ideally, as students learn more in each of these areas, they will begin to integrate insights and strategies from one domain with those learned from another, accelerating their progress. Although most of the approaches we advocate were not developed with the needs of students with autism labels specifically in mind, we are confident that they can be adopted and adapted to suit students with these profiles by knowledgeable and flexible teachers.

At the same time, none of these approaches will have much power unless they are implemented in a classroom environment where students can develop identities as readers and a passion for print. In his autobiography, Luke Jackson, the 13-year-old author whose reading history we profiled at the beginning of this chapter, had valuable insights about the need for reading to be personalized, unintimidating, and self-motivated. One of his suggestions, for example, was aimed directly at his peers with autism-spectrum labels: "Look at books with lots of pictures and pick ones that look fun" and "Just look at it [a book about one's fascination] and realize that books and words will help you learn more about your favorite topic" (2002, p. 121).

Jackson's recommendations remind us that the most important step toward improving reading for any student, but particularly for those with disabilities, is often not about selecting the exactly right instructional method—though we do hope that you'll be deliberate and planful as you work toward doing that—but rather about encouraging a particular child to join what Frank Smith (1988) calls the "literacy club," a metaphor to describe all those who identify themselves as readers. The same membership invitation has to be extended with warmth and the expectation of success where students' development of competencies in writing and other forms of representation are concerned, which we discuss in the next chapter.

Recommended Resources
Alphabet books for younger and older students
For Younger Students (Pre-School–Grade 2)
Aylesworth, J. (1992). *Old black fly*. New York: Henry Holt.   Starting with apple pie, a pesky fly buzzes through a house and lands on objects representing the letters of the alphabet.

(continued)

Recommended Resources *(continued)*

Ehlert, L. (1989). *Eating the alphabet: Fruits and vegetables from A to Z.* Orlando, FL: Harcourt Brace & Company.

Bright colors and bold lettering, trademarks of the work of this author and illustrator, are featured throughout this staple of the K–1 classroom.

Kellogg, S. (1987). *Aster aardvark's alphabet adventures.* New York: Morrow Junior Books.

Children are charmed by this alliterative text and all the humorous pictures of their favorite animals.

Martin, B. & Archambault, J. (1989). *Chicka chicka boom boom!* New York: Simon & Schuster.

Young children will love this rhythmic story as much as they do the fun illustrations of the letters racing to the top of the coconut tree.

Pienkowski, J. (1993). *ABC dinosaurs.* New York: Lodestar Books.

Prehistoric times come to life in this pop-up book that will please those who love dinosaurs (as so many little ones with autism do) and other prehistoric creatures.

Serensits, J. (2001). *The alphabet train coloring book.* Hanover, PA: Railroad Press.

This list would not be complete without a book about trains. This coloring book, appropriate for the youngest learners, will be attractive for those with a passion for these machines. Both capital and small letters are found on the pages and bonus material on signs, signals and locomotives is included.

Seuss, D. (1963). *Dr. Seuss's ABC.* New York: Random House.

This popular book combines rhythm, rhyme, classic illustrations, and general silliness to teach and reinforce important concepts such as the names of the letters, alphabetic order, and phonics.

For Older Students

Base, G. (1986). *Animalia.* New York: Harry N. Abrams.

Base's fantasy world of silly and amazing animals is complex, interesting, artistic, and for all ages.

Bryan, A. (1997). *Ashley Bryan's ABC of African-American poetry.* New York: Simon & Schuster.

Bryan's book is highly creative and captures the essence of 25 poems, making it ideal for a language arts poetry unit for students in any age group.

Johnson, S. (1995). *Alphabet city.* Viking.

Urban America is the setting for this book that features stunning artwork and a sophisticated look at the ABCs.

Mullins, P. (1993). *V for vanishing: An alphabet of endangered animals.* New York: Harper-Collins.

This consciousness-raising book would be a perfect complement to a unit on ecology, animals, or related topics.

Musgrove, Margaret W. (1976). *Ashanti to Zulu.* New York: Dial Books for Young Readers.

This examination of the traditions and customs of 26 African tribes beginning with letters from A to Z features content that will be new even to those in middle and high school classrooms.

Pelletier, D. (1996). *The graphic alphabet.* New York: Scholastic.

Graphic designer David Pelletier has created a stunning alphabet book that explores both the function and the form of letters. Although some students might use this book to polish up on phonics, others may be interested in the inventive designs featured throughout. Art teachers in both elementary and secondary classrooms may want to teach from this unique text.

Pallotta, J., Stillwell, F., & Bolster, R. (1999). *Airplane alphabet book.* Watertown, MA: Charlesbridge Publishing.

Brightly colored pictures of mostly vintage airplanes will attract young aviation enthusiasts as well as those who just love machines, transportation, and technology. A paragraph of text describes the plane featured on each page, making this an appropriate choice for those just beginning to read as well as those who have more experience and skill.

Rankin, L. (1991). *The handmade alphabet.* New York: Penguin.

This introduction to American Sign Language is appropriate for all ages and can work as a primer in reading and in the learning of another language.

Smith, M., & Queener, C. (2006). *The alphabet and the automobile.* Phoenix, AZ: David Bull Publishing.

A great choice for fans of racers, roadsters, sports cars, or sedans. Even adults will find this beautifully illustrated text appealing.

Chapter 6

Focus on Writing
and Representation

onna Williams is a woman with autism whose career has included work as a writer, educational consultant, screenwriter, musician, artist, and public speaker. In addition to providing an insider's view on the difficulties of oral communication for some people with autism, including those with functional speech, Williams's best-selling memoirs *Nobody Nowhere* (1992) and *Somebody Somewhere* (1994) provide detailed descriptions of both her purposes for writing and her processes. Her first book, in particular, shows how writing can be a vehicle for self-discovery and expression:

> At home I had bought a cheap plastic typewriter and begun to type. I began with the center of my world as far back as I could remember. The nights got longer as one page rolled into the next and I relived each moment, staring straight ahead and letting the words come from my fingers. . . . As the pages mounted up, so did my visits to the library, where I buried my head in books on schizophrenia and searched desperately to find a sense of belonging within those pages that would give me a word to put to all of this.
>
> Suddenly it jumped out at me from the page. It was the first time since my father had said it four years ago that I'd hear the word. "Autism," it read, "not to be confused with schizophrenia." My heart jumped, and I shook. Perhaps this was the answer or the beginning of finding one. I looked for a book on autism.
>
> There upon the pages I felt both angered and found. The echoed speech, the inability to be touched, the spinning and jumping, the rocking and repetition mocked my whole life. . . . I wanted an opinion once and for all as to why I was like this. I decided to take my book to a child psychiatrist who could read it and tell me why. During my lunch break I asked for directions to the child psychiatry department of the hospital. I looked for and found a door with the appropriate label on it and knocked.
>
> "I've written a book," I said to the professional behind the desk, "I want you to read it and tell me why I'm like I am." (1992, pp. 187–188)

In other sections of the same book, Donna discusses her use of writing as a practical tool to organize information. For example, she reports arriving at a therapist appointment with a written list of concepts such as the word *friend,* for which she wanted explicit definitions from another perspective than her own. Similarly, she found it helpful when her landlords, a couple with whom she became close friends, used writing and graphics to help represent her relationships with the publishers who had accepted her manuscript:

> Out came the diagrams and stick figures, scales, connecting lines, and talk bubbles. We moved from emotions to sketching out relationships between people. I saw where words like 'friend,' 'acquaintance,' and 'stranger' fit on a scale. With the concepts neat and labeled, it began to emerge just how much I had taken on faith. (1992, p. 118)

Although Williams found considerable success as a writer, it's important to note that composition wasn't always easy for her. Some of the difficulties she faced were tied to the idiosyncrasies of her autism, as this reflection on a college writing assignment shows:

> The psychology teacher handed back our work. She had marked it purely on content rather than on presentation. She got to mine and announced that she had to give me the highest mark in the class even though she had never had to read from so disgusting a piece of paper. I had used white typing fluid to go over an entire page of previous work before writing my new work on it and handing it in. I was poor, it was true, but it never occurred to me that the whitener cost more than the paper I had used it on. (1992, p. 120)

In her English class, Williams reported, the issues were not related to the physical presentation of her ideas. Instead, she struggled to address the teacher's assigned topics:

> I'd spend the time writing evasively about something that disturbed me. I'd write in such a way that it almost needed to be decoded to be understood, and I would always finish the work off with a lightly penciled sketch drawn over the writing, covering the length of the page, which I felt would more adequately capture what I was trying to express. (1992, p. 56)

Williams eventually learned to write so well that her texts need little decoding at all, but she did not come to this facility without considerable persistence and feedback from interested others.

We use Williams's story to begin our discussion of teaching writing to students with autism spectrum labels because we think it demonstrates some key themes of the chapter, including the benefits that writing can offer students with autism as well as the various challenges that they may face in this area. Moreover, Williams's predilection for graphic organizers and her forays into music, sculpture, and painting remind us that constructing meaning with text can, and often should, be a multimodal process—a stance consistent with the multiple literacies perspective we discussed in Chapter 2. In the workplace, in the political arena, and on the Internet, people increasingly communicate their ideas using forms of representation beyond traditional print. By aligning literacy instruction with these trends, teachers can ensure that their pedagogy remains in step with the world beyond the schoolhouse door. They can also create space for students with even more significant disabilities than Williams's—including those who struggle to write or communicate in traditional ways—to use various technologies or symbol systems to make meaningful contributions to the classroom community and their own learning (Bedrosian, Lasker, Speidel, & Politsch, 2003; Copeland & Keefe, 2006).

The remainder of the chapter begins with an overview of purposes and contexts for writing, then turns to several key components—fluency, planning and organization, revision and editing—that recent scholarship (Farnan & Dahl, 2003; Graham & Perin, 2007; MacArthur, Graham, & Fitzgerald, 2006; Smagorinsky, 2006) leads us to suggest may be foundational to success with composition for students with autism. For clarity's sake, we tackle these components one at a time, although some of them overlap in practice, and we use the same organizational structure that we employed in the previous chapter. Each section begins with reference to its research base, explains how each topic might be experienced by learners with autism, and recommends some teaching practices designed to promote greater competence and confidence in that area for these students.

PURPOSES AND CONTEXTS FOR WRITING INSTRUCTION

Researchers dating back to the early 1970s presented the idea that writers' purposes for writing influence the processes they use and the choices they make about form or genre, regardless of whether those writers are children or adults (Bissex, 1980; Chapman, 1995; Donovan & Smolkin, 2006; Emig, 1971). *Writing Next*, a recent review of research on writing that has received a good deal of attention from literacy educators, framed students' awareness of the purposes for their writing, and their ability to adjust their writing to those purposes, as a central goal for writing instruction:

> Most contexts of life (school, the workplace, and the community) call for writing skills, and each context makes overlapping but not identical demands. Proficient writers can adapt their writing to its context. Writing is also produced in different formats, such as sentences, lists, outlines, paragraphs, essays, letters, and books. Proficient writers can flexibly move among most, if not all, of these formats. Proficient writers are also able to move among purposes that range from writing solely for themselves (as in a personal diary) to communicating with an external audience. (Graham & Perin, 2007, p. 22)

When we read autobiographies and memoirs by people with autism spectrum labels, we see many different purposes for composing. Consider the range of purposes—from the creation of order to persuasion, from the learning of new content to personal reflection—revealed in the following excerpts, all taken from the autobiographies of those with autism:

> I used to write labels for various things. I wanted everything to be orderly, clear and separate. This was not some way of keeping an inner chaos under control, but an attempt to arrange the external world according to the same system as the inner world, a way of establishing a slightly better accord between me and everything else. Inside me were already closed compartments with labels attached for events, rooms and worlds. Like a computer, these did indeed have a great many ramifications and sub-departments, but the cross-connections were few. Clearly, the worlds outside me would be easier to relate

to if I was able to sort them out in a similar way. So I made labels which said what everything was and where it belonged. (Gerland, 1996, p. 53)

It is my hope that through this book not only students of anthropology and autism but everyone else as well will see gorillas as teachers, too. It is my hope that we will all become students of the gorillas' gentle care, fierce protectiveness, love, and acceptance. Perhaps if human people learn these same things . . . then a "culture of one" will mean a culture of all. (Prince-Hughes, 2004, p. 223)

Writing about my life has given me the opportunity to get some perspective on just how far I've come, and to trace the arc of my journey up to the present. (Tammet, 2007, p. 12)

I wanted to write before I [had a formal communication system]. I would sit and watch others do things and became an observer of humanity . . . It was when I wrote my first poem with Mom that a whole new world opened up for me. People liked it and I was off the starting blocks and still in the race. (Page, 2003, p. 114)

When one of my scientific papers is accepted for publication, I feel the same happiness I experienced one summer when I ran home to show my mother the message I had found in a bottle. I feel a deep satisfaction when I make use of my intellect to design a challenging project. It is the same kind of satisfied feeling one gets after finishing a difficult crossword puzzle or playing a challenging game of chess or bridge; it's not an emotional experience so much as an intellectual satisfaction. (Grandin, 1995, p. 88)

When I first heard I had A[sperger]S[yndrome] I was sure God must have had a reason for making me different. I am still convinced about this. I also wondered what God's special mission was for me. I was quite determined to find out and I still am. Perhaps writing this book is a part of it but I don't know. (Hall, 2001, p. 16)

In contrast to these varying accounts of authors' purposes, writing in school is often reduced to pleasing the teacher, getting a good grade, or finishing a task quickly in order to move on to something more personally satisfying. We think that teachers need to be aware of the many reasons why people write outside of school so that they can tap the motivation that writing in such varied ways generates.

In addition to establishing clear and varied purposes for different kinds of writing, teachers need to create classroom environments where writing can flourish. Composition scholar Karen Bromley (1999) identified the following as key components of a sound writing program:

- *Standards and assessments that guide teachers and students*: Teachers need to have clear targets for student learning and growth, and students need to be involved in assessing their own progress toward these targets.

- *Large blocks of time for reading, writing, talking, and sharing*: Students need time to practice composing within a print- and language-rich environment that inspires connection-making.

- *Direct instruction in composing and conventions*: Teachers provide students with carefully orchestrated modeling and guidance in how to master specific aspects of composing.

- *Choice and authenticity in writing for a variety of purposes and audiences:* Motivation increases for students who make choices about how to communicate, and with whom, especially as Internet technologies widen the scope of potential audiences.

- *Writing to construct meaning across the curriculum in a variety of forms*: Students use writing to learn and communicate their learning in all disciplines, not just language arts, providing them with additional practice as writers.

As we see it, these components, combined with the key principles for inclusive classrooms that we outlined in Chapter 3, are the foundation for the instructional recommendations that follow.

FLUENCY

We discussed fluency in Chapter 5 in the context of teaching reading, but the concept also applies to writing, so we consider it here as well. Fluent writers are able to encode their messages comfortably and smoothly, with few interruptions or difficulties. According to cognitive scientists, fluency is important to writers because "more fluent text-production processes free working memory resources, allowing the writer to move beyond knowledge telling and engage in higher-level processes, such as planning and reviewing" (McCutcheon, 2006, p. 126). Writing teacher William Strong explained this phenomenon in simpler, more evocative terms, asking his students to compare the experience of writing a summary sentence in their dominant hand (something they can likely do with fluency) with their experience of writing with the other:

> [W]riting with the opposite hand makes us focus on handwriting, rather than on the content of our thinking. It saps mental energy. And that's why it's so important to develop writing fluency with daily practice. . . . Fluency releases brain power, giving us access to the good ideas between our ears. (2006, p. 64)

Some of the most compelling information about fluency comes from research using data from large-scale assessments. For example, the National Assessment of Educational Progress (NAEP) periodically tests a national sample of 4th, 8th, and 11th graders in a variety of subjects including writing (http://nces.ed.gov/nationsreportcard/writing/). Students taking the NAEP are asked to write in three different genres: narrative, informative, and persuasive. In 1996, their papers were scored in several different ways, including holistically for overall fluency using a 6-point rubric. This procedure allowed examiners to compare trends in student writing over time, regardless of the task or genre, with modest gains in fluency being reported between 1984 and 1996 for both fourth and eighth graders.

Other research with a fluency emphasis has considered the social contexts for writing along with the products themselves. For example, Mina Shaughnessy's (1977) classic study of basic writers at the college level was among the first to show that inexperienced writers were often so stymied by their fear of making errors that they often wrote very little. When they did produce text, it was often stilted or nonsensical because of their confusion about what appeared to them to be arbitrary rules and conventions. They had not internalized a sense of how written language works, and the kinds of error corrections they had experienced silenced their voices.

More recent research shows that students' fluency can be increased with targeted instruction (Eckert, Lovett, Rosenthal, Jiao, Ricci, & Truckenmiller, 2006; Graham, Harris, & Larsen, 2001; Quinlan, 2004). What's striking to us is how simple some of these effective interventions are. For example, a team led by psychology professor Tanya Eckert and her colleagues (2006) studied the effects of a writing fluency intervention for third graders, including some with learning disabilities, in an urban school district. Once a week for 8 weeks students were asked to write in response to a story stem like the following: "I never dreamed that the door in my bedroom would lead to. . . ." Before they began drafting, they received individual feedback sheets listing the following: 1) the number of words they produced during the previous week's writing session, 2) the number of sentences they wrote during the previous session, and 3) the number of correctly spelled words from the previous session. Each of the three numbers was accompanied by an arrow symbol to represent visually whether the numbers had gone up or down from the previous week. Students who received the individual feedback achieved statistically significant gains in both fluency and spelling when compared with the performance of students who received a similar writing task but no instructor feedback.

The results from Eckert and colleagues suggest to us that setting fluency goals explicitly for students and involving them in tracking their own progress can go a long way toward supporting improvement in these areas. Students with autism who love numbers (and there are many) will be especially interested in this exercise that allows them to use their quantifying skills.

Other researchers have shown that writing fluency increases for many students, including some with disabilities, when they are provided with access to assistive and augmentative technologies. Quinlan (2004), for example, reported gains for less fluent writers, ages 11–14, when they used speech recognition technology rather than handwriting four narratives. The length of their pieces increased when they used the software and the number of surface-feature errors decreased. Graham, Harris, and Larsen (2001) found that technologies such as word processing, semantic mapping software, word prediction programs, and speech synthesizers aided students with learning disabilities in writing more easily. And Bedrosian, Lasker, Speidel, and Politsch (2003) reported that written output for a nonverbal middle school student with autism increased over time during an intervention that involved him and his writing partner, a same-age peer with a cognitive disability label, in using a story writing software program in conjunction with an AlphaTalker communication device. Although students still need responsive instruction in how to employ various technologies for composing purposes—the technologies themselves are not enough—these researchers suggest that such tools are making fluency a more attainable goal for a wider range of learners than it has ever been before.

 ## Considering Students with Autism

The communication and movement differences often associated with autism can make it difficult for many individuals with this label to achieve writing fluency.

Even writers who eventually learn to create significant amounts of text may approach fluency using different perspectives and different strategies than do learners who are neurotypical. For example, when Lucy Blackman, an Australian woman with autism who is largely nonverbal, began to generate written language by typing, she reported that her mother, who served as her most frequent communication partner, did not quite understand Lucy's approach to typing:

> [She] thought I was using it like other teenagers do. She did not realise that I typed more fluently if I imagined I was sitting above my own body, watching, as another Lucy would, a new character, also called Lucy, going through the motions that all other literate people did. It was as if I were role playing. (1999, p. 105)

At the same time, some learners on the autism spectrum report little difficulty with writing fluency (Grandin, 1995; Williams, 1992, 1994). Some of them appear to process and produce written text more easily than speech. For example, Wendy Lawson, a woman with autism, wrote the following:

> I find the written word much easier to comprehend than the spoken word. It takes me a lot longer to process conversation and work out the meaning behind the words than it does to scan the words on a written page. I think this is because I must also read the expressions on a person's face and study their body language. (1998, pp. 9–10)

Lawson's sentiments are echoed by Gunilla Gerland, another woman with autism, in her autobiography:

> First of all, I learned to write, which was easier, and then I learnt to read. I liked words, and needed new challenges for it to be fun. I wanted to learn more and more complicated words. When I heard a new one, I always grabbed at it, and even if I had seen a word in writing only once, I usually knew how it was spelt. I enjoyed writing and being good at it. Expressing words in writing was much easier for me than taking the long way round, as I experienced it, via speech. (1996, p. 53)

Likewise, Daniel Tammet, a man with Asperger syndrome who was a self-proclaimed "savant," shared that, as a child, fluent writing was one of his many academic gifts. He recalled that, around age 8, he wrote compulsively (often for hours at a time), using up endless reams of computer paper and covering all of the paper's surface with "tightly knit words" so tiny that a teacher complained about having to change the prescription on her glasses just to read the text:

> The stories I wrote, from what I can remember of them, were descriptively dense—a whole page might be taken up in describing the various details of a single place or location, its colors, shapes, and textures. There was no dialogue, no emotions. Instead I wrote of long, weaving tunnels far underneath vast, shimmering oceans, of cragged rock caves and towers climbing into the sky.
>
> I didn't have to think about what I was writing; the words just seemed to flow out of my head. Even without any conscious planning, the stories were always comprehensible. When I showed one to my teacher, she liked it enough to read parts of it out loud to the rest of the class. (2007, p. 44)

Given the heterogeneity of experiences with fluency that Blackman, Lawson, Gerland, and Tammet describe, you will need to observe student writers with autism closely in multiple composing contexts to see whether they struggle with fluency and, correspondingly, whether they might benefit from the kinds of fluency-focused instructional approaches we present in the next section. As we suggested in Chapter 4, you will also want to supplement your observations with assessments such as conferences with students, and possibly their caregivers, to get a sense of their own perspective on their writing fluency as well as to ascertain whether their fluency in school approximates their fluency in other contexts.

Instructional Approaches

According to many composition experts, students need ample amounts of practice in low-anxiety contexts to develop fluency as writers (Kirby, Liner, & Vinz, 1988; McCutcheon, 2006; Strong, 2006). Ungraded daily journal writing of one kind or another is frequently cited as one way to provide that practice (Fulwiler, 1987; Kirby et al., 1988), and we support that approach wholeheartedly for learners with and without disabilities. (Table 6.1 includes brief descriptions of different kinds of journals that might be implemented in inclusive classrooms.) We also advocate the following approaches that may be less familiar to you: language experience approach; scribing; tracking text quantity; silent discussions; differentiating materials; writing "here, there, and everywhere"; and offering handwriting alternatives—each of which is discussed in this section.

Language Experience Approach

Like Copeland and Keefe (2006), we see the language experience approach (LEA) originally conceived by Stauffer (1970) as a method of developing writing fluency that is appropriate for students with wide-ranging needs, including those with significant disabilities. The steps of this approach are fairly simple:

1. Engage the students in a shared experience such as a teacher read aloud of a picture book, a field trip, a cooperative activity, or a classroom visit from a community member that will give them something meaningful and interesting about which to write.

2. Record individual students' contributions to the text on the board or on a projected screen as the ideas are dictated, rereading them for each contributor to make sure you transcribe them accurately.

3. Reread the text periodically from the beginning to help students see how it is progressing, editing and revising as necessary.

4. Continue taking individual contributions and rereading the draft of the text until the students are satisfied that it is complete.

5. Read the text aloud in its entirety so that students can hear what it sounds like, then ask them to reread it chorally with you (see Chapter 5 for more on this approach).

6. Invite students to engage in follow-up activities such as illustrating the text, rereading it in class, and/or taking it home to share with families.

LEA is often used by teachers in inclusive classrooms because it is typically collaborative and students can add a contribution in any number of ways, such as

Table 6.1. Variations on journal writing appropriate for inclusive classrooms

Dialogue journal: Students write entries in the form of a friendly letter about their reading and/or their lives, and their partners, who may be peers (Kirby, Liner, & Vinz, 1988) or a teacher (Atwell, 1998), write back.

Double-entry journal: Students divide the page into two columns, noting information from the text— quotations or paraphrases—in one column and their own responses (e.g., questions they have, connections they make) in the other column (Daniels & Zemelman, 2005).

Family literacy journal: Students and their families read literature or tell stories together and then record their responses with writing, drawings, photographs, and/or captions (Parker, 1997).

Sketch journal: Students sketch, draw, or include images in their journals, sometimes using the visual material alone to capture an idea but often using it as a springboard for writing items such as captions or labels (Ernst, 1994).

Writer's notebook: Students make entries about all aspects of their thinking about writing, including observational notes, lists of potential topics, questions they have, interview notes, favorite quotations, and so forth; they often review these entries for ideas or drafts that they can add to, polish, and share (Hindley, 1996).

choosing a picture to represent an idea, pointing to a choice of a few words or a sentence, or verbally sharing a word or short utterance that can be weaved into the group story. And Downing (2005) suggested that for students with the most significant disabilities, objects related to the story might be used to draw students into the activity and to help them express ideas.

Recently, Labbo, Eakle, and Montero (2002) adapted the LEA approach to tap the potential of digital photography and computer software to promote student learning, even for the youngest writers. In the kindergarten classroom this team studied, the digital language experience approach (or D-LEA) still began with a stimulus experience, but that experience was photographed with digital cameras as students participated. Students then used the photographs to prepare for their compositions by 1) importing them into creativity software such as Kidpix (available from Learning Company, http://www.learningcompany.com), which allowed them to add text to the images; 2) discussing which images to select that best represented the experience; and 3) sequencing those images, sometimes with a storyboard. Next, teachers typed students' contributions into the digital document (or helped students to do so, if they had enough facility with writing and the software). In addition to editing the print aspects of the text, students had the option of adding multimedia effects such as music, sound effects, or animation. The final phase of the approach was also enhanced by the features of the technology because students could read the text on screen, with or without the voice synthesizer.

We think that this adapted LEA has even more potential to support students with autism than the traditional version because it allows for multimodal representation that can build on the visual strengths many learners with autism possess as well as tie in to the fascination with computers that some of these same learners report. It also allows students with fewer verbal skills to participate meaningfully because they can select and sequence images even if they cannot produce written text to caption them.

Scribing

The language experience approach we've described can be implemented in a small- or large-group setting because students benefit from the opportunity to hear others' perspectives on a shared experience and see how that experience is represented in print. Students who are more skilled oral communicators or who know more about how print works therefore serve as models for peers who need additional support in those areas. (This is, in our view, yet another academic benefit of students' participation in inclusive classrooms.) It can sometimes be beneficial to an individual student's writing fluency, however, for a teacher, parent, or peer to serve as his or her scribe while the student plans and drafts a piece of writing aloud. For students with autism who have relatively reliable speech but who find the physical act of writing to be difficult because of their lack of experience or problems with fine motor control, scribing can free them to compose more quickly and, in some cases, in more complex ways. The scribe may simply invite the author of the text to begin talking and then record the words as they are said; or the two may engage in a multistep process together, in which the author brainstorms possibilities recorded by the scribe in list form or on a graphic organizer, and then tells the scribe what to include in the actual draft while using the brainstormed notes as a reference. The approach to select depends on the purpose, length, and complexity of the text: a student's quick response to a poem read by a peer may not require advance planning, but a research paper in science most likely will.

One specific adaptation we have used often in inclusive classrooms is collaborative journaling or "writing buddies" support in which the student with a disability chooses photographs or pictures from magazines to use as writing prompts and glues them into a spiral notebook. He or she then invites peers to "write" with him or her during workshop or free writing time. To be sure that the students talk about ideas together and that they remember key components (e.g., generating a title), we place simple age-appropriate directions right into the front cover of the notebook (see Figure 6.1 for an example) so that partners are reminded of the exact steps to take to support their classmates. For instance, a notebook created for a fifth-grade student contained the following directions:

1. Pick a picture and talk about it with your buddy. Think about a story you can write about the picture. You can also make up a story on your own without using a picture.

2. One person should write the story in the journal.

3. Think of a name for the story together.

4. Write the title at the top of the page.

5. Write your names at the top of the page.

We should note that some educators resist scribing because they fear it does not provide students with enough independent practice with writing. Others—especially those working with students with severe disabilities—may come to depend on the practice too much. We believe that there are plenty of learning situations in which the most important concern is using writing to participate; in those cases, scribing is vastly preferable to silencing a student who has something valuable to say. At the same time, we're aware that some writers lack comfort with the physical act of writing simply because they have had too few opportunities to develop that comfort.

Because our goal is always to help literacy learners do as much on their own as possible, we recommend that teachers who scribe for students try to fade their

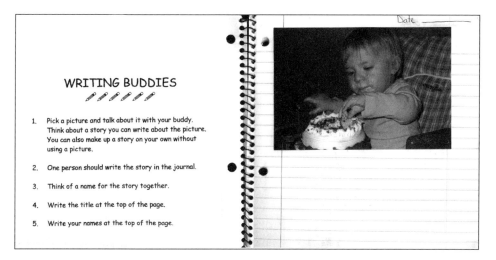

Figure 6.1. A "writing buddies" journal for fifth-graders.

level of support over time, as they observe students gaining more control as writers. When Kelly used this approach, she began by scribing complete texts for students that they could then use for reading practice. (These students' own language structures are so familiar to them that this helps them to develop reading fluency.) When students' texts got longer, and they appeared to compose them orally with greater comfort, she began to scribe only the topic sentences for each paragraph, leaving blank spaces between the paragraphs to cue students about how much text they might include to support those topic sentences. Eventually, she would scribe only an outline or just a few key words to serve as a reminder to students as they wrote independently.

Tracking Text Quantity

The study by Eckert and her colleagues (2006) that we mentioned previously suggested that one way to promote writing fluency is to involve students in tracking how much text they produce over time. Fisher and Frey reported similarly positive results with older learners who engaged in what they called *power writing*, "a fluency activity that requires students to write as many words as they can on a topic as fast as they can" (2003, p. 402). In the ninth-grade English classroom these authors described (in which 75% of the students were English language learners and all tested between the third- and sixth-grade reading level on a diagnostic assessment), power writing was organized such that all students wrote for 1 minute each class on a topic or choice of topic assigned by the teacher. When the minute was up, students counted how many words they had written and recorded the number on a personal chart.

Another key aspect of power writing was that it generated text that students could use for revision-focused activities. Students were assigned to one of five groups per class, and each group was selected once per week to take their power writing home to revise and edit it for homework. Fisher and Frey reported that this component of the approach had two benefits: It encouraged students to "take the power writing activity seriously" because they "never knew which day they would be providing an edited version to the teacher" and it reduced teacher work-load because only 20% of students in each class needed responses per night. Al-though this team did not engage in statistical analysis like Eckert and colleagues (2006), they reported that individual students made dramatic progress because the "act of writing every day for a defined period of time allowed [them] to under-stand the flow more accomplished writers experience" (2003, pp. 402–403).

Although tracking text quantity has been employed most often with tradi-tional print, our expanded conceptions of literacy suggest that it might also be practical to quantify the number of images or symbols a student includes in a composition. Although this, too, is only a gross measure of the complexity of the student's thinking, it gives teachers an initial way to acknowledge improvements in communication, even when the student in question doesn't write convention-ally. In our view, a student who communicates by choosing a single symbol in September but who can link two, three, or even four symbols that tell a story or communicate an idea by May has certainly shown growth as a composer. By ac-knowledging this kind of growth to students and engaging them in reflection on it, teachers can help sustain students' motivation as well as assist them in reaching new goals that might otherwise be invisible if the only indicator for fluency progress is an increased word count.

Using Silent Discussions

Sometimes students struggle with writing not because they can't organize their thinking but because they're not sure what to say. One way to help them practice generating written text in a social context is the "silent discussion," an instruc-tional activity developed by Kelly's friend Tanya Baker, an English and literacy teacher. As Tanya organized it, each student in the class received a blank piece of paper on which he or she wrote a question about a shared reading. After students passed their papers to the right, they answered the question, then added a ques-tion of their own before passing the paper again. Tanya usually ended the passing after five or six turns, at which time she invited students to "report one interesting thing from the paper they have in their hands" (Wilhelm, Baker, & Dube, 2001, p. 141). In Tanya's classroom, students typically generated their own questions, but the basic structure of the activity could be retained with a teacher-designed prompt or question to begin the conversation, followed by students' responding to that question in turn.

We speculate that this activity has the potential to promote fluency because students are cued by their peers' questions and previous answers about what to write. Except for during the first turn, they are not expected to compose from scratch. But a silent discussion doesn't need to be a group task. It can take place with only two participants, and one of them can even be the teacher. Michael, a student with autism whom Paula taught, often asked her to converse with him on paper. During even the shortest exchanges, he preferred to write rather than talk. He would type short answers and Paula would respond in longhand. Although they could not engage in conversations in this way every time he requested it (it was time-consuming, and she had other students to tend to), she tried to dialogue this way with him whenever time allowed. He found these exchanges on paper to be more calming, comforting, and easier to comprehend than those he partici-pated in verbally.

When Paula shared the success of this approach with Michael's middle school teachers, they found that written conversations were not only perfect opportuni-ties to build fluency but also they could be used to develop other skills. For in-stance, each week, Michael's teachers made an effort to add new vocabulary to the written messages they exchanged with him. They also modeled how to use punc-tuation, type size, and font to indicate tone, inflection, and emotion in his writ-ing—all aspects of communication that are conveyed differently in oral communi-cation than they are in print. After working on these conversations for several weeks, Michael became interested in sharing his new skills with classmates and was able to teach them (via three mini-presentations) about communicating clearly using written language, which helped all students improve their own e-mail messages.

Differentiating Writing Materials

Still another way to encourage fluency is to use a wide range of materials and pro-vide choice in how the learner will complete writing tasks. Teddy, a young man with Asperger syndrome, for instance, was often much more willing to write longer passages when he could use markers or colorful paper. Another student we know did higher quality work when he wrote on the chalkboard instead of on notepaper or the computer. Still another learner was motivated to write when his teacher honored his passion for kitchen utensils by attaching his pencils to small cooking ladles and allowing him to, in essence, write with a spoon (see Table 6.2 for more ideas on differentiating writing materials).

June Downing described her student Joannie, who profited from both choice activities and from using different materials during writing exercises. This learner, who, previous to being included in a first-grade classroom had been in a room for students labeled as "trainable mentally retarded," made gains when she was given materials that allowed her to construct text and participate in typical class-room activities:

> When asked to write in her journal, she was given choices of pictures from which to select. She tended to select topics around her classmates, in particular, her friend, Monica. Initially starting with pictures and then fading to word cards alone, Joannie was able to complete sentences by using index cards placed sequentially in separate boxes following the sentence pattern of "Monica is _____." Joannie seemed to take great delight in choosing the adjectives (a choice of three) to complete the sen-tence, which were then read to her and written in her journal. She held a pencil but used the word cards to put in the sequential boxes to form her sentences about her friend. (2005, p. 68)

Assistive technology should also be considered for each learner with autism. Students may need low-tech options such as a slant board or pencil grip or high-tech options such as software programs and augmentative communication devices. Common writing supports for students with autism include word prediction soft-ware, voice recognition software, "talking" dictionaries, teacher-created letter or picture boards, alternative keyboards (with larger keys that can be arranged to suit the learner's needs or preferences), and even typewriters (a favorite for students who are sensory learners and like to "feel" what they are writing).

Table 6.2. Differentiating writing materials

Implements	Surfaces	Related tools
Pencils	Paper	Magazines
Markers	Computer screen	Glue sticks
Rubber stamps	Chalkboard	Stickers
Crayons	Wipe board	Post-it notes
Paintbrushes	Magnetic board	Etch-a-Sketch
Chalk	Sidewalk	Language Master
Vibrating, novelty, or textured pens	Chart paper	Correction fluid
	Paper with raised lines	Stencils
Stylus	Index cards	
Label maker	Cardboard	
Computer mouse or touch screen	Note pad	
	Paper plates	
Letter or word magnets	Carbon paper	

Sometimes students will need a combination of assistive technology supports. For instance, Erickson and Koppenhaver (2007) shared an example of a student with significant physical disabilities who typed slowly on a keyboard equipped with a keyguard. He often typed letters of words out of order (CTA for CAT), causing his teacher to question whether he had spelling difficulties or was simply fatigued from typing. Working with her special education colleague, the teacher replaced the learner's keyboard with a joystick, an on-screen keyboard, and Co:Writer 4000 (Don Johnston), a software program that assists the user with both writing and spelling. These authors reported that after implementing these adaptations, the student was able to type more easily and spell more accurately. See Figure 6.2 for examples of assistive technology that can be used for supporting literacy and communication skills and competencies.

Writing Here, There, and Everywhere

Although all writing researchers recommend giving students meaningful opportunities throughout the school day to write for enjoyment, different audiences, and authentic reasons, we believe this recommendation may be even more critical for students with disabilities who may not only need practice with writing but also with communication, in general. Students may be asked to write any number of things throughout the day including notes to friends, requests to teachers, or e-mails to pen pals anywhere in the world, but, in any of these instances, the purpose should be clear, the time commitment should be manageable, and the experience should be fun. In one seventh-grade class, for instance, Robert, a student with autism, comes into his classroom, takes an index card from his teacher's desk that is always left in the same spot, and copies the "fun fact" (that usually begins "On this day in history. . . .") from the card to the board. He often adds a second sentence that serves as a greeting or inspiration to his classmates (e.g., "Have a great day!"). In a second-grade classroom, Diego, a young man who has the label of fragile X syndrome, is responsible for e-mailing the school secretary to notify her of classroom absences, changes in the schedule, or students who may be leaving for appointments. See Table 6.3 for other examples of how students can practice writing across the school day.

a) Single-level device.   b) Multilevel device.   c) Comprehensive device.

Figure 6.2.   Examples of assistive technology that can be used for communication and participation in literacy activities. (*Key:* a) iTalk2™ Communicator from AbleNet, Inc. b) Tech/Talk, by EnableMart; and c) Mercury II™, by Assistive Technology, Inc. [see http://www.assistivetech.com/p-mercury.htm for more information].)

Offer Handwriting Alternatives

We can't conclude our discussion of promoting students' fluency as writers without giving some attention to handwriting. Even Hans Asperger, the man responsible for characterizing students with the disability that now bears his name, noted that the individuals he saw had great struggles with penmanship. In a description of a student he called Fritz, he wrote the following:

> In his tense fist, the pencil could not run smoothly. A whole page would suddenly be covered with big swirls, the exercise book would be drilled full of holes, if not torn up. In the end it was possible to teach him to write only by making him trace letters and words which were written in red pencil. (Asperger, 1944/1991, p. 49)

This characteristic is one that is oftentimes very frustrating for learners on the spectrum, especially when teachers are not aware of or sensitive to it. In fact, this was one of the most striking commonalities we discovered in our research on autobiographies written by people with autism (Grandin, 1995; Hall, 2001; Mukhopadhyay, 2000; Prince-Hughes, 2004; Shore, 2003; Tammet, 2007). All of these authors lament their difficulties with neatness and legibility, even in those situations in which they were highly motivated to achieve those goals (Grandin, 1995). Teachers can sometimes be confused when students' lack of success with handwriting is accompanied by prowess in other domains requiring precision and care. That people on the spectrum do not experience fine motor issues uniformly is

Table 6.3.   Ideas for integrating writing opportunities across the school day

Younger students can	Older students can
Write social notes to peers	Record the names of students who are absent
Write to a class pet or mascot	Write the daily schedule on the board
Sign autograph books or slam books	Create or copy a joke, quote, or fact of the day and write it on the board
Sign up for centers, playground equipment, or for class jobs	Sign yearbooks
E-mail home to family members to share daily happenings	E-mail friends, cyber pen-pals, or teachers
	Write assignments in their daily notebook

demonstrated by these comments from Stephen Shore, an author and musician with an autism label:

> I have always wondered how I can have the fine motor control to take apart a watch's gears while my drawing and penmanship when writing in script is so poor. Perhaps it is because the structure is inherent within the watch innards themselves, whereas when writing or drawing in freehand, I am forced to provide the structure. Even though I am well aware of my difficulties in penmanship and drawing, having to provide that structure from within myself makes it impossible for me to do these activities well. (2003, p. 60)

Shore goes on to say that the "computer serves as a wonderful assistive device for me" in creating texts that would otherwise be "labor-intensive and time-consuming" (2003, p. 144). As he explains it, "The relative ease of creating a good-looking document may determine whether or not the document is produced at all rather than being considered as something that will be too arduous to create" (2003, p. 144). We urge you to allow students with autism to compose on the keyboard as much as possible, as many of them will achieve fluency with this piece of adaptive technology that they simply could not while using a pen or pencil. (Quite honestly, we sympathize with these students' needs and preferences; as more and more of our own composition takes place on the keyboard, both of us find it increasingly difficult to draft fluently by hand!) Numerous K–12 teachers with whom we work find the AlphaSmart™ 3000 (Don Johnston), a word processor that is relatively inexpensive, to be a terrific tool for encouraging writing fluency for a wide range of learners, both with and without disabilities.

Please don't misunderstand our point here. In advocating for a greater emphasis on electronic composition, we're not advocating that students with autism, at least not all of them, should be exempt from learning to write legibly by hand. For some learners, however, support in this area might best be coordinated with occupational therapy services. Classroom teachers tend to receive little research-based training, if any, in how to support the development of fine motor skills in students with disabilities, making teachers' efforts, not surprisingly, often less effective and more time-consuming than those of an experienced specialist. We see little evidence that students' handwriting is improved by many of the copying and tracing activities teachers typically require them to do, and we're convinced that the valuable instructional time devoted to such activities could be better used to promote writing fluency.

A final recommendation we have in relation to handwriting is a bit of a departure from our earlier discussion. It is worth mentioning that while some students will need to move away from handwriting to find success in their expression and fluency, others may find that handwriting can be a doorway to communication. Some students have had success with a technique that might be called facilitated handwriting. In the 1960s, a woman named Rosalind Oppenheim (Crossley, 1997) taught a group of nonverbal students with autism to communicate through writing. The students, previously assumed to have mental retardation, were soon able to "talk" on paper. Oppenheim noted that putting pressure on the student's hand seemed to be the key to writing success for those in her group:

> We believe that the autistic child's difficulties stem from a definite apraxia . . . There seems to be a basic deficiency in certain areas of his motor expressive behaviour. So, in teaching writing, we find that it is unusually necessary to continue to guide the

child's hand for a considerable period of time. Gradually, however, we are able to fade this to a mere touch of a finger on the child's writing hand. We're uncertain about precisely what purpose this finger-touching serves. What we do know is that the quality of the writing deteriorates appreciably without it, despite the fact that the finger is in no way guiding the child's writing hand. "I can't remember how to write the letters without your finger touching my skin," one nonverbal child responded. (Oppenheim, as cited in Crossley, 1997, p. 40)

While writing is not a common augmentative communication strategy used by those with autism, Oppenheim is not the only person to discover success with it. Tito Rajarshi Mukhopadhyay (2000), a young man with autism, has been writing independently since age 6. Mukhopadhyay's story is interesting because he does not have verbal communication that is well understood by others:

> I can speak although many people cannot follow because it is not clear. Sometimes I need facilitation to begin my speech like opening a speech door in my throat. To facilitate me mother has to wave her hands. (p. 76)

Mukhopadhyay's first attempts at augmentative communication involved typing on a letter board. Eventually, however, his mother introduced pencil and paper to her son. Mukhopadhyay also needed facilitation and support to write before he was able to do so on his own. He describes how he moved from typing on a communication board to learning to write:

> Mother placed my communication board next to a page. She asked me to write the spelling of "cat."
>
> I pointed at the letter c and I copied it.
>
> Next I pointed at the letter a and I copied it.
>
> Then I pointed at the letter t and I copied it.
>
> That was the beginning and that was my passport to make people believe that my words are no one's but my own. . . . after that I was believed. (http://www.cureautismnow.org/tito/memories/my_memory.pdf., p. 22)

In the foreword of Mukhopadhyay's book, *Beyond the Silence*, Lorna Wing, a noted psychiatrist, describes her first impression of this young man and his use of these multiple systems of communication:

> When [I first met him], Tito's observable behaviour was exactly like that of a mute child with classic autism, ignoring people but exploring the objects that took his attention. [His mother] settled him down and wrote the alphabet on a piece of paper. We asked questions and Tito pointed to the letters to spell his replies. He did this independently, without any physical guidance from his mother. He replied to questions in full sentences, including long words used appropriately. He also spontaneously told us, in handwriting, that he wanted the book he had written to be published and demanded a promise that this would happen. (2000, p. 2)

For some students, then, particularly those who do not have reliable communication, facilitated handwriting may be an option not only for writing but also for communication in general.

PLANNING AND ORGANIZING TEXTS

The previous section of this chapter focused on assisting students to become writers who can generate text in a variety of forms. That, in our view, is the foundation for all other writing-oriented efforts, but it is only the beginning. Once learners have taken crucial steps toward fluency, they need to be introduced to a variety of tools and strategies to help them plan and organize their texts more effectively, given their purposes and audiences.

Several researchers cite significant differences in the planning processes of experienced writers compared with novices (Bereiter & Scardamalia, 1987; Langer, 1986; McCutcheon, 2006). Expert writers use a variety of approaches to planning their writing, often devoting considerable time to this phase of the writing process before they even put pen to paper. In contrast, many young children jump immediately to drafting upon being invited to write, although some do rehearse their ideas orally first, speaking either to themselves or to others around them (Dahl & Farnan, 1998). Artifacts of their planning are often indistinguishable from their drafts. Older writers, typically those in the middle grades, appear to delineate their planning from their drafting more easily than younger children, expanding upon their notes and discussing how their decisions related to the overall purpose of their pieces (Bereiter & Scardamalia, 1987).

These broad developmental trends notwithstanding, researchers also indicated that writers with varying levels of experience can learn to plan better if they are taught explicit strategies for doing so (Chapman, 2006; Graham, 2006; Graham & Perin, 2007). Collaborative talk among teachers and students may play a key role in supporting this sort of strategy acquisition. For example, in a frequently cited study, Bereiter and Scardamalia (1987) found evidence that group interactions can promote a higher level of planning, even in very young children. The researchers found that when various alternative ideas were presented in a collaborative setting, children were forced to weigh and analyze ideas before writing. In these cases, planning was much more conceptual and did not represent simply a mirror image of the composition itself (Dahl & Farnan, 1998).

Given this body of scholarship, it is suggested that teachers pay deliberate attention to incorporating planning and organizing into their writing instruction, and they would do well to embed that instruction in meaningful social interaction. This is especially vital for students with autism, who may have less experience with writing for a variety of reasons than their age peers, and who may, due to their communication and movement differences, be less able to facilitate informal social interaction around their writing for themselves without a teacher's careful assistance.

 ## Considering Students with Autism

Very little empirical research has been conducted on composing processes used by students with autism, but our personal experiences and reading of the autobiographical literature suggests that some individuals on the spectrum struggle to plan and organize their writing. Some authors with autism report taking a stream-of-consciousness approach to their writing, making it difficult for them to predict or control where the text will take them (Blackman, 1999; Williams, 1992). Conversely, others have experienced difficulty veering from a writing plan when the act of composing suggests a new direction that might be fruitful but that was not laid out in their original scheme.

Despite these trends, several authors have reported that assistance from other people has helped to scaffold them in approaching their writing planfully, rather than too spontaneously or rigidly. For example, when Lucy Blackman's mother discovered that her daughter (who uses an augmentative communication device to communicate) was bored and disengaged in her segregated classroom, she set Lucy a new challenge: "While you are sitting around doing nothing in the Special School classroom, get your mind working. Every evening I expect you to have planned part of a story ready to be typed out" (Blackman, 1999, p. 124). Lucy resisted her mother's suggestion at first ("Silly woman! That is not how I write. I flash up paragraphs and hook up phrases as I require them"), but she soon discovered that her mother's idea had merit: "[I]n my misery I daydreamed an image of me typing at home, and later that day found some of her assumptions were true. A little planning does make language more effective" (1999, p. 124).

Similarly, when 10-year-old Kenneth Hall decided that he wanted to write a book explaining Asperger syndrome to people working in schools, the Education Department in Northern Ireland, where he lived, sent a student to work with him weekly on planning and structuring the text. In the book, Kenneth reported with noticeable self-satisfaction that

> Michelle helped me by using index cards. First I had to decide all my section headings and have an index card for each one. This meant that all the proper information and ideas could be sorted into their proper sections. Later on I opened folders on the laptop for them all instead. (2001, p. 85)

With clear headings and subheadings for its various topics, Hall's finished text manifests the organizational help he received, suggesting that teachers who model and scaffold the use of such strategies explicitly can have a significant impact on the quality of students' composing.

Instructional Approaches

Most people, including those without disabilities, need explicit instruction from more experienced writers to develop a repertoire of strategies for planning and organizing the compositions that works best for them (Dahl & Farnan, 1998; Graham, 2006; Graham & Perin, 2007). The instructional approaches that we see as having the most potential for helping students with autism acquire and refine these strategies include the following: speak and write, framed paragraphs, graphic organizers, story kits, and color-coded notes.

Speak and Write

Because some students with autism may find the initiation or the idea-generation aspect of writing difficult, teachers may want to seek strategies that simply get students to put something on paper (or on the computer screen). One such strategy that we call *speak and write* involves listening to students' conversations or engaging in conversation with learners and suggesting which pieces of the discussion might be starting points for an essay, story, or other written product. Whereas many learners plan better on paper and with visuals in front of them, others may find this method too restricting in the early stages of organization. Some learners may want to do initial idea generation aloud and then move to traditional planning on paper for the next steps.

The speak and write strategy (or at least an unintentional form of it) is illustrated in Debra Ginsberg's memoir, *Raising Blaze*, about her adolescent son and her life's journey with him. The author tells of how Blaze came home from school and, as usual, began sharing stories of the day. Like many busy mothers, Ginsberg was distracted by another task and was only half listening to her persistent son until he caught her attention, finally, with his lyrical description of a classmate:

> "Breanna was crying yesterday, Mom," he told me. "She was really upset."
>
> "Oh, uh-huh?" I said, distractedly editing a poem about the color red.
>
> "Mom, really," Blaze went on. "She cried and it was like a storm. Her face was all dark and light and quiet. She didn't make any sound but there were all these clouds and rain in her face."
>
> This I paid attention to. "Blaze," I told him, "why don't you write that down? Write down what happened to Breanna yesterday. Just like you told me."
>
> "Oh, okay," he said, as if this was a good idea that hadn't occurred to him. Blaze's difficulty with the physical act of writing inclined him toward brevity, so he was finished very soon after he started. He handed me his paper and when I read it, I had the same surge of joy that I felt whenever I had read anything particularly good.
>
> *When Breanna cried it looked like a storm*
> *She didn't make any sound*
> *but there was rain*
> *and clouds*
> *and sun*
> *and darkness in her face*
>
> Blaze hadn't used any punctuation, so I added a couple of commas and periods. That was the extent of my edit.
>
> "That's a really great poem, Blaze," I told him. "I love it."
>
> "Really?" he said, disbelieving. (Ginsberg, 2002, pp. 185–186)

Ginsberg then told her bewildered son that he needed a title and provided several suggestions such as "The Quiet Storm" and "Raining Tears," but Blaze, once again, surprised his mother with his well-chosen words: "'Breanna Crying," Blaze said simply. 'That's what it's called.' Yes, I thought. Yes, indeed" (2002, pp. 185–186).

Similarly, in her memoir, Olga Holland, the mother of a young man with autism, recounted how she got her son, Billy, to "write" stories, make music, and create poetry in the most creative way. Holland shared that Billy often vocalized for long periods of time, often replicating the sounds of bullets, tanks, and helicopters. Because she knew making the sounds pleased Billy, Holland was reluctant to ask him to stop. Instead, on those occasions when the family was growing weary of battle sounds, Holland simply suggested to Billy that he turn his noises into stories or songs. She recalled Billy's reaction the first time she tried this approach:

> The next time Billy was making a noise, I approached him and said, "Billy I think there is a story in your mind."
>
> No reaction.
>
> "Billy, I think you have a story about a dinosaur in your mind."

"No," he said. "It's about a dragon."
"Oh. It must be about a pink dragon."
"No mom! A green dragon."
"He must be asleep, that green dragon."
"No, Mom. He is fighting. Fire comes from his mouth! Psh-sh-sh!" (Imitation of fire.)
(Holland, 2003)

Holland shared that Billy then began singing a song about his dragon. These kinds of interactions continued until Billy began spontaneously sharing songs and crafting stories on a regular basis. We can imagine a teacher capitalizing on this family habit and either audiorecording or scribing as Billy wove his tales or belted out his ballads.

Notice that this strategy is different from scribing alone because with speak and write, the "subject" is not necessarily setting out to write or share. Instead, an adult or peer listens for utterances, conversations, exchanges, monologues, or even songs that can be recorded and used as a springboard for writing.

Framed Paragraphs

The term *framed paragraph* is used to refer to a paragraph with sentences that include carefully chosen blanks for students to fill in. Some instructors use framed paragraphs to help inexperienced readers understand how expository text structures such as description, comparison/contrast, or problem/solution are organized (Olson & Gee, 1991). Others use them to help scaffold students' writing by modeling what a successful paragraph in a genre or on a topic should include. Although framed paragraphs are most often used in language arts classrooms, they have applicability across the curriculum (see Figure 6.3 for a sample framed paragraph on butterfly migration appropriate for a primary-level science class).

Framed paragraphs are a common way for teachers to engage students in writing for whom the production of much text would be difficult. For example, in their book on teaching literacy to students with significant disabilities, Copeland and Keefe (2006) described an approach to framed paragraphs that has the potential to build home–school connections, especially for students who lack reliable communication. The teacher they profiled sent home a weekly questionnaire for families to complete that included check-off items such as the following:

This weekend I went to:
___ mall
___ toy store
___ grandparents
___ the lake. . . . (p. 117)

This teacher then used the families' responses to construct framed paragraphs for journal writing for those writers needing the most intensive support. Some learners filled in the blanks independently, others used a model to write or trace the words, and still others selected pictures to complete the sentences. This approach allowed all students to produce some text about their lives that could be shared with others in the group.

Although we support the use of framed paragraphs, we do have some concerns about this strategy that we want to share. We have seen increased emphasis on this approach in the K–12 schools we visit as researchers and consultants. In

Migration is when an animal moves from one area to another for food or to have babies. A monarch butterfly migrates in _____. It _____ to where its _____ have gone before. Monarchs often _____ together. At _____, they _____ in trees. They can fly up to _____ miles in a day. They fly to places like _____, _____, and _____. I would feel _____ if I saw a group of butterflies fly by my _____.

Figure 6.3. Sample framed paragraph using information from Gibbons (1989).

some cases, teachers have chosen framed paragraphs to make the inner workings of composition more explicit for learners, and they embed these texts in a print-rich environment where students have opportunities to write under a variety of conditions. In other settings, however, concerns about the written forms that students will encounter on high-stakes tests have led to teachers tightening control on both the format and the content of students' writing. Students in these class-rooms, including some who could likely compose more independently if given the chance, are being asked to memorize structures and then replicate the kinds of paragraphs that their teachers see as likely to yield acceptable test scores. To guard against this pitfall, the use of framed paragraphs, like nearly all of the highly scaf-folded approaches we recommend in this book, should be faded as soon as pos-sible. If students have learned to organize a paragraph for themselves, they should be encouraged to do so. They should also be engaged in conversation with their teacher and each other about how a framed paragraph is put together and what effect it has on the reader, to ensure that they are learning to organize their writing in general, not simply learning to fill in the blanks of a worksheet.

Graphic Organizers

Graphic organizers are visual displays of knowledge that structure information by arranging important aspects of an idea or topic into a pattern that shows relation-ships between its components (Bromley, Irwin-DeVitis, & Modlo, 1995). These representations are effective teaching tools because they help students to express abstract ideas in concrete ways, store and recall information, demonstrate rela-tionships among facts and concepts, and organize ideas (Billmeyer & Barton, 1998; Buehl, 2001; Ridgeway & Cochran, 2002). Examples of graphic organizers include Venn diagrams, cause-and-effect frameworks, semantic webs, network trees, cycle maps, timelines, and flow charts.

Graphic organizers can be used to support nearly any aspect of the literacy curriculum (you may recall that we discussed their benefits for comprehension and vocabulary acquisition in Chapter 5), but they have special usefulness as a tool to support students, both with and without disabilities, in planning and or-ganizing their compositions. To see a wide range of possibilities, you might visit the Tools for Reading, Writing, and Thinking page sponsored by the Greece Cen-tral School District in New York (http://www.greece.k12.ny.us/instruction/ela/6-12/Tools/Index.htm) or conduct a Google search of your own using *graphic or-*

ganizers and *writing* as your search terms. We guarantee that such a search will yield tools you can adopt or adapt for use with students with autism, even if these students are not explicitly mentioned as the audience for the samples.

Like nearly any aspect of writing, the use of graphic organizers needs to be modeled and guided by teachers before students can be expected to take it up independently. Students will need demonstrations on how to match specific organizers with specific writing tasks as well as how to integrate material from a completed organizer into a draft. If you devote time to these skills, however, we think you'll see increased sophistication in students' decision-making, as did Pat Ciotoli, an elementary teacher profiled by Bromley, Irwin-DeVitis, and Modlo (1995), whose students used an organizer focused on the five senses to brainstorm possibilities for richly detailed poems.

Students can also be taught to use technology to create and complete graphic organizers as part of their writing process. For example, the popular computer software program Inspiration® (or Kidspiration®, a version from the same publishers aimed at learners in Grades K–6) allows students to create web diagrams of ideas, with different colors, shapes, and links helping to reinforce connections among the pieces of information they include. Once they have created a web on a given topic, a click of the mouse can turn that web into a hierarchical outline for students to use in drafting a composition with more extended text. (Although neither of us sees it as advisable to spend a lot of instructional energy drilling students on the fine details of outline conventions, we do think it can be beneficial for students to see how their material might be sequenced using that format.) The map and outline give students two different tools for conceptualizing the components of a particular composition, increasing the chances that one will suit the task and their preferences. We also think that this software can be an effective tool for students with autism because it allows authors to integrate multimedia resources such as audio and video into their compositions as well as to incorporate images and symbols from a searchable library of more than 1,000 items.

Before we leave this topic, we want to make it clear that although graphic organizers do serve pre-writing purposes admirably, they can also serve as a legitimate final product for students in their own right. Depending on what skills you want to focus on or who the audience will be, a primarily visual representation of ideas may even be the best choice, not merely an acceptable substitute, for a print text with a beginning, middle, and end. See Table 6.4 for other suggestions for adapting and using graphic organizers in inclusive classrooms.

Story Kits

Another way to help students plan their writing is to engage them with a story kit, a term we use to describe a bag or box of items related to a particular text, concept, genre, theme, or even author. A story kit for the popular intermediate-grade novel *The Island of the Blue Dolphins* (O'Dell, 1960/1999), for instance, might contain a stuffed dog, a small toy canoe, a rock, some sand or water in a vial, and a dolphin figurine. Such a kit has multiple uses; it can be used to introduce, enrich, or review the story for student readers/listeners. Students can also participate in creating such kits. One teacher we know asked her first graders to help construct kits that could be used by all learners in the classroom, especially a child with Down syndrome who needed help understanding abstract concepts. One kit that the class spent weeks assembling and modifying was the one representing fairytales, a

Table 6.4. Using graphic organizers in the inclusive classroom

If some students in the classroom are emerging readers, then icons, images, or pictures should be paired with words whenever possible. The teacher should be sure to teach the meaning of the icons, images, or pictures as students may be even more confused when unclear or unfamiliar graphics are used to make text easier to comprehend.

Many students will need practice and guidance as they learn to use organizers. Students should have many opportunities to see the teacher develop and use a range of different graphic organizers before they are asked to use them as learning tools. Because it is sometimes hard for a teacher to talk and illustrate her discussion at the same time, many teachers rely on another adult to co-teach this type of lesson with them. A general educator might work with a special educator, paraprofessional, speech-language pathologist, or even another student to "show and tell" about graphic organizers.

Teaching students how to create graphic organizers will help them learn how to approach complex text on their own. Students should be given plenty of time and ample opportunity to learn how to create organizers before they are asked to attempt this with partners or on their own.

When students are taught to read and develop graphic organizers, they can also learn critical thinking, organization, and communication skills. Consider the needs of individual students and determine if graphic organizers might assist them in meeting their goals (e.g., IEP objectives). If a student with a disability is working on note taking skills, for instance, he or she might be taught how to do so using a graphic organizer such as a semantic web. Or a learner might be taught how to follow along with a whole-class discussion by tracking topics on a flow chart or series-of-events map.

theme they explored across different areas of the curriculum. The kit contained finger puppets of a princess, a frog, three bears, a wolf, and a grandma; a "magic" wand; a plastic beanstalk; and a red cape. Students then used the kit as the catalyst for writing their own fairytales. Each child chose an item from the kit and wrote a story that was in some way related to that item. One student who chose the red cape developed a story about a flying princess who only had her special powers when she remembered to accessorize her cape with matching shoes or bag!

In addition, the contents of an entire kit can give student writers cues about what should be included in writing about the topic. Students who are asked to draft a book review of a text like *The Island of the Blue Dolphins* that has a story kit associated with it might set the objects out in front of them as they write to ensure that they mention each of these important story elements in their summaries. Some might even sequence the items in a particular way, perhaps explaining their choices to a peer or teacher who could take notes on their rationales, before generating text in that order. Such a combination of visual and verbal cues would give inexperienced or struggling writers a good deal of support to compose their story.

Color-coded Notes

As we discussed, some individuals with autism demonstrate a keener awareness of visual cues than their peers who are neurotypical. These learners may be aided by planning and organizational tools that incorporate the visual cue of color to make the relationship between ideas more salient. Stephen Shore, a man with Asperger syndrome, wrote about his use of visually oriented strategies both to learn and to communicate complex ideas. For example, he shared the following insights about color coding his notes during one of his college courses:

An information technology class I took as an undergraduate was highly structured. I took notes in a multilayered outline format using up to six different-colored pens. For example, the main idea was in black, subtopics in red, divisions of those in green and further prose-based explanations in light blue. The levels of indentation combined with the different colors helped me to map and retain key information for class. (2003, p. 91)

Although not all students will be able to grasp such a complex system as Stephen's, it could be quite practical to teach even young students to take notes in two different colors, based on main categories of information, or—even simpler—to return to their notes while studying and color code them at that time.

Students may also use colored tape flags—the sticky kind that most people use to bookmark ideas in their reading—to help them organize information for a sustained piece of writing drawing on research. The procedures for this approach are as follows:

- Invite students to review highlighted readings and/or notes from their research to identify between two and five main categories in the information (tape flags are often sold in packs of five different colors). More categories than this are often hard to manage.

- Have students write these categories on a single sheet of paper, or write them yourself while the students talk or indicate what they might be with predetermined symbols; this will serve as their code sheet.

- Help students to assign each of the categories a specific colored tape flag (e.g., a student pursuing a project on the rainforest might assign green tape flags for information about plants, blue tape flags for information about animals, and orange tape flags for information about threats to the rainforest).

- Direct students to return to their research sources to put tape flags of the appropriate color next to material related to each of the topics they've identified.

- When it's time to compose, help students to locate all of the tape flags of one color and review the material to make sure they include all of the details they see as important in the text they generate (some may choose to compose directly after this review; others may want to make an outline or some other kind of graphic organizer before they begin).

We suggest introducing this approach to students with autism in the context of a topic that interests them—a fascination, if they have one—and about which they have a lot of knowledge. This will help them to focus their attention on the new strategies, rather than unfamiliar content. Later, as they become more accustomed to the color-coding process, they can certainly apply the steps to curriculum-focused content that they are in the midst of learning.

REVISION AND EDITING

Since the 1980s, the terms *revision* and *editing* have entered literacy teachers' everyday lexicons to such a degree that many classrooms have posters on the wall listing them as discrete steps of the writing process, with revision usually preceding editing in the numbered sequence. We like that these terms are not used interchangeably because we think that they reflect different ways of thinking about text and require different strategic processes. For us, Gere, Christenbury, and Sassi's distinctions are very useful: Revision is "best thought of as re-vision, re-looking, re-working of a piece of writing" while editing is "a look at a revised piece of writing to review and change word order and sentence structure and to check usage issues" (2005, p. 45). Gallagher makes these distinctions even clearer and perhaps even more child-friendly by associating revision with the acronym

STAR ("substituting, taking stuff out, adding stuff, and rearranging") and defining editing as the process of "fixing mistakes writers make" (2006, p. 179). We think it's beneficial for teachers to talk with students about how revision and editing differ from each other, and we think that writers need explicit instruction about how to do both. The latter may be especially important with revision, because writing instruction—or perhaps more accurately, writing assessment—has historically paid more attention to correcting errors than it has to addressing structure or content (Russell, 2006).

Early proponents of process-oriented writing instruction suggested that students be freed to compose without expending too much energy on the niceties of conventions related to spelling, punctuation, and so forth until late in the process (Calkins, 1986; Graves, 1983). To do otherwise, these advocates believed, risked impeding the flow of students' ideas and focusing their attention on small details rather than the big picture. To a certain degree, this makes sense to us, especially given the research we reviewed earlier on writing fluency. A student writer who spends 3 minutes trying to figure out how to spell a word in the middle of a paragraph may forget what that paragraph was supposed to be about. It may indeed be a waste of time to edit a paragraph perfectly that might be cut from the piece entirely if it gets rearranged with a new opening and a different sequence—decisions that would fall under the category of revision for us, not editing. For these reasons, we subscribe to the general idea that it is more productive for most students to draft first, revise next, and edit later.

That said, we want to point out that our own writing, as well as the writing we've observed students doing in school, has led us to theorize that these processes are not always distinct from each other as they are carried out, and that revision need not always precede editing. For example, when we are working on a major piece of writing (like this book) that requires us to compose over a period of time, sometimes with days intervening between one writing session and another, we find it both comforting and constructive to read the incomplete draft through once, editing any errors we see, before beginning to move, change, or add new text. Rereading to edit, in this case, becomes one of the ways we re-acclimate ourselves to the world of writing after an absence from it. A literal, rigid reading of the writing process "steps," however, would likely invalidate this approach. For this reason, we encourage you to think flexibly about revision and editing, and to acknowledge how these processes are often recursive, rather than linear (Dahl & Farnan, 1998; Routman, 1994; Strong, 2006).

Considering Students with Autism

Students with autism spectrum labels vary greatly in their profiles where revising and editing are concerned. In our experience, those students who struggle to produce written text using conventional methods tend to have few experiences with revision and editing and receive little instruction in these areas. Some students with autism who draft with a fair degree of fluency report difficulties with revising and editing their compositions that are similar to those they experience with planning and organizing them. Lucy Blackman, a young woman with autism, wrote about how, as a teenager, she had problems with envisioning how a reader would make sense of her text:

As a rule writing came in response to visual stimuli which had stirred up my internal lan-guage enough to link words spontaneously with what I had seen, rather than typing obliquely about what I had felt. Really, it never occurred to me, in spite of what I heard from teachers and friends, that the prime purpose of poetry was not to make word-pictures of my linked vocabulary, but to rework this so as to let someone else have the il-lusion they were sharing whatever it was I composed. (1999, p. 176)

Blackman tied growth in this area to general education literature classes requiring her to participate in a variety of peer-response activities, including one in which she went over her poems line by line with a partner, explaining what she wanted to change about each one. As she recalled, "This conversation was kept, printed out, and included with the drafts in the completed project when it was handed in" (1999, p. 209). Although Blackman resisted making changes in some of the poems she considered to be most appealing in their current form (and what writer, with or without autism, doesn't engage in that sort of resistance from time to time?), she re-ported that these lessons made an impact on her thinking about her compositions:

This was the first time that I had corrected finer details in my own creative writing, as op-posed to correcting factual or grammatical errors I had made. I could now start to see that it was the path to other people getting more pleasure and therefore more impact from my stories. (1999, p. 210)

Other individuals with autism report paying too much attention to what Black-man calls the "finer details" of their writing. Liane Holliday Willey, for instance, reported that

Sometimes the care I give to words can throw me into an obsessive compulsive ritual. I typ-ically end up spending far too much time on selecting which word to use and too much time reworking a sentence so that it looks and feels and sounds right. This all translates into a fixation that can grind my thought process to a halt. When I get like this, I cannot con-centrate on anything else, not a thing, until I have found the perfect term or phrase I need. This tendency can make my experiences with the written word tedious, at least in terms of time and other missed opportunities, but never meaningless or futile. (1999, p. 36)

David Tammet reported getting stuck not on word choice but on the mechanics and surface features of writing itself:

Whenever I wrote, I poured over every letter and word and period. If I noticed a smudge or error I would erase everything and start over. This stream of perfectionism meant that I sometimes worked at a snail's pace, finishing a lesson in a state of near exhaustion, yet with little to show for it. (2007, p. 50)

Jerry Newport pointed out that this tendency toward perfectionism can stymie writers with autism. In his book, *Your Life is Not a Label*, he speaks directly to people with autism about this characteristic:

The best writers misspell words. People make mistakes on national TV on quiz shows. Mistakes are an important part of life, so relax and stop trying to control your world be-cause you are sick and tired of always being corrected and don't want to ever make a mistake again. (2001, p. 36)

This direct way of addressing the problem, and the person with autism, may be one effective strategy for supporting that individual.

At the same time, some individuals with autism demonstrate unusual prowess with conventions of writing, making them natural editors of their own work and perhaps of others' work as well. Spelling, for example, came prodigiously easy to Gunilla Gerland—so easy, in fact, that one of her teachers questioned the validity of her skill:

> In that teacher's world, you simply couldn't be as good at spelling as I was. The way she saw it, I was afraid to make mistakes, so I looked things up in the book when we had spelling tests. But the fact was that I would never even have dreamt of cheating. I always observed the rules made for me as long as they didn't conflict with my most important needs. And I had no need to look in the book—I knew the words anyway. The teacher told me that it was all right to make mistakes. That was allowed. I didn't understand what she wanted, but so as to please her and be left in peace I started deliberately making spelling mistakes. I used my talent for language to calculate which mistakes would be the most likely—to forget one of the double consonants, confuse "sleep" and "slip," or use *sh* instead of *ch*. I made an effort to make plausible mistakes, and I varied the number of mistakes between one and three each time. I thought that was just about right. . . . The rules you lived by in this world were very strange. You had to do it as it wasn't, write "cheep" when it should be spelt "cheap." But the teacher was pleased and I was still top of the class at spelling, so I was left in peace. (1996, pp. 93–94)

Gerland's experiences remind us of the importance of teacher expectations in framing what can be seen about a particular learner in the classroom. They also point out that students with autism may be blessed with gifts related to writing as well as, or instead of, hurdles and obstacles.

One last recommendation we want to share about autism and editing is to keep in mind that the process may be tricky for students who have difficulties with language and communication. Some teachers may think that the revision or editing processes for these learners might be too challenging or frustrating, but we see it as perhaps the most important part of literacy instruction for students with significant disabilities.

In their valuable and teacher-friendly text *Children with Disabilities: Reading and Writing the Four-Blocks® Way*, Erickson and Koppenhaver (2007) emphasized how critical the revision process is for students who do not communicate in conventional ways. When students write or type slowly or express themselves in incomplete phrases or thoughts, revision, they explained, can accomplish a number of instructional goals. Revision and editing of writing can help students, among other things, expand on their ideas, consider their word choices, and practice using any of their assistive technology supports or devices. These researchers share the story of a boy with autism named Eric who views an image of a wounded bird and proceeds to write a story about it:

> At first the child wrote "BIRDS OWIE HERTS." The following day a classroom aide worked with Eric to revise his text, asking questions such as: "How did the bird get hurt?" and "What do you think will happen next?" Eric's revision read as follows:
>
> BIRDS OWIE HERTS
> ARROW IN THE BIRD

BOY IS SADE
XSNDINT
AMBULINS

Eric then continued to add to his story with the aide supporting him in this work.
   Eric wrote another text for a subsequent picture that was very confusing to readers:

BIRD DINNER EATING BOY.

His teacher, aide, and mother could not determine if he meant the boy and the bird
were eating together, the boy was eating the bird's dinner, or the boy *was* the bird's
dinner. After revision, his text read:

BIRD DINNER EATING BOY
BIRDS EATING WERMS

While this didn't clarify all the questions entirely, it suggested that he was writing
about the boy eating dinner with the bird, who was eating worms. (Erickson & Koppenhaver, 2007, p. 91)

   The researchers shared that the aide's support during this activity was critical
and that she was able to move Eric along in his writing because she understood
key principles about beginning writing. She knew, for instance, to avoid putting
words in Eric's mouth and to help him share his own message. She also asked several open-ended questions and gave Eric time to answer them. Finally, she understood that revision for many emerging writers involves adding new ideas and she,
therefore, did not ask Eric to reorder and organize his text before he was ready to
do so. This savvy educator also took notes on what kind of instruction Eric would
need to be more successful as a writer (e.g., help with sentence expansion). In sum,
she understood the purposes of and knew the tools associated with the successful
revision and editing of student work.

Instructional Approaches

A number of approaches we've discussed in other chapters of this book can help
students learn to revise and edit their writing. For instance, a one-to-one conference with a teacher that we discuss in Chapters 3 and 4 can focus on either of these
processes and help students improve a particular composition on the spot, with
the teacher providing instruction calibrated to her immediate observations of and
interactions with the learner. Other instructional approaches that can be advanta-
geous with these dimensions of writing that we have not previously profiled include the following: authentic audiences, teacher think alouds, peer conferences,
and editing checklists.

Authentic Audiences

One of the most important suggestions we have for helping students with revising
and editing is to make sure that they have authentic audiences for their texts. Revising and editing are difficult processes for all writers, regardless of their experience level or dis/ability status. If the teacher is the sole audience for classroom
writing (as is most often the case), it's a rare student writer indeed who can accept

critical feedback and settle down to solving the problems in his or her text simply because those are skills that will earn a good grade or translate into success in some distant work or college setting. In our experience, students work the hardest—and for the most sustained periods of time—when the piece in question has an audience whom they want to impress or convince. Here are some scenarios you might consider, some of which require advance planning but some of which are fairly simple to facilitate:

- Invite students to create picture books on a theme or within a content area with younger children as their audience. Many young people feel a special responsibility to "get it right" when placed in a tutoring or mentoring role, and the opportunity to share the text personally with the younger children can also create authentic motivation for developing reading fluency through multiple practice sessions.

- Exchange a batch of student writing on the same topic or in the same genre with another class at your school or invite each group to write pen pal letters about what they liked about each other's writing, as well as what questions they have. In this setting, we don't recommend inviting recipients to critique or make suggestions for the authors because we're concerned about the ability of students who don't know each other well to provide appropriately pitched feedback, but we think the questions these readers ask are likely to point out where the authors need to clarify or add more information.

- Assign students to write a text in a particular genre—we've found that poetry and memoir work well—as a gift for a friend or loved one, possibly around a holiday or celebration (e.g., Mother's Day, a birthday). Some students write about an aspect of their relationship with the recipient; others simply want to produce their best work for someone who is important in their lives.

- Post samples of student work on a class or district web site. This option is appealing to many students because it allows students to use links, graphics, images, and sound effects in addition to print text.

- Encourage your students to submit their writing to local newspapers, which often publish texts authored by young people on their editorial pages, neighborhood sections, or school beats. You can also be on the watch for contests that students can enter or calls for online publications to which they might submit.

If writing by students with autism includes a substantial number of technical errors unusual for their grade level, you will need to decide whether to mediate those differences for the audience of their texts. Some teachers resist making writing public beyond the classroom unless it is conventionally edited; consequently, they confer with students to edit their writing together as much as possible before correcting the remainder of students' errors on their own (often, the rationale here is that even published authors have a copyeditor to find those mistakes that are hard for the author of a text to see him- or herself). Other teachers feel comfortable sharing or displaying student writing that is less than conventional.

For us, the audience of the text makes a difference in how much editing of a student's text we are likely to do. If an individual piece of work (regardless of whether the student who authored it has autism) is going to be displayed in the hall outside the classroom, where a range of people not familiar with the student may see it, we typically advocate editing that piece to conventional quality to make the message to the audience as clear as possible. If the piece is going home as a present for a family member, we might send an unedited version if the meaning is clear (or include the draft with the edited piece) so that the recipient, who is likely not to make negative judgments about the writer solely based on errors, can see which editing skills the student is controlling and which he or she is not.

Teacher Think Alouds

Just as teacher think alouds are a useful way to demonstrate to students how to use comprehension strategies (see Chapter 5), they can also be a good instructional tool for teachers to model various approaches to revising and editing one's writing (Anderson, 2005; Atwell, 1998; Robb, 2004). Think alouds are flexible because they can be done with nearly any size group, ranging from a whole-class modeling session to an individual conference, and with learners of any age. What's important is that the teacher makes his or her own composing processes both audible and visible to students by explaining his or her decision-making in language they can understand while simultaneously demonstrating with an overhead transparency or a projected computer the changes being made in the text. Successful revision and editing depend on such decisions, but learners (both with and without disabilities) typically receive very little explicit modeling about how to make them.

You might consider using a think aloud to model any of the following aspects of revision and/or editing with a text of your own, including how to

- Reread a text aloud to oneself to see if any necessary words have been left out

- Insert a caret (^) or asterisk (*) into a text to indicate that a word or sentence should be added in that spot

- Note missing words or sentences in the margin of the original text or on a Post-it to be attached to the page

- Choose a different image or symbol than was originally selected from a communication overlay to convey a change in your thinking

- Decide on a spelling for a word from a set of choices generated by a word-completion software tool (e.g., the kind used in personal digital assistants such as a PalmPilot or in other kinds of assistive technologies)

- Reread a text looking for one kind of error (e.g., to make sure that all sentences end with a punctuation mark or to check that the right form of *their/they're/there* is used)

- Use the find-all function within a word-processing program to locate all of the instances of words that serve as particular spelling "demons" (those you habitually misspell)

- Use circled text and marginal arrows to indicate which parts of a text you would like to move to another part of the page

- Highlight and copy/cut text within a word processing program to move it to another location in the text

- Open up and toggle between two word-processing files for a given piece of writing: one for the draft itself and another for "scraps" that don't fit in the main text but that you might not want to delete, just in case they could be useful later

As we hope you can see from our list, these possibilities include skills that are appropriate for beginning writers as well as those that require students to have more experience and sophistication. Consistent with our "presuming competence" stance, we urge you to model skills around revision and editing that students might not be ready to use on their own yet but that they may need in the future, as their skills change (or as those skills are understood better, with more sensitive or appropriate assessment tools). Learners need to see these approaches as possibilities, and to understand *why* they might use a particular approach in their writing, even before they take them up in their own compositions.

In addition to a teacher-led think aloud, you may want to consider engaging students in peer think alouds, an activity requiring students to explain their thought processes to each other. Students can take turns sharing their texts and their decision-making in front of the whole class, or the think alouds can be structured to be what Robb calls "dialogues, in which partners talk out loud to each other" (2004, p. 44). In either case, we think that students with autism will benefit from the chance to hear about their peers' problem solving as writers as well as from the opportunity to articulate their own revision and editing strategies for an audience beyond themselves and their teachers. You will also benefit from these interactions because circulating to take notes while students talk yields useful information about what students know about revision and editing as well as what they need to learn next.

Peer Conferences

In addition to giving writers a space to voice their own thoughts about a piece of writing to a partner, peer conferences can help students realize that their ideas aren't always perceived by a reader as they intended. This sort of collaborative work has a "strong impact on improving the quality of students' writing" (Graham & Perin, 2007, p. 16), and it can help them to be more metacognitive about the processes they use (Dahl & Farnan, 1998).

Classroom-based research with a sociocultural orientation reveals, however, that students don't automatically know how to give each other useful feedback (Finders & Hynds, 2003; Gallagher, 2006). Moreover, inequities that are present in the classroom around social status and ability can be reproduced or even magnified in peer conferences or sharing sessions if these interactions are not carefully structured, supported, and monitored (Lensmire, 1994). How the school day is organized can further contribute to these inequities, as teacher researcher Jo Ann Pryor Deshon (1997) discovered when she took a close look at writing in her first-grade classroom and realized that students who were identified with special needs were marginalized during peer conferences and whole-class sharing time because of their absences for pull-out reading instruction.

In order to harness the positive power of peer conferences in inclusive classrooms, we offer the following suggestions:

- Create a list of concrete behaviors you want to see students demonstrate during peer conferences (e.g., feedback that makes specific reference to the text, suggestions that leave the final choice up to the author, questions that are genuine), and make that list public to all members of the class.

- Include in that list explicit consideration of how students who do not communicate in conventional ways might participate in peer conferences (e.g., "Some members of the group may need a partner to read their work aloud. . . .").

- Model your expectations for those behaviors by performing a peer conference in front of students, either with colleagues or with students who exhibit those behaviors already.

- Debrief that modeling with the class, pointing out and naming what made the conferences beneficial for the author.

- Keep the group size for conferences small, especially at first. (We recommend groups of between two and four students, with pairs used most often until students demonstrate familiarity with the desired conferring behaviors.)

- Group students deliberately (not randomly or by student choice), drawing on information you have about student profiles (e.g., who is tolerant, who often needs to be redirected, who is patient, who gets frustrated easily) to create balanced teams.

- Confer in advance with students for whom peer conferences might be stressful, to elicit names of partners with whom they might be most comfortable.

- Take notes as you observe peer conferences in action, then share your observations with students about what was successful as well as what needs to be problem solved by the group.

- Regroup students or provide additional models of desired behaviors if conferences function poorly, or if you want students to take on increasingly challenging roles in those conferences.

Be sure that all students have a way to participate in the conference. When Ms. Greene, a teacher we observed, conducted conferences in her classroom, she created adaptations for Hollen, a student with autism who is nonverbal. Hollen facilitated the conference by drawing a card to indicate who would read first, second, and last in the group. She also pointed to items on a phrase board that represented appropriate questions for the conference (e.g., "That is interesting," "I don't like that part," "I don't understand that," "Can you read it again?")

Like Gallagher (2006), we believe that peer conferences are likely to be more successful when they are focused on the "big picture" of a text—the choices writers make that communicate meaning, rather than aspects of grammar, spelling, or usage. In most situations, we teach students to direct their attention to the aspects of another person's text that engage, confuse, or provoke them—all concerns that might aid in revision—rather than to correct discrete errors. We think that peers can aid each other best by providing genuine feedback as interested readers. (Quite honestly, most K–12 students are not good-enough editors to locate most of the errors their peers make, much less identify patterns in those errors that would help another person stop making them!) We're willing to grant an exception to this revision-first rule of thumb for peer conferences, however, if a student with autism (or another student in a class who might otherwise be marginalized from participation) demonstrates skill with editing that might position him or her in a favorable way for others.

Editing Checklists

Editing checklists are a useful scaffolding tool for student writers as they review their own work. When they are made public in the classroom, editing checklists serve as a concrete reminder of teacher-directed lessons, among other benefits. Jeff Anderson, a teacher in San Antonio, Texas, has written extensively about his use of the editor's checklist in his middle school English classroom. He posts a large piece of butcher paper on the wall and adds items to it such as "Check homophones: *there, their, they're*" or "Capitalization rules!" as he teaches them. He often enlists students' help in wording the items before they are posted, and he and his students occasionally decide to create additional posters with more specific information about a particular rule. For instance, he teaches the seven rules for capitalization (see Figure 6.4) over several days before hanging them in the classroom to serve as a permanent reference. Once a rule has been discussed enough that students understand it, Anderson explains that students should now be accountable for checking it:

> From now on, every time you finish a piece of writing, instead of saying, "I'm finished," I want you to look at this list and reread your work, correcting it for whatever area of focus has been added to the checklist. (2005, p. 46)

You might also consider engaging students in developing a classwide editing checklist collaboratively, as Routman did with a group of fourth graders. According to her, this process was valuable because when "students came up with the items, as opposed to being told them by the teacher, they became more engaged in the editing process and took more responsibility for their papers" (1994, p. 179). Routman and her teacher collaborator insisted that students make their own corrections as much as possible, and they frequently referred students to the language arts textbook to check conventions.

Seven Capitalization Rules

1. Proper names (e.g., San Antonio, Brittany)
2. Proper adjectives (e.g., Sony television, Chinese food)
3. Title with a last name (e.g., Coach Anderson, President Lincoln)
4. First word in a direct quotation (e.g., Vanessa asked, "What can I write about?")
5. Titles (e.g., *The Giver*, *Seventeen*)
6. Letter opening (e.g., Dear Mr. Anderson:)
7. First word of a letter closing (e.g., Yours truly)

Figure 6.4. Example of a poster stating explicit rules to share with students. (From *Mechanically Inclined: Building Grammar, Usage, and Style into Writer's Workshop* [p. 46], by Jeff Anderson, © 2005, with permission of Stenhouse Publishers.)

In other classrooms, especially at the elementary level, teachers help students develop personal editing checklists in addition to or instead of classwide tools. We see these as useful tools for students with autism because they can be tailored to the peculiarities that these students sometimes exhibit in their writing. A writer like Dawn Prince-Hughes (2004), a woman with Asperger syndrome who capitalizes all nouns in her poetry, might be taught to isolate these words in her writing as she edits, adding Anderson's seven capitalization rules to her checklist. A student with less sophisticated writing skills than Dawn's could have a checklist with questions like "Do all of my words have a vowel (*A, E, I, O, U,* and sometimes *Y*) in them?" and "Do all my sentences start with capital letters?" As students learn to control new conventions, some questions can be deleted to keep the process manageable and others can be added. The key consideration here, as with most aspects of teaching writing and other forms of representation to diverse populations, is to be willing to adapt the editing expectations to reflect students' current level of competence while stretching them toward new levels.

Consider that some learners may need desktop or portable versions of these checklists. One student we supported liked to have certain editing rules stuck to his desk with Velcro tape. Whatever rule he was focusing on at the moment would be secured to the top right corner of his workspace. He rotated several rules throughout the year, making and attaching new cards as needed.

CONCLUDING THOUGHTS

In a recent review of research, Chapman lauded Glenda Bissex's (1980) 5-year case study of her own son as the richest description of a student's learning to write that the field has to date. According to Chapman, Bissex's key finding in that book was that the "development of writing must be seen as part of the development of the person rather than merely as the product of an instructional writing sequence" (2006, p. 22). We think this finding actually applies to far more than just writing; any aspect of literacy development needs to be seen in terms of its impact on a whole person, especially given the importance of literacy success in the development of positive self-images for students with autism spectrum labels.

At the same time, writing seems to have a special power of its own for many individuals with autism, including Donna Williams (1992, 1994), the author we profiled at the beginning of this chapter. Among its other benefits, writing became a way for Williams to integrate the disparate and often conflicting identities she experienced. Although she reports often being terrified at the prospect of revealing what she called "my world" to others, her prolific production of published texts, and her candor in those texts, indicates that she also craved that intimacy.

Similarly, Lucy Blackman, whose book has taught us as much about literacy as it has about autism, included a vignette in her autobiography that reminds us about the potential for writing competence to aid individuals in constructing new identities. The episode recounts how Blackman first learned that she could use writing to effect change in her environment and underscore her own agency as a person:

> The Easter school holidays were looming, and so were five days for me in respite care to give Jay [her mother] a break. More than anything I wanted not to be in a group with a whole lot of people who were even more incomprehensible than my school-mates, and with staff who were kind but thought my understanding was mirrored by echolalia. (1999, p. 92)

When her mother canceled the booking after reading Lucy's adamantly expressed written message ("IDONTWANTTOGOTOTHATHOUSEATEASTER"), Lucy reported that she was "more than pleased. I was suffused with achievement. I had discovered that the word, as spread by my finger on that [communication device], was mightier than my most unpleasant behaviour had been to date" (1999, p. 92).

We hope that the suggestions in this chapter, as well as elsewhere in this book, help your own students with autism to be "suffused with achievement" as the written and multimedia texts they compose make changes in the world for themselves and for others. We turn in Chapter 7 to further explicit discussion, intended to build on and extend ideas from this and previous chapters, of how to provide support for this goal for students with significant physical, movement, sensory, and communication problems.

Chapter 7

Literacy Learning for Students with Significant Disabilities

Yes, Those Students, Too

In his landmark book, *Schooling Without Labels* (1990), Doug Biklen described a boy, Melvin, who lived in an institution during some of his childhood years. Many at the institution saw Melvin, who did not have reliable speech, as "severely retarded" and a "hellion." One of the most striking aspects of Melvin's story is how he was viewed as incapable of learning even though he demonstrated complex literate behaviors from an early age. For instance, while he was still living in the institution, Melvin managed to escape from his ward and order lunch from a neighborhood restaurant, despite knowing only a few words in sign language:

> When he was still only five years old, he left his unit at the institution, went down to the ground level on the elevator, got past the receptionist at the admin desk and out the door. An hour later the receptionist took a call from the local McDonald's, two blocks away but across two busy streets. "There is a little boy here demanding a hamburger and I think he is one of the kids that has come down here with your folks," the caller announced. When the institution staff went to retrieve him, they found him making the sign for "eat." Obviously he knew where he was going. He knew what he wanted. (p. 21)

Melvin was soon adopted and moved from the institution to his new family's home. There, according to his adoptive mother, he emerged as a "bright little kid" (1990, p. 24). She noticed that her son began paying close attention to church ser-

177

vices (they were augmented with sign language) and that his communication, in general, was blossoming. Within 3 months of moving in with his mother, Melvin's repertoire of signs had gone from 5 to more than 200.

On one occasion, Melvin's mother observed her son examining a book and stared at him, stunned at his engagement in the process. Once again, he was demonstrating literate behavior, and more importantly, confirming his mother's suspicions that he was an aware and intelligent person:

> He was sitting on the couch quietly with a book open, just crying. I couldn't imagine what was happening. He had never had quiet moments like that at that point or at least very rarely. I just looked and didn't say anything. He was looking at Burt Blatt's book, *Christmas in Purgatory* [1966, an exposé of abuse in mental retardation institutions]. He looked up and said "big house." It was like he recognized that this was about where he had been. I sat down and we went through the book together. He just cried. At this point he had very little language. It was just amazing to me. . . . He has shown me time and time again, "Don't underestimate me and don't judge me by your outside perceptions." (Biklen, 1990, p. 28)

Melvin's story is an example of the power of an inclusive philosophy. It is also a story of the need for all of us to see student strengths, question what we *think* we know about learners, and follow the lead of a student, even when he or she has limited ways to show us what he or she knows (Kliewer & Biklen, 2001). It illustrates how critical it is to support the literacy development of students with significant disabilities, no matter how tentative the process may be.

WHY A CHAPTER ON SIGNIFICANT DISABILITIES?

Even though we have included numerous examples related to students with significant disabilities throughout this book, we feel that stories like Melvin's are so rich, compelling, and complicated that they need a chapter of their own. We feared that some readers might finish reading this text without understanding that when we insist that *all* learners must gain access to literacy, we do mean *all*— including students with the most significant physical, movement, sensory, and communication problems.

When we suggest that all students with autism should have access to literacy instruction; inclusive classrooms; and challenging, standards-based curriculum, we are hoping that our readers understand that, yes, we mean students with significant disabilities, too. Unfortunately, we find that when we offer a variety of suggestions on a topic, teachers may be prone to discount some ideas that can work for their students if the suggestions appear to include other strategies that might not apply. For instance, we were talking to a student teacher about how she could adapt the teacher read aloud, and we shared ideas ranging from using adapted books or having students read with the teacher to allowing learners to manipulate puppets or objects during the story. When we observed the student teacher in her classroom, however, she did not include Chase, a boy with significant disabilities, in the read aloud. When we asked her about this decision, she exclaimed, "Oh, he doesn't talk or use books appropriately, so he couldn't do most of the things you suggested. I didn't think you meant Chase."

We realize we may have added to that confusion by writing a book that tries to address the needs of a very diverse population. In this quest, we undoubtedly offer many ideas and suggestions that apply much better to some students than they do to others. For instance, some of our adaptations apply best to students who use some speech or have reliable communication. We did not choose to include this material because we believed that these were the only students capable of learning. Rather, we wanted to offer as wide a range of suggestions as possible to meet the needs of as many classroom teachers as we could. This chapter is our attempt to address those of you who feel you did not recognize your students enough in the previous pages.

LITERACY FOR STUDENTS WITH SIGNIFICANT DISABILITIES: ADDRESSING COMMON QUESTIONS

In these times of inclusive schooling, NCLB, and high standards, it should be obvious that all learners deserve an appropriately challenging literacy education. But we find that questions still arise continually when it comes to students with significant disabilities. After fielding so many of these queries, we thought that some of our readers might need more information to help them think and talk about how to design literacy experiences for these learners. For this reason, we have constructed responses to some of the most common questions we hear related to students with significant disabilities and literacy.

How Can We Teach Him to Read? He Can't Even Hold a Pencil.

Many students with autism are seen as incapable of learning either because they cannot use materials in typical ways (e.g., a student may be unable to hold a pencil or turn the pages of a book) or because they cannot communicate reliably. As a group, individuals on the spectrum are not alone in being doubted as competent (or dismissed). As Crossley pointed out, there is a long history of making conclusions about intellect based on assessments of speech, communication, and the normative perspective:

> In the eighteenth century society discovered it had been making a mistake about one group of people who behaved like idiots. These people weren't intellectually impaired at all, they had a sensory problem; they were deaf. The true nature of their impairment was discovered and an educational system developed to capitalize on the language of sign. (1997, p. 274)

Other groups who have been negatively affected by low expectations include those with physical disabilities and/or sensory impairments, and those with the label of mental retardation. When people cannot communicate reliably, when they move in unusual ways, and when they exhibit unexplained behaviors (e.g., screaming that seems unprovoked), we often assume they are not competent, and in many ways "less than" (Donnellan & Leary, 1995) other people.

Julia Tavalaro, a woman who awoke from a coma to find herself paralyzed and unable to communicate, experienced this bias firsthand. When she tried to use her eyes to communicate, none of her caregivers noticed her attempts for several years. Tavalaro describes the experience of being both cut off from typical experiences and being seen as incompetent as unbearable. She shared, for instance, the horrible and degrading experience of having her personal care issues discussed in front of her, with her body treated like an object. Many of her care providers appeared to dismiss her humanity altogether:

> A white dress comes close to me, lifts me, laughs to another white dress who makes a sucking sound between her teeth and says, "The vegetable needs changing." I realize with sudden terrible knowledge that I am a grown woman about to experience what it's like to be a baby. (Tavalaro & Tayson, 1997, p. 22)

During this episode, the workers exchanged insulting remarks about Tavalaro and even shared opinions on how long she would live.

Only years later did a therapist notice Tavalaro's communication abilities and restore dignity, control, and intimacy to her life. This story, however moving and shocking, is hardly rare. Many people with significant disabilities gain access to augmentative and alternative communication and demonstrate their complexity and ability in ways never dreamed by those in their lives. Helen Keller may be the most famous example of this, but there are countless other similar tales throughout history and around the world (Biklen, 2005; Blackman, 1999; Brown, 1989; Crossley, 1997; Donnellan & Leary, 1995; Sellin, 1995).

So what does this mean for literacy instruction and people with significant disabilities? It means, in part, that when people with autism have severe problems with movement, communication, and learning, it can be extremely challenging for them to show what they know. This means that if students do not appear to have any literacy skills at all we do not wait for them to demonstrate such skills before providing instruction. Instead, we must teach "as if" students are capable of understanding us (a topic we will discuss later in this chapter) and continue to explore ways to connect with, communicate with, and support them.

But His IQ Is 16. Why Would We Focus on Literacy Instruction for Him?

Only a dozen years ago or so, many textbooks claimed (and some still do) that most students with autism are "mentally retarded." Over time (and as technology and teaching methods improved), that percentage dropped, leaving researchers, practitioners, and families alike to question the supposed link between autism and low cognition (Biklen, 2005; Donnellan & Leary, 1995; Edelson, 2006; Wallis, 2006). Many researchers now see those symptoms that brought on a diagnosis of mental retardation (e.g., hand flapping, failure to respond to cues, pacing, vocalizing) as symptoms of *autism*, not as indicators of cognitive disability. As Claudia Wallis reported in a recent issue of *Time*, much of our thinking about autistic behavior has changed:

> Many classic symptoms of autism—spinning, head banging, endlessly repeating phrases—appear to be coping mechanisms rather than hard-wired behaviors. Other classic symptoms—a lack of emotion, an inability to love—can now be largely dismissed as artifacts of impaired communication. The same may be true of the supposedly high incidence of mental retardation. (2006, p. 44)

We have seen this theory of low IQ scores being a result of unreliable communication tested when students get access to their voices for the first time. In these instances, we often see that the better our supports and the better the match between the learner and his or her new system or device, the higher a student's IQ score jumps! Perhaps no person is more suitable to illustrate how cognition "suddenly" improves with communication than Sue Rubin. Rubin, subject and writer of the Oscar-nominated documentary *Autism Is a World* (Wurtzburg, 2004), was believed to have mental retardation until age 13, when she began communicating via facilitated communication (supported typing). After gaining access to communication, Rubin was tested to have an IQ score of 131, well above average. She reinforced the notion that her early "problems" were related to expression, not intellect:

> As a person with autism I have very limited speech and lack motor control governing my body movements. When I was in school autistic people like me were usually placed in separate schools or special day classes with other disabled students [and] were not allowed to learn academic subjects. Because of the way we move and our lack of speech we were assumed to be retarded. But all this changed when I could type without support. . . . (Rubin et al., 2001, p. 419)

Rubin has every classic symptom of autism. She rocks. She flips her fingers in front of her face. At times, she vocalizes incoherently. She shares that her body is often hard to control and, in fact, it took her several *years* to get her movement under control to the point where she could type on her device without physical support. For these reasons, people who do not know her or have access to her communication often believe that she IS her body. In other words, they understand all of those markers of autism as markers of low cognition. But as Rubin herself points out, her "very existence" challenges these beliefs: "When people see me they are forced to admit that their assumptions about mental retardation are wrong" (2001, p. 419).

Clearly, for many students like Rubin, a test does not exist that can measure what they know and what they can do; most of the instruments that are used in evaluations measure autism symptoms as much as or more than these students' abilities. In addition to the instruments used in these assessments being inadequate, many aspects of the evaluation process itself make accurate assessment challenging if not impossible. As we shared in Chapter 4, there are many barriers to accurate testing for students with autism, including problems with language. Tests that are highly dependent on language comprehension, for example, are biased against students with autism because lengthy verbal directions are almost always challenging for these learners. Even tasks that require performance and not verbal responses often depend on receptive language skills to understand the directions.

In addition, many children and adults with autism cannot participate as they are asked to due to movement problems, sensory differences, or related difficulties. It is not terribly uncommon for a student with significant disabilities to get a low score on an instrument because he or she did not have a reliable pointing response (but was able to point). In other words, students may be asked to point to a monkey and actually know which image represents the monkey but point to a giraffe instead. This type of problem with motor planning is widely reported by people with autism (Donnellan & Leary, 1995; Leary & Hill, 1996; Marcus & Shevin, 1997; Rubin et al., 2001).

What does all of this IQ critique have to do with literacy learning? Seeing how intelligence has been understood and measured is crucial to understanding how so many students, to this point, have been left out of academic learning and literacy experiences. IQ scores often determine where a child receives his or her education, how rigorous that education is, what materials are used, and whether or not an academic curriculum is pursued. So we implore our readers to question the construct of IQ, not only for students with autism but also for all learners (Gould, 1981), and to teach to student strengths and abilities versus perceived limits.

He Seems So Low, I Don't Know Where to Begin.

When we do not have a way to assess what students know, we have to make some guesses. Too often the guesses or assumptions we make about learners lack generosity, creativity, and introspection. Instead of assuming, for instance, that a student who is nonverbal is expressing everything he or she knows, we should assume the individual knows more than he or she can show us. That is, we should be making decisions for students with significant disabilities based on what Anne Donnellan, a prominent scholar in both autism and special education, calls the "least dangerous assumption." According to Donnellan, experiences should be designed with the belief that the "individual with a disability is a 'person first,' deserving the same considerations and concern as would be given a person without a disability" (Donnellan & Leary, 1995, p. 98). The Least Dangerous Assumption principle asks us to consider, "What if we later learn that the person is more competent than we ever imagined . . . what curriculum and instruction will we wish we had provided?" This principle is critical during this time when we know so little about autism and significant disability. Therefore, even in cases in which we do not know what a student understands or how or if he or she is communicating, we have a moral obligation to provide him or her with literacy experiences that are varied, interesting, challenging, and connected to peers and general education curriculum.

A teacher operating from the Least Dangerous Assumption should always be asking, "What would an education for this student look like if I viewed him as a literacy learner?" and "What does it mean to give this student the benefit of the doubt educationally?" All students, regardless of label, must be provided with opportunities to communicate through drama, art, and movement; to explore a range of augmentative communication strategies and techniques; to socially interact with peers; and to see, hear, and examine a range of books and other materials. And in the case of literacy instruction, this means that every student with significant disabilities should have IEP objectives related to literacy and learn alongside their peers without disabilities in general education classrooms.

TEACHING STUDENTS WITH SIGNIFICANT DISABILITIES: RECOMMENDED PRACTICES

Nearly nonverbal, Tito Rajarshi Mukhopadhyay has significant physical, communication, and sensory problems. His body does not always move as he wants it to. He cannot use spoken words to express himself. Some of his behaviors are unusual and puzzling (e.g., running around the room, rocking vigorously back and forth). He has difficulties modulating, predicting, and controlling perception, expression, postures, and emotions. For all of these reasons, people meeting Tito often assume he has significant cognitive disabilities. . . until they observe him communicating on his keyboard or writing messages in his notepad. Not only can Mukhopadhyay communicate his thoughts, feelings, and ideas using a letter board or a pencil and paper but also, at a relatively young age, he became a celebrated author and public "speaker." He has written several books, gained national recognition for his poetry, and toured the world to share his journey and provide guidance to others.

Mukhopadhyay is, then, an enigma. His body sends one message, in a sense, and his words another. He alludes to this challenge in one of his many introspective poems:

> Men and women are puzzled by everything I do
> Doctors use different terminologies to describe me
> I just wonder
> The thoughts are bigger than I can express
> Every move that I make shows how trapped I feel
> Under the continuous flow of happenings
> The effect of a cause becomes the cause of another effect
> And I wonder
> I think about the times when I change the environment around me
> With the help of my imagination
> I can go places that do not exist
> And they are like beautiful dreams
> But it is a world full of improbabilities
> Racing towards uncertainty (Mukhopadhyay, 2000, p. 99)

Mukhopadhyay's mother, Soma, always felt he was more capable than he appeared to be. She believed in her son's ability to communicate and grow intellectually, and she put tremendous effort into educating and supporting him, especially in the area of literacy. She was instrumental in Mukhopadhyay's success with augmentative communication and his more recent success as an author and public figure.

When people learn of Mukhopadhyay's story, it is easy for them to believe that this young man must have somehow signaled his literate ability at an early age. The truth is, actually, quite the opposite. As a child, Mukhopadhyay demonstrated so little skill and ability with communication and literacy that it is a wonder his mother pursued any instruction at all. But pursue she did. In his book, *Beyond the Silence* (2000), Mukhopadhyay detailed how his mother trained him to write. At first she brought him a pencil and paper and conducted a simple lesson:

> She drew a line. The boy showed reluctance to hold the pencil. Any new activity terrified him. He kept his grip on the pencil so loose that every time his mother gave it to him, he dropped it. . . . But [his] mother was equally stubborn. She tied the pencil to his hand with a rubber band, so that he could not shake it off. She kept him sitting in the same place, until he drew the lines. By the end of the day, the boy was drawing not only horizontal lines, but vertical lines too. A notebook was given to him and he soon filled it up with lines. But there was more to be done. He needed to move onwards. He needed to write. (2000, p. 32)

Mukhopadhyay shares how the lessons frustrated both participants. Mukhopadhyay did not initially succeed with the copy work, but his mother did not want to give up. Finally, his mother suggested a unique physical support—holding his shoulder. Mukhopadhyay reported that the physical cue gave him exactly the help he required: "This time it was easy for the boy to write, as he could feel the presence of the hand, his own hand linked to his body, at the shoulder point, where his mother was holding him" (2000, p. 32). This unique hand-to-shoulder physical support is one of many examples of effective personalized adaptations Mukhopadhyay's mother created for her son. She also provided him with motivating materials, read him interesting stories, and expected him to rise to her expectations in every instance.

Mukhopadhyay's story is, in many ways, a remarkable one, but we feel it could and should be a far more common one. Too often, this young man is portrayed in the media as a miracle of sorts; his abilities have been described as extraordinary and even as unparalleled for a person with his needs and challenges. We reject these characterizations of Mukhopadhyay. Although we certainly are fans of his work, we do not feel that his abilities are necessarily unique. In fact, what Soma and others (e.g., Jamie Burke, Sue Rubin, Michael Ward, Lucy Blackman), described throughout this book, demonstrate is that *many* (if not all) people with autism are capable of much more than previously thought, including high levels of literacy.

In the examples we share in this chapter, teachers, family members, and people with autism illustrate in many ways that behind every extraordinary pupil there are usually extraordinary expectations and teaching practices to match. To this end, we offer five recommendations to keep in mind as you plan for and structure literacy experiences for students with significant disabilities. They are 1) act "as if," 2) study the practice of parents, 3) rely on the classroom community, 4) follow "small cues," and 5) prioritize communication.

Act "As If"

When teachers assume that their students are competent and, most likely, know more than they can demonstrate (even when they may not have formal evidence that this assumption is true), we call this behavior acting "as if." For some learners this means providing instruction even when you are unsure of what the student understands. In the touching memoir, *Running with Walker*, Robert Hughes shared how, when he walked around Chicago with his son during their home-schooling outings, he kept up a running commentary to teach his son about his hometown: "I'd talk to him—sometimes nonstop—about the things we saw. I'd spot what he seemed to be looking at and say something about it. Or I'd point out things—traffic, clouds, advertisements, ice on the lake, architecture—and give mini-lectures" (2003, pp. 103–104).

For her part, Walker's mother bought him a coffee table book filled with beautiful images of Chicago from the air. According to Walker's parents, the boy who was able to communicate so little in a conventional way demonstrated his interest of the book in ways all his own. Their son would "devour" the book every night in bed: "He'd turn the pages, spot something he recognized, smile, put his fingers in his ears, and stare wide-eyed at the picture" (2003, p. 104). Walker's father explained how the book not only gave Walker comfort and enjoyment but also that it taught him about geography, his own community, and perspective: "He knew what Lincoln Park and Michigan Avenue and Belmont Harbor looked like from the ground; this book showed him the same terrain from the sky" (2003, p. 104). This family demonstrated perfectly what it means to act "as if" and how literacy might be used not only to give students independence or daily living support but also to make life itself more interesting and rich.

Walker's story (and the work of his parents) reminds us of Randall, a little boy with significant disabilities who spent many of his days rearranging books in the library of his first-grade classroom. As Randall picked up or paged through various books, the teacher or paraprofessional working in the classroom would comment on them. If he picked up the classroom book on rattlesnakes (a favorite of many of the students), his teacher would give him information about reptiles, try to read short passages as he held his finger on them, or ask other students to tell Randall their favorite parts. If Randall sat in place for a few moments, a teacher (or sometimes a classmate) would read him a book from cover to cover even if the "audience" did not look over or appear to notice the reader. Furthermore, as Randall picked up objects in the classroom, toured the hallways, and examined posters, his teachers kept up a running impromptu monologue based on the topic of the day or week. If he touched a yellow wall, they would tell him, "Oh, yes, Randall, remember when we were learning Spanish yesterday? Yellow is 'amarillo' in Spanish. And maybe you also remember that 'azul' is the word for blue." This team of savvy teachers taught "as if" Randall understood them, was smart, was learning, was interested in a variety of topics, could learn from peers, could learn experientially, and was demonstrating understanding in the only ways he could. Other ways to teach "as if" are featured in Table 7.1.

Study the Practice of Parents

It is not uncommon for students with disabilities, especially those with more significant needs, to be taught to read or to write by their parents instead of by their teachers. Perhaps this phenomenon is due to the fact that schools have not traditionally seen some students as potential literacy learners, or perhaps it is because parents have such a specialized set of skills and abilities when it comes to the unique learner that is their child that they are able to develop effective personalized techniques and strategies that teachers would not.

For instance, Sam, a child with the diagnosis of Down syndrome and autism, was presumed to be a nonreader by his teachers. Although the teachers felt that Sam was interested in reading, they also felt they had "tried everything" to engage him in literacy instruction. Every time they tried to start a lesson, Sam insisted on paging through his book from front to back and stopping on random pages to point to words or to comment on the illustrations. In response to this odd behavior, the teachers created a reading "window" by cutting a small hole in a manila folder. They then asked Sam to move the window as he read so he could focus on one word at a time. This practice not only proved unsuccessful at boosting his reading performance but also it created so much anxiety that he began to refuse to read altogether during the school day.

When the frustrated teachers asked Sam's mother for help, they made progress for the first time all year. She began by collecting boxes of materials on his favorite topic, bats. When Sam's mother was unsuccessful at getting him to

Table 7.1. Ideas for acting "as if"

Talk to students even if they cannot reliably communicate with you. Do more than ask questions or give directions; share ideas, give information, read, show, demonstrate, and communicate respect for the learner.

Always use age-appropriate materials and activities. Too often, students who do not demonstrate competence are given curriculum and instruction more appropriate for younger children (e.g., farm animal flashcards, first-grade primers). If an older student cannot demonstrate literacy ability, resist using primary books or preschool activities. Instead try magazines, coffee table books (with pictures and few words), or comic books appropriate for all ages.

Give many opportunities for students to practice new skills. Many times students are given a communication device, a new curricular adaptation, or a strategy and asked to use it (and master it) without much opportunity for practice. Acting "as if" means giving students plenty of time, support, and opportunity to practice and demonstrate their competencies. We know of one student who joined a school choir and was not able to stand on the risers and attempt to sing until she had observed the group over a dozen times. The first 4 days of the class, she ran out of the room and down the hall. It took her weeks to sing a few words, but eventually she could stand with the group and use sign language to "sing" three songs. This outcome would not have been possible if her teachers had seen her as incapable of learning through repeated practice.

Look for alternative opportunities to integrate literacy skills, especially for older students who may not have many chances to practice literacy skills across the school day in their inclusive classes. For instance, consider extracurricular activities that allow for reading, writing, speaking, and listening opportunities. When Gregg, a student with autism, joined his school newspaper staff, his role was to bundle and deliver copies to homerooms with a peer. An unexpected outcome was that he began "browsing" through the paper like his peers and, therefore, encouraged his peers to read it to him.

---

slowly examine one piece of material at a time, she allowed him to explore several pieces of literature at once. This process often looked strange and very unlike a reading lesson because it involved him blanketing the kitchen table with posters, pamphlets, video boxes, pages printed off the Internet, and magnetic pictures and words. He moved quickly from one piece of material to the next.

Sam's mother provided instruction by highlighting certain vocabulary words in the materials and pointing to them as he perused the stacks of papers and books. She also read aloud from some of the texts as he worked on his own. Finally, she created scrapbooks and posters about bats and placed them around the house (including on the refrigerator, in the bathroom, and on the walls) so she could give him as many opportunities as possible to see and review the content. Eventually, she found that her son could answer a handful of questions about the topic using magnetic pictures instead of spoken words; could read a passage fluently; and, with help from her and his sister, could even act out a scene from *Stellaluna* (Canon, 1993), a picture book about a lost baby bat.

What can we learn from Sam's mother and her reading instruction? Many teachers would read this scenario and throw their hands up in the air, exclaiming, "That's great for the home, but I don't have the time or the energy to do all that in my classroom!" The trick, we propose, is not necessarily to replicate all of the supports of the home environment but to ask what pieces of this lesson *could* be easily replicated in the classroom. For instance, could Sam be provided with a curriculum built, at least partially, around his areas of interest? Might the teachers be able to give him less linear and more "creative" instruction as he develops new skills in reading and writing? Would observing Sam give us the information so necessary to teach him effectively? Could we ask Sam how he learns and work those ideas into his program? And finally, might Sam's mother serve as an informal consultant to our work with him so that we might take the best of what was discovered at home and build on it in our classroom?

The bottom line really is that we must learn from parents because they—out of sheer necessity, passion, and love—often persist when teachers do not. Parents work from a more intimate understanding of the student and they may be more motivated to try a variety of different approaches to get their child to learn. Furthermore, parents are often very eager to share what they know with professionals. Consulting with these partners, therefore, provides teachers with additional help for instruction, curriculum, and support, and it also moves the school–home collaborative relationship forward. See Table 7.2 for additional ideas on studying the practice of parents.

Rely on the Classroom Community

If you have read this far in the book, it is no secret that we believe that the general education classroom is the best learning environment for students with autism. In fact, we believe that inclusion might be the most critical component of an educational program for students with significant disabilities. Among the essential elements of the inclusive classroom are peer interaction, support, and modeling. Consider the example of Rebecca, a "primarily nonspeaking" fifth-grade student with autism considered "preliterate" by professionals who had evaluated her (Kliewer & Biklen, 2001). Determined to include their new student in classroom life, teachers asked the class to brainstorm ways to include Rebecca throughout the day. Some of the girls thought of using notes (the type students typically pass to each other during class to socialize). One teacher recalls that students started passing notes to Rebecca, unfolding them for her and then reading them to her. Over time, the teachers noted how interested Rebecca became when notes were read to her. Sometimes the notes would include questions such as, "Do you like James? Yes? No?" and the stu-

Table 7.2.   Ideas for studying the practice of parents

Observe students at home to see all of the ways they communicate, socialize, and interact with materials and demonstrate literacy-related abilities, interest, and skills. Take particular note of how family members encourage or support the child as they engage in various tasks and routines.

Invite families to come to the school and observe their child. If the student is uncomfortable or confused by seeing a parent at school, you can videotape a lesson or segment of time. Invite parents to give suggestions or offer observations that might increase the student's communication opportunities, access to literacy learning, or interactions with peers.

Ask the family for materials that might be motivating for the learner with significant disabilities including favorite books, menus from frequently visited restaurants, photo albums, programs from special events, and cards or letters from loved ones. One student we taught loved his junior high school yearbook and carried it with him for 4 years. His mother suggested that the school use this text to inspire a love of reading and to help the student interact with peers at the same time.

Work together to teach new skills. For example, if the team decides to convert a picture schedule to words and phrases, parents and teachers can work together to devise a system to teach and reinforce the transition.

Use family photographs to create books that students will find irresistible. Many learners enjoy seeing pictures of themselves, especially if the photos show them having fun, interacting with loved ones, or looking capable. Begin by finding or taking some photos of a preferred activity or event. Then, create captions (using repetitive text for emerging readers) for the photos, securing them in a photo album or laminating the pages with clear contact paper.

dents would ask Rebecca to answer. After Rebecca started nodding her head at some of the questions, the teaching team constructed a yes/no board and built a range of literacy experiences around the note-passing experiences. As Kliewer and Biklen pointed out, this type of academic growth could not occur without Rebecca first having access to the general education classroom:

> Within the course of a single school year, Rebecca had gone from being perceived as nonsymbolic to constructing symbolic interactions with her classroom friends. Rather than requiring proof of symbolic competence prior to the development of relationships, [the teacher] had turned the traditional equations on its head. Entrance into interaction constituted the terrain on which symbol literacy was recognized. In this sense, social engagement in specific, localized situations preceded demonstrations of intellectual competence and a more abstract definition of Rebecca as a thoughtful, engaged, and engaging human being. (2001, p. 6)

As Rebecca's teachers demonstrate, educating students in a general education environment is not really inclusion unless there are targeted goals, appropriate curriculum, individualized instruction, and appropriate personal supports. The peers in this situation made instruction work.

  This same phenomenon of community support is highlighted in a study by Sonnenmeier, Jorgensen, and McSheehan. These authors engaged in a multiyear case study of Jay, a 10-year-old child with autism, who, previous to their research activities, was seen as having an "18 months to 24 months" academic level (2005, p. 103). The Test of Auditory Comprehension of Language-3 (Carrow-Woolfork, 1999) indicated Jay's receptive language to be below the first percentile for his age. Interventions based on the study consisted of supporting this young man with augmentative communication, technology, curriculum adaptations, teaching strategies, and personal supports such as peer assistance. Jay made gains in engagement and communication, and in his ability to demonstrate knowledge of the general education curriculum. These strides were due, in part, to the team's commitment to understanding Jay's inclusion as a contribution to the class, particularly as an opportunity to teach other students about technology, expression, and community.

  One element of the inclusion process was to use an "immersion approach" with Jay's voice output communication aid or VOCA (which, simply put, is an augmentative communication device that "speaks"). All of the students in the classroom were given the same overlay or set of symbols that covered Jay's VOCA, so they, too, could communicate by pointing to communication symbols. Jay's communication system, in many ways, was everywhere:

> All students were encouraged to use their communication boards during class discussions, writing activities, and teacher-directed lessons. The classroom teacher used an enlarged copy of the core vocabulary overlay during whole class instruction. The team used the VOCA and/or paper overlays to provide modeling, restatements, and expansion of what Jay communicated during classroom activities. This immersion approach created a classroom culture of rich communication for Jay. (2005, p. 110)

The types of supports used in Jay's classroom have the potential to provide for several learners, not just Jay. In this classroom, adaptations, different methods of communication, and a variety of educational materials were seen as a necessary part of the inclusive classroom and as a learning tool for every student. These adaptations, particularly the technology-related materials, were designed not only to support Jay's academic growth but also to connect him socially to his peers and to classroom experiences. So, in this example, as in the one featuring Rebecca, peers not only were key to a student's social, communication, and academic gains but also beneficiaries of the experience as well. They profited both from learning new skills and from having a wider range of experiences and learning new ways of "doing business" in their inclusive classroom from their classmate with disabilities.

Of course, peers are an important part of any child's educational experience. A responsive classroom community is even more critical, however, for those who need others in order to understand text or use materials and for those who learn by observing competence in others. But one of the most important ways that peers inspire literacy growth is nearly ignored in the literature on this subject: the idea that access to peers gives students richer and more varied experiences, thus inspiring their communication, social growth, and, of course, their literacy development.

Ian Martin, a young man with autism, demonstrated how motivating classmates can be when he began using typed communication to interact during his first years of elementary school. Although he relished opportunities to show everyone how smart he was, he appeared even more excited to share with, learn from, and interact with his classmates and, thus, needed little encouragement to practice literacy when such exercises involved writing stories for or letters to friends. A letter written to his classmates during the first week of school illustrates this intersection of literacy, social, and communication goals:

DEATR KIDS,
IHAD AMN AMAZINBNG SUMMER. I ASTARTED TTAKING A NEW MREDICINE AND I AM GWWETTING WELL. I XCAN DSO ALL SOERTS OF THINHGS I COUKLDNT DO BEIORE, LOIKE I WENT TO HORNBECK HOMWESTHEAD AND I WPORE A COSTUME AND I ASCTED KLIKE A SREGULAR KID. AND EDDIE SSOPENT THRE NIGHT AND IAM EATHING ATT THE YTABLE WITH MY FA, MILY. I CVAN PLAY MORE TOO. PKLEASE P;LAY WITH ME LOTS. BUT RTHE MOST EZX-CVITING THUING IS MNY PET SNAKE. I NSAMED HIM JOHNNYO. ISNT BTHAT A GREAT MNAME? IGOT HIM ON AHIKE WITH MY DAD SAND SISTER. IAM SO HAP-PUY TO BE BACK QAND IGREATLY HOPE YTO BE YOOUR FRIEND.
IAN (Martin, 1994, p. 270)

Even more touching than these words typed by Ian and read by his mother to classmates is the description of how students reacted upon hearing the letter. They applauded their friend's words despite the fact that he was not able to stand at the front of the room and read the text himself or even respond to their cheers. Instead, as he often did, Ian "sat on the floor with a book between his legs . . . his face bent over the pages that he busily flapped from side to side" (p. 270). Peers who had been educated with Ian for so long, and who had grown to understand his needs and idiosyncrasies, saw this not as a lack of interest in them or in the letter but simply as "Ian's way." The classroom community accepted and understood Ian's manner of interacting and responding and profited from it as Ian showed his classmates that there are many ways to communicate, interact, demonstrate interest and attention, and be a friend. See Table 7.3 for more ideas related to capitalizing and relying on the classroom community.

Table 7.3.   Ideas for capitalizing and relying on the classroom community

Have students read to each other. Have students who need practice with fluency read to those who cannot read aloud. For students in upper grades, look for opportunities to encourage reading in natural ways. For example, a high school drama teacher might have students read monologues to one another in pairs and then switch pairs several times so they can practice their "performance" repeatedly (and the student with significant disabilities can listen to the work of peers while possibly being asked to respond or critique using a yes/no board or picture board).

Ask students for their help in devising adaptations and supports for their peer with a disability.

Consider all of the ways students connect with one another through literacy. Create constant opportunities for students to share information, socialize, and connect via reading, writing, speaking or listening. For instance, have students share a joke of the day, keep a classroom newsletter going throughout the year, or structure a classroom pen pal system.

Keep the student involved in *all* aspects of classroom life (e.g., sharing secrets, being the "student of the week," going on fieldtrips, voting for Prom Queen). Evaluate all of the structures and routines of the school, especially those that might have a link to literacy learning, and consider how you might increase the participation of students with significant disabilities. In a junior high school, a vice principal and former special educator designed a picture board of the entire ninth-grade class so that Emiko, a young woman with autism and significant communication struggles, could vote for classmates in the yearbook's annual "Mr./Ms." Awards (e.g., Mr. & Ms. Dimples, Mr. & Ms. Bookworm).

Following Small Cues

One strategy that some teachers and families employ is to follow what we call "small cues" (Chandler-Olcott & Kluth, 2006). Following small cues means that educators look for evidence of ability, growth, or understanding and teach to those suspicions. For example, a teacher is following a small cue when she notices that her student always puts the classroom DVDs in the right cases even though she "can't read." Or when a teacher notices that a child always runs to the chalkboard when he posts new classroom jobs. Or when a teacher observes that the child who bangs on the keyboard is making choices that do not seem random. Educators who see and build on small cues are perpetually open to the idea that students are more capable than those around them may assume they are.

In our own experience, we have seen that families are particularly skilled at this work of following small cues. They sort through distracting or even contradictory data to identify opportunities for literate engagement, celebrate even the smallest indications of progress, and make sensitive adaptations as needed. One example of this parental persistence comes from Lucy Blackman, an Australian teenager with autism who has notoriously unreliable speech:

> [My mother] still was not sure whether I could store narrative long enough to read a full-length novel. To date I had yelled every time she had tried to get me to sit still while she turned pages, and when I picked up a book I read what was on the open page in front of me, and then just fanned through the leaves. (1999, p. 121)

Convinced that her daughter had both the desire and the ability to sustain an interaction with text but that her sensory difficulties prevented her from doing so, Lucy's mother boxed Lucy into a corner of the sofa with her body, put a book across both their laps, and moved Lucy's hand to help her track the print. Lucy later described the discovery of this position, which led to her becoming a voracious reader of novels, as "wonderful for me because I always feel so much more competent when I am squashed" (1999, p. 121).

We have noticed that parents like Lucy's mother who are successful at teaching their children with autism to read and write often come to the task without the expectation that they will impose new learning on the "student." Rather, these savvy educators follow the lead of the pupil, observing his or her learning style and often idiosyncratic behavior, work with the individual's needs and strengths, and take cues from the learner as the "lesson" progresses.

A school-based example of following small cues comes from Heather Ruiz, a colleague Paula collaborated with during a multiyear grant project focused on including students with autism. Paula met with Heather over a period of 2 years and, therefore, had an opportunity to see the young teacher make great strides with Luz, a young woman with significant disabilities who was nonverbal. A literacy journey began when Heather started noticing that whenever she was sitting at her desk working on her laptop, Luz would circle around the workspace. Mostly she would just walk in circles around Heather's desk. Other times, though, she would crouch near her teacher and occasionally try to put her face close to the computer (sometimes getting so close, in fact, that her nose was touching the screen). For years, Luz had had a reputation of circling the teacher's desk in this way, but others had seen this as an indication that the young woman wanted her teacher's attention. Heather, a new teacher, was curious about this "circling" almost immediately and began to wonder if Luz was trying to read or at least to imitate Heather. She followed this small cue and began typing messages to Luz such as, "Hi Luz. Are you reading this?" Although Luz often did not seem to react, other times she seemed to laugh or respond to the text. Heather reported that after several weeks of this cooperative computer dialogue, she typed, "I LOVE YOUR NEW SHIRT" and Luz giggled, looked down at the floor, and then tugged at her sleeves.

Luz's reaction to the typed message provided an incredible piece of evidence of her literacy potential. Heather began reading newspapers and magazines to her student (who previously had no targeted literacy goals whatsoever). She also launched a collaborative journaling exercise with her student that involved talking to Luz about a variety of topics and writing the conversation on paper. She then began passing simple notes to Luz containing messages such as "Stand up" and "Take a pencil." Luz did not respond to these particular notes but when Heather wrote, "Will you bring Dan a drink?" Luz looked up, waved her fingers, made a soft noise, got up from her chair, walked to Heather's desk, grabbed a juice box, and put it at her classmate's feet. Heather reported that she yelped aloud at this moment and that "everything changed" in her expectations for her student then and there.

This is an example of a teacher who responded to a small cue and ended up with a large window in which to view her student's ability. For so many of our students with significant disabilities, the small cues come first, so it is imperative that teachers are prepared to be pleasantly surprised by their students' abilities and ready to act on the smallest indicators of ability, interest, and skill. See Table 7.4 for additional ideas on following small cues.

Make Communication a Priority

In many ways, access to communication parallels access to a literate life. One does not necessarily need to be linked to the other, but it is hard to work on communication without working on literacy, and it is a challenge to support literacy growth

Table 7.4.   Ideas for following "small cues"

Videotape the student for an extended period of time (1 hour or more) during a literacy lesson or even during a free period. Watch the tape to determine how the student may be demonstrating literacy skills and abilities in subtle ways (e.g., "experimenting" with a pencil and paper, peering at the work of other students).

Give the student a variety of materials to explore, activities to participate in, and environments to learn in and from. Take notes on how his or her habits, behaviors, or responses change or differ.

When you have success following a student's small cues and teaching from them, document the steps you took in doing so. This process may be very helpful in understanding how, when, and under what circumstances the student learns.

Have a "small cue conversation" with the family and a colleague or two. Ask participants to share any of their own observations about the learner and subtle ways he or she has shown interest, growth, or understanding.

if we are not simultaneously working to give students improved access to their voices. If the student does not have a reliable way to communicate, the educational team will need to experiment with strategies, systems, materials, or devices that might be effective. If the student does have reliable ways to communicate, the team should focus on building the student's communication skills and competencies and giving the student opportunities to participate in class, engage in curriculum, and socialize using those skills and competencies. Supporting a student's communication is critical; if a teacher in an inclusive classroom wants to develop better curriculum and instruction for a student, find more effective and sensitive ways to support his or her behavior, learn more about the student's social needs, or provide more sophisticated literacy supports, he or she needs to be able to access that student's voice.

One way to help students build literacy skills and abilities is to consider your role and responsibility as a communication partner. Too often we put ourselves in the role of teaching communication skills without considering what skills students already possess and how we might be more sensitive and effective on our side of the equation. In other words, we must consider how *we* communicate before we can expect students to better their skills. Too many teachers expect students to initiate communication without modeling much communication themselves. Some teachers may feel uncomfortable or unsure of how to interact with a student who does not speak or one who communicates in a way unfamiliar to him or her. This is understandable, but feeling uncomfortable is no excuse for not learning new ways of being with our students with communication differences.

One of the most important ways to make a student feel included in the classroom is to communicate with him or her and expect the student to communicate with you. Gillingham stressed the importance of holding these values:

Whenever I am with an autistic person, I communicate with them and I fully expect them to communicate with me. The fact that they do not respond in the exact way that I approach them, does not mean that I cannot understand them. When I go into a home and say "hello" to an autistic person, they do not have to reply "hello" for me to feel that they are responding. Whether they approach me or withdraw to another room tells me something. I read an increase in repetitive behavior as an indication that they are excited to see me, and I verbally tell them that it feels good to see their excitement. I follow their lead if they take my hand to show me something. If they speak with garbled sounds, I acknowledge their efforts and openly admit that I don't quite understand what they are trying to say. As I spend time with them, I am continuously aware of what they are doing and how they are responding to me. (2000, pp. 111–112)

These beliefs and behaviors inspire trust in relationships and allow teachers and students to get to know each other. As Gillingham went on to share, "Concentration on acceptance of what is, instead of trying to fix what appears wrong, leads to improved communication" (2000, p. 112).

When communicating with students and expecting communication, it can be helpful to reflect on what assumptions a teacher might have about his or her student. Shevin & Kalina (1997) have shared that in their role as communication allies, they always begin with "default values" that they act on until receiving specific information to the contrary. Their own assumptions about individuals with communication differences are the following:

- They are highly intelligent.

- They have a deep interest in fostering relations with others (and possibly with me).

- They have stories they would like to tell, if the circumstances are right.

- They have positive images of themselves that they wish to present as part of their communication.

- Regardless of appearances, they are paying attention to me when I interact with them.

Whereas every teacher will want to establish his or her own values and assumptions, those offered here can inspire positive actions. For instance, a teacher who believes his or her student is intelligent will creatively include that student in lessons and respond to that learner in moments when he seems interested in a topic or idea.

Another way teachers can support and teach communication is to give students with autism time to interact, share, and communicate with the teacher and peers throughout the day. In some classrooms, a handful of students dominate small-group conversations and whole-class discussions. Although it is important for these verbal and outgoing students to have a voice in the classroom, it is equally important for other students—including shy and quiet students, students using English as a second language, and students with disabilities—to have opportunities to share and challenge ideas, ask and answer questions, and exchange thoughts. To ensure that all students have opportunities to communicate, teachers need to put structures and activities in place that allow for interaction.

For instance, in one middle school classroom, a social studies teacher asks students an open-ended question at the beginning or end of class. One morning she asked students to report on something they learned on the previous day's fieldtrip to an art museum. After a few moments of "think time," students were expected to given an answer in five words or less as their teacher pointed to each student and invited his or her response. Responses ranged from "Picasso was a sculptor" to "Dancing is art" to "Kids can be artists." This structure was initially put in place for one student, Walter, because his teachers noticed that he was more

Figure 7.1. BIGmack® communicator from AbleNet, Inc.

engaged and interested in using his augmentative communication device when it was used in the context of classroom activities.

For this reason, all four of Walter's teachers made an extra effort to provide more opportunities for interaction between students in their classes. His math teacher began to allow students to turn and talk to each other at various points in the day. After giving mini-lectures of 15 to 20 minutes, she would ask students to turn to a partner and answer a specific question or re-explain a concept she had taught. For instance, after giving a short lecture on decimals, she asked students to discuss how they used decimals in their own lives.

For both of these exercises, Walter was given time to prepare a response in advance either with a partner or with a teachers. The response was either programmed into a BIGmack switch, a large one-hit switch that holds a 20 second message (see Figure 7.1) or it was written on index cards that were traded and shared with classmates. Often Walter would answer questions and ask others. For instance, he might select a response from a set of cards and give it to peers to read and discuss and follow up by hitting his switch to say, "WHAT IS A QUESTION YOU HAVE ABOUT WORKING WITH DECIMALS?"

In all of these examples, it should be clear that supporting communication cannot be extricated from supporting literacy growth. Helping students learn a new gestural communication system also teaches a learner new words. Teaching a student to spell on a letter board also teaches letter knowledge and, possibly, letter–sound relationships. And sharing weekend experiences with students can help them learn the structure of stories and motivate them to share their own. For more ideas on prioritizing and supporting communication, see Table 7.5.

CONCLUDING THOUGHTS

Think of a student with significant disabilities you know. Maybe he's the one who flaps his fingers in front of his face or dances alone in a corner or spends hours on end gazing out the window at passing trains. We want to be clear that, yes, we

Table 7.5.   Ideas for prioritizing and supporting the communication growth of students with significant disabilities

Put students in situations in which they can profit from hearing multipartner dialogue, can eavesdrop on and participate in student-to-student conversations, and learn from the communication habits and abilities of others.

Encourage a "total communication" approach for students with significant disabilities. Even if students have a formal communication system, encourage them to use informal strategies as well. If a student uses pictures to communicate, for instance, he or she can also be introduced to gestures and signs.

Encourage students to support each other, talk to each other, share ideas with each other. Liberally use think–pair–share structures (Kagan, 1993), cooperative learning, class meetings, and small group structures. These provide opportunities for all students to practice communication and social skills and allow students with autism to interact, move, share, and practice new skills (e.g., new sign language vocabulary).

Include words/labels on picture schedules and communication systems. Often, students with significant disabilities work with pictures, icons, or symbols for years without having the opportunity to learn the words represented by these images.

Teach and use augmentative and alternative communication with all students. Incorporate a few American Sign Language words into your teaching, have all students hold up communication cards (instead of shouting out answers) for some lessons, or have all students occasionally dialogue on paper with a partner.

Model the use of augmentative and alternative communication. Infuse a handful of sign language "words" or phrases into your vocabulary (e.g., "Let me get your attention," "We are finished," "Good morning"). And make sure that students using devices or systems have ample opportunities to see others using them. Students are often asked to access their communication systems without ever seeing others use it in context (if at all). If a child has a multilevel device that allows him or her to have access to a range of ideas to answer fill-in-the-blank questions (e.g., *Sounder was* _____), it will help the student's learning immensely to see the teacher use it in a presentation to the class and to observe as his or her small-group members use it before he or has to make a selection of his or her own.

mean that learner too when we implore teachers to have higher expectations and to provide meaningful and varied educational experiences for all students in inclusive settings.

It is our belief that the next several decades of research on autism will illuminate just how much students with significant autism know, can understand, and have been trying to show us. For this reason, we hope that we have offered encouragement in this chapter to try something new and to be creative as we approach an area of curriculum and instruction that is largely unexplored. To this end, it might be inspiring to learn of a commitment Anne Sullivan made regarding her pupil with significant disabilities. Though she had little in the way of precedent, could not possibly know what to expect of her pupil, and, incidentally, was only 21 years old, Sullivan moved forward in her work with Helen Keller with both conviction and remarkable expectations. Certainly as we are waiting to learn more about significant disability, technology, communication difficulties, and autism itself, it will serve our students well if we hold high expectations while employing practices that might bring the most promising results. Sullivan herself lived and taught by this philosophy:

> I shall assume that she has the normal child's capacity of assimilation and imitation. I shall use complete sentences in talking to her, and fill out the meaning with gestures and her descriptive signs when necessity requires it, but I shall not try to keep her mind fixed on any one thing. I shall do all I can to interest and stimulate it, and wait for results. (Lash, 1980, p. 56).

Bibliography

REFERENCES

Adams, M.J., Foorman, B.R., Lundberg, I., & Beeler, T. (1998). *Phonemic awareness in young children: A classroom curriculum*. Baltimore: Paul H. Brookes Publishing Co.

Afflerbach, P., Blachowicz, C., Boyd, C.D., Cheyney, W., Juel, C., Kame'enui, E., et al. (2005). *Scott Foresman Reading Street*. Glenview, IL: Pearson Scott Foresman.

Allen, J. (2002). *On the same page: Shared reading beyond the primary grades*. Portland, ME: Stenhouse Publishers.

Allen, J., & Gonzalez, K. (1998). *There's room for me here: Literacy workshop in middle school*. Portland, ME: Stenhouse Publishers.

Allington, R. (2002). *Big Brother and the national reading curriculum: How ideology trumped evidence*. Portsmouth, NH: Heinemann.

Allington, R., & Johnston, P. (2002). *Reading to learn: Lessons from exemplary fourth-grade classrooms*. New York: Guilford Press.

Alvermann, D., Hinchman, K., Moore, D., Phelps, S., & Waff, D. (1998). *Reconceptualizing the literacies in adolescents' lives*. Mahwah, NJ: Lawrence Erlbaum Associates.

American Psychiatric Association. (1994). *Diagnostic and statistical manual of mental disorders* (4th ed.). Washington, DC: Author.

American Psychiatric Association. (2000). *Diagnostic and statistical manual of mental disorders* (4th ed., rev.). Washington, DC: Author.

Anderson, C. (2000). *How's it going? A practical guide to conferring with student writers*. Portsmouth, NH: Heinemann.

Anderson, J. (2005). *Mechanically inclined: Building grammar, usage, and style into a writer's workshop*. Portland, ME: Stenhouse Publishers.

Arnberg, A. (1999). A study of memoir. *Primary Voices, 8*(1), 13–21.

Asperger, H. (1991). Die autistischen psychopathen im kindesalter. In U. Frith (Ed. & Trans.), *Autism and Asperger syndrome* (pp. 37–92). New York: Cambridge University Press. (Original work published in 1944)

Atwell, N. (1998). *In the middle: New understandings about writing, reading, and learning* (2nd ed.). Portsmouth, NH: Heinemann.

Au, K. (2000). A multicultural perspective on policies for improving literacy achievement, equity, and excellence. In M. Kamil, P.B. Mosenthal, P.D. Pearson, & R. Barr (Eds.), *Handbook of reading research* (Vol. 3, pp. 835–851). Mahwah, NJ: Lawrence Erlbaum Associates.

Baker, L. (2002). Metacognition in comprehension instruction. In C. Collins Block & M. Pressley (Eds.), *Comprehension instruction: Research-based best practices* (pp. 77–95). New York: Guilford Press.

Bakhtin, M.M. (1981). *The dialogic imagination*. (C. Emerson & M. Holquist, Trans.). Austin: University of Texas Press.

Barone, D., Hardman, D., & Taylor, J. (2004). *Reading First in the classroom*. Boston: Allyn & Bacon.

Barron, J., & Barron, S. (1992). *There's a boy in here*. New York: Simon & Schuster.

Barton, D., Hamilton, M., & Ivanic, R. (2000). *Situated literacies: Reading and writing in context*. New York: Routledge.

Baumann, J., Jones, L., & Seifert-Kessell, N. (1993). Using think-alouds to enhance children's comprehension monitoring abilities. *The Reading Teacher, 47*, 184–193.

Bauer, S. (1996). *Asperger syndrome*. Retrieved July 8, 2007, from http://www.udel.edu/bkirby/asperger/as_thru_years.html

Beck, I., McKeown, M., & Kucan, L. (2002). *Bringing words to life: Robust vocabulary instruction*. New York: Guilford Press.

Bedrosian, J., Lasker, J., Speidel, K., & Politsch, A. (2003). Enhancing the written narrative skills of an AAC student with autism: Evidence-based research issues. *Topics in Language Disorders, 23*(4), 305–324.

Bereiter, C., & Scardamalia, M. (1987). *The psychology of written composition*. Mahwah, NJ: Lawrence Erlbaum Associates.

Berndle, E. (2001). Choral reading: Miss Berndl's fabulous fours and fantabulous fives. Retrieved July 7, 2007, from http://www.rocksforkids.com/FabFours/choral_reading.html

Biancarosa, G., & Snow, C. (2004). *Reading next: A vision for action and research in middle and high school literacy: A report to the Carnegie Corporation*. Washington, DC: Alliance for Excellence in Education. Retrieved May 26, 2006, from http://www.all4ed.org/publications/ReadingNext/ReadingNext.pdf

Biklen, D. (1990). Communication unbound: Autism and praxis. *Harvard Educational Review, 60*(3), 291–314.

Biklen, D. (with Atfield, R., Bissonette, L., Blackman, L., Burke, J., Frugone, A., Mukhopadhyay, T.R., & Rubin, S.) (2005). *Autism and the myth of the person alone*. New York: New York University Press.

Biklen, D., & Burke, J. (2006). Presuming competence. *Equity & Excellence in Education, 39*, 1–10.

Billmeyer, R., & Barton, M.L. (1998). *Teaching reading in the content areas: If not me, then who?* Aurora, CO: Mid-continent Research for Education and Learning.

Bissex, G. (1980). *Gnys at wrk: A child learns to write and read*. Cambridge, MA: Harvard University Press.

Bissonnette, L. (2005). Letters ordered through typing produce the story of an artist stranded on the island of autism. In D. Biklen (Ed.), *Autism and the myth of the person alone* (pp. 172–182). New York: New York University Press.

Blachman, B. (2000). Phonological awareness. In M. Kamil, P.B. Mosenthal, P.D. Pearson, & R. Barr (Eds.), *Handbook of reading research* (Vol. 3, pp. 483–502). Mahwah, NJ: Lawrence Erlbaum Associates.

Blachman, B.A., Ball, E.W., Black, R., & Tangel, D.M. (2000). *Road to the code: A phonological awareness program for young children*. Baltimore: Paul H. Brookes Publishing Co.

Blachowicz, C., & Fisher, P. (2000). Vocabulary instruction. In M. Kamil, P.B. Mosenthal, P.D. Pearson, & R. Barr (Eds.), *Handbook of reading research* (Vol. 3, pp. 503–523). Mahwah, NJ: Lawrence Erlbaum Associates.

Blackburn, J. (1997). *Autism? What is it?* Retrieved on February 15, 2006, from http://www.autistics.org/library/whatis.html

Blackburn, M. (2003). Exploring literacy performances and power dynamics at The Loft: Queer youth reading the world and the word. *Research in the Teaching of English, 37*, 467–490.

Blackman, L. (1999). *Lucy's story: Autism and other adventures*. Brisbane, Australia: Book in Hand.

Blatt, B. (1966). *Christmas in purgatory: A photographic essay on mental retardation*. Boston: Allyn & Bacon.

Boulineau , T., Fore, C., Hagan-Burke, S., & Burke, M. (2004). Use of story-mapping to increase the story-grammar text comprehension of elementary students with learning disabilities. *Learning Disability Quarterly, 27*, 105–121.

Broderick, A., & Kasa-Hendrickson, C. (2001). "Say just one word at first": The emergence of reliable speech in a student labeled with autism. *The Journal of the Association for Persons with Severe Handicaps, 26*, 13–24.

Bromley, K. (1999). Key components of sound writing instruction. In L.B. Gambrell, L.M. Morrow, S.B. Neuman, & M. Pressley (Eds.), *Best practices in literacy instruction* (pp. 152–174). New York: Guilford Press.

Bromley, K., Irwin-DeVitis, L., & Modlo, M. (1995). *Graphic organizers: Visual strategies for active learning.* New York: Scholastic.

Brophy, J., & Evertson, C. (1981). *Student characteristics and teaching.* Boston: Addison Wesley.

Broun, L.T. (2004). Teaching students with autism spectrum disorders to read: A visual approach. *Teaching Exceptional Children, 36*(4), 36–40.

Buehl, D. (2001). *Classroom strategies for interactive learning* (2nd ed.). Newark, DE: International Reading Association.

Burke, J. (2002). *"Inside the edge": A journey to using speech through typing* [video]. Syracuse, NY: Facilitated Communication Institute.

Burke, Jamie. (2005). The world as I'd like it to be. In D. Biklen (Ed.), *Autism and the myth of the person alone* (pp. 248–253). New York: New York University Press.

Burke, Jim. (2002). It's all in the cards. *Voices from the Middle, 10*(1), 54–55.

Calkins, L. (1986). *The art of teaching writing.* Portsmouth, NH: Heinemann.

Calkins, L. (1991). *Living between the lines.* Portsmouth, NH: Heinemann.

Callahan, J. (1990). *Don't worry, he won't get far on foot.* New York: Vintage Books.

Carrow-Woolfolk, E. (1999). *Test for Auditory Comprehension of Language* (TACL). Austin, TX: PRO-ED.

Centers for Disease Control and Prevention. (2007). *CDC releases new data on autism spectrum disorders (ASDs) from multiple communities in the United States.* Retrieved June 12, 2007, from http://www.cdc.gov/od/oc/media/pressrel/2007/r070208.htm

Chandler, K. (1996). 'Making it more real': Book groups, make lemonade, and the school nurse. *ALAN Review, 24*(1), 16–19.

Chandler, K., & Gibson, G. (1998). Making reading partners an integral part of the reading-writing curriculum. *Journal of the New England Reading Association, 34*(2), 3–10.

Chandler, K., & The Mapleton Teacher-Research Group. (1999). *Spelling inquiry: How one elementary school caught the mnemonic plague.* Portland, ME: Stenhouse Publishers.

Chandler-Olcott, K. (2003). Seeing all students as literate. In P. Kluth, D. Straut, & D. Biklen (Eds.), *Access to academics for all students: Critical approaches to inclusive curriculum, instruction, and policy* (pp. 69–84). Mahwah, NJ: Lawrence Erlbaum Associates.

Chandler-Olcott, K., & Hinchman, K. (2005). *Tutoring adolescent literacy learners: A guide for volunteers.* New York: Guilford Press.

Chandler-Olcott, K., & Kluth, P. (2006, November). *"Mother's voice was the main source of all learning": Parents' role in supporting the literacy development of students with autism.* Paper presented at the annual meeting of the National Reading Conference, Los Angeles, CA.

Chandler-Olcott, K., & Mahar, D. (2003). Tech-savviness meets multiliteracies: An exploration of adolescent girls' technology-mediated literacy practices. *Reading Research Quarterly, 38*, 356–385.

Chapman, M. (1995). The sociocognitive construction of written genres: Some findings from an examination of first grade writing. *Research in the Teaching of English, 29*, 164–192.

Chapman, M. (2006). Preschool through elementary writing. In P. Smagorinsky (Ed.), *Research on composition: Multiple perspectives on two decades of change* (pp. 15–47). New York: Teachers College Press.

Clagett, F. (1996). *A measure of our success: From assignment to assessment in English language arts.* Portsmouth, NH: Heinemann.

Coalition of Essential Schools. (2007). *The CES Common Principles*. Retrieved March 7, 2007, from http://www.essentialschools.org/pub/ces_docs/about/phil/10cps/10cps.html

Colasent, R., & Griffith, P.L. (1998). Autism and literacy: Looking into the classroom with rabbit stories. *The Reading Teacher, 51*, 414–420.

Copeland, S.R., & Keefe, E.B. (2007). *Effective literacy instruction for students with moderate or severe disabilities*. Baltimore: Paul H. Brookes Publishing Co.

Craviotto, E., Heras, A., & Espindola, J. (1999). Cultures of the fourth-grade bilingual classroom. *Primary Voices, 7*(3), 25–37.

Crossley, R. (1997). *Speechless: Facilitating communication for people without voices*. New York: Dutton.

Cunningham, A., & Shagoury, R. (2005). *Starting with comprehension: Reading strategies for the youngest learners*. Portland, ME: Stenhouse Publishers.

Cunningham, J.W. (2001). The National Reading Panel report. *Reading Research Quarterly, 36*(3), 326–335.

Cunningham, P.M., & Cunningham, J.W. (1992). Making Words: Enhancing the invented spelling-decoding connection. *Reading Teacher, 46*, 106–115.

Dahl, K., & Farnan, N. (1998). *Children's writing: Perspectives from research*. Newark, DE: International Reading Association and National Reading Conference.

Daniels, H. (1994). *Literature circles: Voice and choice in the student-centered classroom*. Portland, ME: Stenhouse Publishers.

Daniels, H., & Bizar, M. (2005). *Teaching the best practice way: Methods that matter, K–12*. Portland, ME: Stenhouse Publishers.

Daniels, H., & Zemelman, S. (2005). *Subjects matter: Every teacher's guide to content-area reading*. Portsmouth, NH: Heinemann.

Darling-Hammond, L. (1997). *The right to learn*. San Francisco: Jossey-Bass.

Delano, M.E. (2007). Video modeling interventions for individuals with autism. *Remedial and Special Education, 28*, 33–42.

Deshon, J. (1997). Innocent and not-so-innocent contributions to inequality: Choice, power, and insensitivity in a first-grade writing workshop. *Language Arts, 74*, 12–16.

Dole, J. (2002). Comprehension strategies. In B. Guzzetti (Ed.), *Literacy in America: An encyclopedia of history, theory, and practice, volume one* (pp. 85–88). Santa Barbara, CA: ABC-Clio.

Dole, J., Duffy, G., Roehler, L., & Pearson, P.D. (1991). Moving from the old to the new: Research on reading comprehension instruction. *Review of Educational Research, 61*, 239–264.

Donnellan, A., & Leary, M. (1995). *Movement differences and diversity in autism/mental retardation: Appreciating and accommodating people with communication and behavior challenges*. Madison, WI: DRI Press.

Donovan, C., & Smolkin, L. (2006). Children's understanding of genre and writing development. In C. MacArthur, S. Graham, & J. Fitzgerald (Eds.), *Handbook of writing research* (pp. 131–143). New York: Guilford Press.

Downing, J.E. (with invited contributors). (2005). *Teaching communication skills to students with severe disabilities: Strategies for the K–12 inclusive classroom* (2nd ed.). Baltimore: Paul H. Brookes Publishing Co.

Duffy, G. (2003). *Explaining reading: A resource for teaching concepts, skills, and strategies*. New York: Guilford Press.

Dynamic Measurement Group. (2006). Position paper on use of DIBELS for diverse learners. Retrieved February 15, 2007, from http://www.dibels.org/papers/Appropriateness_2006-11-22.pdf

Eastham, M. (1992). *Silent words: Forever friends*. Ottawa, Ontario: Oliver Pate.

Eckert, T.L., Lovett, B.J., Rosenthal, B.D., Jiao, J., Ricci, L.J., & Truckenmiller, A.J. (2006). Class-wide instructional feedback: Improving children's academic skill development. In S.V. Randall (Ed.), *Learning disabilities: New research* (pp. 271–285). Hauppauge, NY: Nova Sciences.

Edelson, M.G. (2006). Are the majority of children with autism mentally retarded? A systematic evaluation of the data. *Focus on Autism and Other Developmental Disabilities, 21,* 66–83.

Edwards, E., Heron, A., & Francis, M. (2000, May). *Toward an ideological definition of literacy: How critical pedagogy shaped the literacy development of a fifth-grade social studies class.* Paper presented at the annual meeting of the American Educational Research Association, New Orleans, LA.

Ekwall, H., & Shanker, J. (2000). *Ekwall-Shanker reading inventory* (4th ed.). Boston: Allyn & Bacon.

Emig, J. (1971). *The composing processes of twelfth graders.* Urbana, IL: National Council of Teachers of English.

Erickson, K., & Koppenhaver, D. (1995). Developing a literacy program for children with severe disabilities. *The Reading Teacher, 48,* 676–687.

Erickson, K., & Koppenhaver, D. (2007). *Children with disabilities: Reading and writing the Four-Blocks® way.* Greensboro, NC: Carson-Dellosa Publishing Company, Inc.

Ernst, K. (1994). *Picturing learning: Artists and writers in the classroom.* Portsmouth, NH: Heinemann.

Farnan, N., & Dahl, K. (2003). Children's writing: Research and practice. In J. Flood, D. Lapp, J. Squire, & J. Jensen (Eds.), *Handbook of research on teaching the English language arts* (2nd ed.) (pp. 993–1007). Mahwah, NJ: Lawrence Erlbaum Associates.

Feldman, R.S., & Theiss, A.J. (1982). The teacher and student as pygmalions: Joint effects of teacher and student expectations. *Journal of Educational Psychology, 74,* 217–223.

Fihe, T. (2000, November). *Speech in an abnormal psychology class.* Paper presented at University of California-Santa Cruz, Santa Cruz, CA.

Finders, M., & Hynds, S. (2003). *Literacy lessons: Teaching and learning with middle school students.* Upper Saddle River, NJ: Prentice Hall.

Fisher, D., & Frey, N. (2001). Access to the core curriculum. *Remedial and Special Education, 22,* 148.

Fisher, D., & Frey, N. (2003). Writing instruction for struggling adolescent readers: A gradual release model. *Journal of Adolescent & Adult Literacy, 46*(5), 396–405.

Fisher, D., & Johnson, C. (2006). Analyzing student work. *Principal Leadership, 7*(2), 37–42.

Fisher, D., Sax, C., & Jorgensen, C. (1998). Philosophical foundations of inclusive, restructuring schools. In C. Jorgensen (Ed.), *Restructuring high schools for all students: Taking inclusion to the next level* (pp. 29–47). Baltimore: Paul H. Brookes Publishing Co.

Fisher, D., Sax, C., & Pumpian, I. (1999). *Inclusive high schools: Learning from contemporary classrooms.* Baltimore: Paul H. Brookes Publishing Co.

Fling, E. (2000). *Eating an artichoke.* Philadelphia: Jessica Kingsley.

Flood, J., Lapp, D., Flood, S., & Nagel, G. (1992). Am I allowed to group? Using flexible patterns for effective instruction. *The Reading Teacher, 45*(8), 608–616.

Fountas, I., & Pinnell, G.S. (1996). *Guided reading: Good first teaching for all children.* Portsmouth, NH: Heinemann.

Fox, B. (2003). Word recognition. In B. Guzzetti (Ed.), *Literacy in America: An encyclopedia of history, theory, and practice* (Vol. 2, pp. 678–682). Santa Barbara, CA: ABC-CLIO.

Freire, P., & Macedo, D. (1987). *Literacy: Reading the word and the world.* Westport, CT: Bergin and Garvey.

Fulwiler, T. (1987). *The journal book.* Portsmouth, NH: Heinemann.

Gaddy, G.D. (1988). High school order and academic achievement. *American Journal of Education, 96,* 496–518.

Gallagher, K. (2006). *Teaching adolescent writers.* Portland, ME: Stenhouse Publishers.

Gallego, M., & Hollingsworth, S. (2000). *What counts as literacy: Challenging the school standard.* New York: Teachers College Press.

Gatti, G. (with Wisconsin Center for Educational Research). (2005). *Scott Foresman Reading Street benchmark item validation study.* Retrieved February 15, 2007, from http://www.scottforesman.com/reading/readingstreet/pdfs/readingstreetbivs.pdf

Gee, J.P. (1996). *Social linguistics and literacies: Ideology in discourses* (2nd ed.). London: Falmer.

Geertz, C. (2000). *Local knowledge: Further essays in interpretive anthropology.* New York: Basic Books.

Gere, A.R., Christenbury, L., & Sassi, K. (2005). *Writing on demand: Best practices and strategies for success.* Portsmouth, NH: Heinemann.

Gerland, G. (1996). *A real person: Life on the outside.* London: Souvenir Press.

Gerland, G. (1999). *Living with an autistic disability.* Retrieved on February 15, 2006, from http://xoomer.virgilio.it/marpavio/Gunilla_Gerland_Living_with_an_autistic_disability.htm

Giacobbe, M. (1986). Learning to write and writing to learn in the elementary school. In A. Petrosky & D. Bartholomae (Eds.), *The teaching of writing* (pp. 131–147). Chicago: National Society for the Study of Education.

Gillet, J.W., & Temple, C. (2000). *Understanding reading problems: Assessment and instruction* (5th ed.). New York: Longman.

Gillingham, G. (1995). *Autism: Handle with care.* Edmonton, Alberta: Tacit Publishing Inc.

Gillingham, G. (2000). *Autism: A new understanding.* Edmonton, Alberta: Tacit Publishing Inc.

Gilroy, D.E., & Miles, T.R. (1996). *Dyslexia at college* (2nd ed.). New York: Routledge.

Ginsberg, D. (2002). *Raising Blaze: Bringing up an extraordinary son in an ordinary world.* New York: HarperCollins.

Good, R.H., & Kaminski, R.A. (2002). *Dynamic indicators of basic early literacy skills* (6th ed.). Eugene, OR: Institute for the Development of Educational Achievement. Available: http://dibels.uoregon.edu/

Goodman, Y. (1978). Kidwatching: An alternative to testing. *National Elementary School Principal, 57,* 41–45.

Goodman, Y., Watson, D., & Burke, C. (1987). *Reading miscue inventory.* Katonah, NY: Richard C. Owen.

Gould, S.J. (1981). *The mismeasure of man.* New York: W.W. Norton.

Graff, H.J. (2001). The nineteenth-century origins of our times. In E. Cushman, E. Kintgen, B. Kroll, & M. Rose (Eds.), *Literacy: A critical sourcebook* (pp. 211–233). New York: Bedford/St. Martins.

Graham, S. (2006). Strategy instruction and the teaching of writing: A meta-analysis. In C. MacArthur, S. Graham, & J. Fitzgerald (Eds.), *Handbook of writing research* (pp. 187–207). New York: Guilford Press.

Graham, S., Harris, K., & Larsen, L. (2001). Prevention and intervention of writing difficulties for students with learning disabilities. *Learning Disabilities Research & Practice, 16*(2), 74–84.

Graham, S., & Perin, D. (2007). *Writing next: Effective strategies to improve writing of adolescents in middle and high schools—A report to the Carnegie Corporation of New York.* Washington, DC: Alliance for Excellent Education. Retrieved June 29, 2007, from http://www.all4ed.org/publications/WritingNext/index.html

Grandin, T. (1995). *Thinking in pictures and other reports from my life with autism.* New York: Vintage Books.

Grandin, T. (1997). *Genetics and the behavior of domestic animals.* San Diego: Academic Press.

Grandin, T. (1999). *Social problems: Understanding emotions and developing talents.* Center for the Study of Autism. Retrieved March 21, 2007, from http://www.autism.org/temple/social.html

Graves, D. (1983). *Writing: Teachers and children at work.* Portsmouth, NH: Heinemann.

Gray, C. (1994). *Comic strip conversations.* Arlington, TX: Future Horizons Inc.

Gray, C. (2000). *The new social story book: Illustrated edition.* Arlington, TX: Future Horizons Inc.

Gray, C., & White, A. (2002). *My social stories book.* London: Jessica Kingsley Publishers.

Gurry, S., & Larkin, S. (2005). Literacy learning of children with developmental disabilities: What do we know? *Currents in Literacy*. Retrieved September 22, 2006, from http://www .lesley.edu/academic_centers/hood/currents/v2n1/gurry_larkin.html

Hall, K. (2001). *Asperger syndrome, the universe and everything*. London: Jessica Kingsley Publishers.

Hamill, L., & Everington, C. (2002). *Teaching students with moderate to severe disabilities: An applied approach for inclusive environments*. Columbus, OH: Merrill Prentice Hall.

Harvey, S. (1998). *Nonfiction matters: Reading, writing, and research in grades 3–8*. Portland, ME: Stenhouse Publishers.

Harvey, S., & Goudvis, A. (2000). *Strategies that work: Teaching comprehension to enhance understanding*. Portland, ME: Stenhouse Publishers.

Hays, H. (1996). *Asperger memories*. Retrieved February 13, 2007, from http://www.inlv .demon.nl/subm-events.html

Hedeen, D.L., & Ayers, B.J. (2002). "You want me to teach him to read?" Fulfilling the intent of IDEA. *Journal of Disability Policy Studies, 13*, 180–189.

Henry, J. (1995). *If not now: Developmental readers in the college classroom*. Portsmouth, NH: Heinemann.

Hill, B., Johnson, N., & Noe, K.S. (1995). *Literature circles and response*. Norwood, MA: Christopher-Gordon.

Hindley, J. (1996). *In the company of children*. Portland, ME: Stenhouse Publishers.

Hockenberry, J. (1996). *Moving violations: War zones, wheelchairs, and declarations of independence*. New York: Hyperion.

Holland, O. (2003). *The dragons of autism: Autism as a source of wisdom*. London: Jessica Kingsley Publishers.

Holliday Willey, L. (1999). *Pretending to be normal*. London: Jessica Kingsley Publishers.

Hopkins, G., & Bean, T. (1998/1999). Vocabulary learning with the verbal-visual word association strategy in a Native American community. *Journal of Adolescent & Adult Literacy, 42*(4), 274–281.

Howlin, P. (1998). *Children with autism and Asperger syndrome: A guide for practitioners and careers*. New York: Wiley.

Hoyt, L. (1999). *Revisit, reflect, retell: Strategies for improving reading comprehension*. Portsmouth, NH: Heinemann.

Hughes, R. (2003). *Running with Walker: A memoir*. London: Jessica Kingsley Publishers.

Institute for the Study of the Neurologically Typical (2002, March). Retrieved March 21, 2007, from http://isnt.autistics.org/

Jackson, L. (2002). *Freaks, geeks, and Asperger syndrome: A user guide to adolescence*. London: Jessica Kingsley Publishers.

John-Steiner, V. (1987). *Notebooks of the mind: Explorations of thinking*. New York: HarperCollins.

Johnson, M.D. & Corden, S.H. (2004). *Beyond words: The successful inclusion of a child with autism*. Knoxville, TN: Merry Pace Press.

Jolliffe, T., Lansdowne, R. & Robinson, C. (1992). Autism: A personal account. *Communication, Journal of the National Autistic Society, 26*, 12–19.

Jorgensen, C. (1998). *Restructuring high schools for all students: Taking inclusion to the next level*. Baltimore: Paul H. Brookes Publishing Co.

Kagan, S. (1993). *Cooperative learning*. San Clemente, CA: Kagan Cooperative Learning.

Karp, S. (2004). NCLB's selective vision of equality: Some gaps count more than others. In D. Meier & G. Wood (Eds.), *Many children left behind: How the No Child Left Behind Act is damaging our children and failing our schools* (pp. 53–65). Boston: Beacon Press.

Kasa-Hendrickson, C. (2005). "There's no way this kid's retarded": Teachers' optimistic constructions of students' ability. *International Journal of Inclusive Education, 9*, 55–69.

Kasa-Hendrickson, C., & Kluth, P. (2005). "We have to start with inclusion and work it out as we go": Successful inclusion for non-verbal students with autism. *Journal of Whole Schooling, 2*, 2–14.

Kephart, B. (1998). *A slant of sun*. New York: W.W. Norton.

Kirby, D., & Liner, T. (with Vinz, R.) (1988). *Inside out: A developmental approach to teaching writing* (2nd ed.). Portsmouth, NH: Heinemann.

Kist, W. (2002). Finding "new literacy" in action: An interdisciplinary high school Western civilization class. *Journal of Adolescent & Adult Literacy, 45*(5), 368–378.

Kliewer, C. (1998). *Schooling children with Down syndrome*. New York: Teachers College Press.

Kliewer, C., & Biklen, D. (2001). "School's not really a place for reading": A research synthesis of the literate lives of students with severe disabilities. *The Journal of the Association for Persons with Severe Handicaps, 26*, 1–12.

Kliewer, C., Biklen, D., & Kasa-Hendrickson, C. (2006). Who may be literate? Disability and resistance to the cultural denial of competence. *American Educational Research Journal, 43*, 163–192.

Kluth, P. (1998). *The impact of facilitated communication on the lives of students with movement differences*. Unpublished manuscript. University of Wisconsin.

Kluth, P. (2003). *"You're going to love this kid!" Teaching students with autism in the inclusive classroom*. Baltimore: Paul H. Brookes Publishing Co.

Kluth, P., Biklen, D., English-Sand, P., & Smukler, D. (2007). Going away to school: Stories of families who move to seek inclusion educational experiences for their children with disabilities. *Journal of Disability Policy Studies, 18*(1), 43–56.

Kluth, P., & Dimon-Borowski, M. (2003). *Strengths & strategies profile*. Retrieved July 9, 2007, from http://www.paulakluth.com

Kluth, P., Straut, D., & Biklen, D. (2003). *Access to academics for all students: Critical approaches to inclusive curriculum, instruction, and policy*. Mahwah, NJ: Lawrence Erlbaum Associates.

Knobel, M. (2001). "I'm not a pencil man": How one student challenges our notions of literacy failure in school. *Journal of Adolescent & Adult Literacy, 44*(5), 404–415.

Kokaska, C.J., & Brolin, D.E. (1985). *Career education for handicapped individuals*. Columbus, OH: Charles E. Merrill.

Koppenhaver, D., Coleman, P., Kalman, S., & Yoder, D. (1991). The implications of emergent literacy research for children with developmental disabilities. *American Journal of Speech and Language Pathology, 1*, 38–44.

Koppenhaver, D., & Erickson, K. (2003). Natural emergent literacy supports for preschoolers with autism and severe communication impairments. *Topics in Language Disorders, 23*(4), 283–292.

Koppenhaver, D., Spadorcia, S., & Erickson, K. (1998). How do we provide inclusive early literacy instruction for children with disabilities? In S. Neuman & K. Roskos (Eds.), *Children achieving: Best practices in early literacy* (pp. 77–97). Newark, DE: International Reading Association.

Krebs, A. (2005). Analyzing student work as a professional development activity. *School Science and Mathematics, 105*(8), 402–412.

Labbo, L., Eakle, J., & Montero, K. (2002). Digital Language Experience Approach: Using digital photographs and software as a Language Experience Approach innovation. *Reading Online, 5*(8). Retrieved April 2, 2007, from http://www.readingonline.org/electronic/elec_index.asp?HREF=/electronic/labbo2/index.html

Ladson-Billings, G. (1994). *The dream-keepers: Successful teachers of African-American children*. San Francisco: Jossey-Bass.

Langer, J. (1986). *Children reading and writing: Structures and strategies*. Norwood, NJ: Ablex.

Langer, G., Colton, A., & Goff, L. (2003). *Collaborative analysis of student work: Improving teaching and learning*. Alexandria, VA: Association for Supervision and Curriculum Development.

Lash, J.P. (1980). *Helen and teacher: The story of Helen Keller and Anne Sullivan Macy*. Boston: Addison Wesley.

Latham, A. (1999). Teacher-student mismatch. *Educational Leadership, 56*(7), 84–86.

Lattimer, H. (2003). *Thinking through genre: Units of study in reading-writing workshops 4–12.* Portland, ME: Stenhouse Publishers.

Lawson, W. (1998). *Life behind glass: A personal account of autism spectrum disorder.* London: Jessica Kingsley Publishers.

Leary, M.R., & Hill, D.A. (1996). *Moving on: Autism and movement disturbance.* Mental Retardation, 34, 39–53.

Lensmire, T. (1994). *When children write: Critical re-visions of the writing workshop.* New York: Teachers College Press.

Lewis, C. (2001). *Literary practices as social acts: Power, status, and cultural norms in the classroom.* Mahwah, NJ: Lawrence Erlbaum Associates.

MacArthur, C.A., Graham, S., & Fitzgerald, J. (2006). *Handbook of writing research.* New York: Guilford Press.

MacIver, D.J. (1991). Enhancing students' motivation to learn by altering assessment, reward, and recognition structures: Year 1 of the incentives for improvement program. Baltimore: Johns Hopkins University, Center for Research on Effective Schooling for Disadvantaged Students.

Mahar, D. (2003). Bringing the outside in: One teacher's ride on the anime highway. *Language Arts, 81*(2), 110–117.

Maifair, L. (1999). (Practically) painless peer editing. *Instructor, 108*(7), 8–10.

Marcus, E., & Shevin, M. (1997). Sorting it out under fire: Our journey. In D. Biklen & D. Cardinal (Eds.), *Contested words, contested science: Unraveling the facilitated communication controversy* (pp. 115–134). New York: Teachers College Press.

Marshall, N., & Hegrenes, J. (1972). The use of written language as a communication system for an autistic child. *Journal of Speech and Hearing Disorders, 2,* 258–261.

Martin, R. (1994). *Out of silence: An autistic boy's journey into language and communication.* New York: Penguin.

McCutcheon, D. (2006). Cognitive factors in the development of students' writing. In C. MacArthur, S. Graham, & J. Fitzgerald (Eds.), *Handbook of writing research* (pp. 115–130). New York: Guilford Press.

McDonald, J. (1991). *Exhibitions: Facing outward, pointing inward.* Retrieved March 3, 2007, from http://www.essentialschools.org/cs/resources/view/ces_res/227

McGee, G., Krantz, P., & McClannahan, L. (1986). An extension of incidental teaching procedures to reading instruction for autistic children. *Journal of Applied Behavioral Analysis, 19*(2), 147–157.

Michel, P. (1994). *The child's view of reading: Understandings for teachers and parents.* Boston: Allyn & Bacon.

Miller, D. (2002). *Reading for meaning: Teaching comprehension in the primary grades.* Portland, ME: Stenhouse Publishers.

Mirenda, P. (2003). "He's not really a reader . . . ": Perspectives on supporting literacy development in individuals with autism. *Topics in Language Disorders, 23,* 270–282.

Moje, E.B. (2000). To be part of the story: The literacy practices of gangsta adolescents. *Teachers College Record, 102,* 652–690.

Mont, D. (2001). *A different kind of boy: A father's memoir about raising a gifted child with autism.* London: Jessica Kingsley Publishers.

Mooney, J., & Cole, D. (2000). *Learning outside the lines.* New York: Fireside.

Moustafa, M. (2006). *Research on phonemic awareness training.* Retrieved on May 22, 2006, from http://instructional1.calstatela.edu/mmousta/Research_on_Phonemic_Awareness_Training.htm

Mukhopadhyay, T. (2000). *Beyond the silence.* London: The National Autistic Society.

Nagy, W., Herman, P., & Anderson, R. (1985). Learning words from context. *Reading Research Quarterly, 20,* 233–253.

National Institute of Child Health and Human Development. (2000a). Report of the National Reading Panel. *Teaching children to read: An evidence-based assessment of the scientific research literature on reading and its implications for reading instruction* (NIH Publication No. 00-4769). Washington, DC: U.S. Government Printing Office.

National Institute of Child Health and Human Development. (2000b). *Summary report: Teaching children to read.* Retrieved August 23, 2006, from http://www.nichd.nih.gov/publications/nrp/findings.htm

New London Group. (1996). A pedagogy of multiliteracies: Designing social futures. *Harvard Educational Review, 66,* 60–92.

Newport, J. (2001). *Your life is not a label: A guide to living fully with autism and Asperger's syndrome.* Arlington, TX: Future Horizons.

Nieto, S. (2000). *Affirming diversity: The sociopolitical context of multicultural education* (3rd ed.). New York: Longman.

No Child Left Behind Act of 2001, PL 107-110, 115 Stat. 1425, 20 U.S.C. §§ 6301 *et seq.*

O'Brien, D. (2001). "At-risk adolescents": Redefining competence through the multiliteracies of intermediality, visual arts, and representation. *Reading Online 4*(11). Retrieved June 28, 2007, from http://www.readingonline.org/newliteracies/lit_index.asp?HREF=/newliteracies/obrien/index.html

O'Brien, D. (2003). Juxtaposing traditional and intermedial literacies to redefine the competence of struggling adolescents. *Reading Online, 6*(7). Retrieved February 24, 2006, from http://www.readingonline.org/newliteracies/lit_index.asp?HREF=obrien2/

O'Connor, I.M., & Klein, P.D. (2004). Exploration of strategies for facilitating the reading comprehension of high-functioning students with autism spectrum disorders. Journal of Autism and Developmental Disorders, 34(2), 115–127.

O'Donnell-Allen, C. (2006). *The book club companion: Fostering strategic readers in the secondary classroom.* Portsmouth, NH: Heinemann.

Oelwein, P. (1995). *Teaching reading to children with Down syndrome: A guide for parents and teachers.* Bethesda, MD: Woodbine.

Olson, M.W., & Gee, T. (1991). Content reading instruction in the primary grades: Perceptions and strategies. *The Reading Teacher, 45*(4), 298–307.

O'Neill, J. (1997). A place for all. *The Pennsylvania Journal on Positive Approaches 1*(2), 1.

O'Neill, J.L. (1999). *Through the eyes of aliens: A book about autistic people.* London: Jessica Kingsley Publishers.

Opitz, M. (1999). *Flexible grouping in reading: Practical ways to help all students become better readers.* New York: Scholastic.

Page, T. (2003). *Caught between two worlds: My autistic dilemma.* Woodbridge, CN: Words of Understanding.

Palinscar, A.S., & Brown, A.L. (1984). The reciprocal teaching of comprehension-fostering and comprehension-monitoring activities. *Cognition and Instruction, 1,* 117–175.

Park, C.C. (2001). *Exiting Nirvana: A daughter's life with autism.* New York: Little, Brown.

Parker, D. (1997). *Jamie: A literacy story.* York, ME: Stenhouse Publications.

Peek, F. (1996). *The real rain man: Kim Peek.* Salt Lake City, UT: Harkness Publishing Consultants LLC.

Perry, A. (2003). PowerPoint presentations: A creative addition to the research process. *English Journal, 92*(6), 64–69.

Phelps, S. (1998). Adolescents and their multiple literacies. In D. Alvermann, K. Hinchman, D. Moore, S. Phelps, & D. Waff (Eds.), *Reconceptualizing the literacies in adolescents' lives* (pp. 1–2). Mahwah, NJ: Lawrence Erlbaum Associates.

Pinnell, G.S., Pikulski, J., Wixson, K., Campbell, J., Gough, P., & Beatty, A. (1995). *Listening to children read aloud.* Washington, DC: Office of Educational Research and Improvement, U.S. Department of Education.

Porco, B. (1989). *Reading: Functional programming for people with autism* (Rev. ed.). Bloomington, IN: Indiana Resource Center for Autism.

Powers, M.D. (2000). *Children with autism: A parent's guide.* Bethesda, MD: Woodbine House.

Prescott, J. (2003). The power of reader's theater. *Instructor.* Retrieved May 26, 2006, from http://www.teacher.scholastic.com/products/instructor/readerstheater.htmx

Pressley, M. (2000). What should comprehension instruction be the instruction of? In

M. Kamil, P.B. Mosenthal, P.D. Pearson, & R. Barr (Eds.), *Handbook of reading research*, Volume III (pp. 545–561). Mahwah, NJ: Lawrence Erlbaum Associates.

Pressley, M. (2002). What I have learned up until now about research methods in reading education. In D. Schallert, C. Fairbanks, J. Worthy, B. Maloch, & J. Hoffman (Eds.), *51st Yearbook of the National Reading Conference* (pp. 33–44). Oak Creek, WI: National Reading Conference.

Pressley, M., Dolezal, S., Roehrig, A., & Hilden, K. (2002). Why the National Reading Panel's recommendations are not enough. In R. Allington (Ed.), *Big Brother and the national reading curriculum* (pp. 75–89). Portsmouth, NH: Heinemann.

Prince-Hughes, D. (2004). *Songs of the gorilla: My journey through autism*. New York: Harmony Books.

Probst, R. (1988). *Response and analysis*. Portsmouth, NH: Heinemann.

Pugach, M., & Warger, C. (2001). Curriculum matters: Raising expectations for students with disabilities. *Remedial and Special Education, 22*(4), 192–196.

Purcell-Gates, V. (2002). Multiple literacies. In B. Guzzetti (Ed.), *Literacy in America: An encyclopedia of history, theory, and practice* (Vol. 1, pp. 376–380). Santa Barbara, CA: ABC-CLIO.

Quinlan, T. (2004). Speech recognition technology and students with writing difficulties: Improving fluency. *Journal of Educational Psychology, 96*(2), 337–46.

Rashotte, C.A., & Torgesen, J.K. (1985). Repeated reading and reading fluency in learning disabled children. *Reading Research Quarterly, 20*, 180–188.

Rasinski, T. (1999). Making and writing words. *Reading Online*. Retrieved on May 16, 2006, from http://www.readingonline.org/articles/words/rasinski.html

Rasinski, T. (2003). *The fluent reader: Oral reading strategies for building word recognition, fluency, and comprehension*. New York: Scholastic.

Richards, J., & Morse, T. (2002). One preservice teacher's experiences teaching literacy to regular and special education students. *Reading Online*. Retrieved September 22, 2006, from http://www.readingonline.org/articles/art_index.asp?HREF=/articles/richards/index.html

Ridgeway, V.G., & Cochran, C. (2002). Graphic organizers. In B. Guzzetti (Ed.), *Literacy in America: An encyclopedia of history, theory, and practice* (pp. 213–214). Santa Barbara, CA: ABC-CLIO.

Robb, L. (2002). Multiple texts: Multiple opportunities for teaching and learning. *Voices from the middle, 9*(4), 28–33.

Robb, L. (2004). *Nonfiction writing from the inside out: Writing lessons inspired by conversations with leading authors*. New York: Scholastic.

Robinson, W. (1999). *Gentle giant*. Boston: Element.

Roe, M., & Burns, P. (2006). *Informal reading inventory* (7th ed.). Boston: Houghton Mifflin.

Roller, C. (1996). *Variability not disability: Struggling readers in a workshop classroom*. Newark, DE: International Reading Association.

Rosinski, D. (2002, June). Literacy on the autism spectrum. *The Spectrum*. WI: The Autism Society of Wisconsin.

Rubin, S. (1998, December). *Castigating assumptions about mental retardation and low functioning autism*. Paper presented at the annual meeting of The Association for Persons with Severe Handicaps, Seattle, WA.

Rubin, S., Biklen, D., Kasa-Hendrickson, C., Kluth, P., Cardinal, D., & Broderick, A. (2001). Independence, participation, and the meaning of intellectual ability. *Disability & Society, 16*(3), 415–429.

Russell, D. (2006). Historical studies of composition. In P. Smagorinsky (Ed.), *Research on composition: Multiple perspectives on two decades of change* (pp. 243–276). New York: Teachers College Press.

Ryder, R.J., & Graves, M. (1998). *Reading and learning in content areas* (2nd ed.). Upper Saddle River, NJ: Prentice Hall.

Ryndak, D.L., Morrison, A.P., & Sommerstein, L. (1999). Literacy before and after inclusion in general education settings: A case study. *The Journal of the Association for Persons with Severe Handicaps, 24*, 5–22.

Salinger, T. (2002). Writing assessment. In B. Guzzetti (Ed.), *Literacy in America: An encyclopedia of history, theory, and practice* (pp. 688–693). Santa Barbara, CA: ABC-CLIO.

Samuels, S.J. (1979). The method of repeated readings. *The Reading Teacher, 32*, 403–08.

Samway, K., Whang, G., & Pippitt, M. (1995). *Buddy reading: Cross-age tutoring in a multicultural school.* Portsmouth, NH: Heinemann.

Sapon-Shevin, M. (2007). *Widening the circle: The power of inclusive classrooms.* Boston, MA: Beacon Press.

Schlosser, R. W., & Blischak, D. M. (2004). Effects of speech and print feedback on spelling by children with autism. *Journal of Speech, Language, and Hearing Research, 47*(4), 848–862.

Schwarz, P. (2006). *From disability to possibility.* Portsmouth, NH: Heinemann.

Sellin, B. (1995). *I don't want to be inside me anymore.* New York: Basic Books.

Shanahan, T. (1999). The National Reading Panel: Using research to create more literate students. *Reading Online.* Retrieved on March 30, 2006, from http://www.readingonline.org/critical/shanahan/panel.html

Shaughnessy, M. (1977). *Errors and expectations: A guide for the teacher of basic writing.* New York: Oxford University Press.

Shevin, M., & Kalina, N. (1997, December). *On being a communication ally.* Paper presented at the annual conference of TASH, Boston.

Shore, S. (2003). *Beyond the wall: Personal experiences with autism and Asperger syndrome* (2nd ed.). Shawnee Mission, KS: Autism Asperger Publishing Company.

Short, K., Harste, J., & Burke, C. (1995). *Creating classrooms for authors and inquirers* (2nd ed.). Portsmouth, NH: Heinemann.

Sinclair, J. (1993). Don't mourn for us. *Our Voice, 1*(3), Autism Network International, 1.

Sizer, T. (1992). *Horace's school: Redesigning the American high school.* Boston: Houghton Mifflin.

Smagorinsky, P. (2006). *Research on composition: Multiple perspectives on two decades of change.* New York: Teachers College Press.

Smith, C., & Strick, L. (1997). *Learning disabilities: A to Z.* New York: Fireside.

Smith, F. (1988). *Joining the literacy club: Further essays into education.* Portsmouth, NH: Heinemann.

Smith Myles, B., Adreon, D., & Gitlitz, D. (2006). *Simple strategies that work! Helpful hints for all educators of students with Asperger syndrome, high-functioning autism, and related disabilities.* Shawnee Mission, KS: Autism Asperger Publishing Company.

Smith Myles, B., & Southwick, J. (2005). *Asperger syndrome and difficult moments: Practical solutions for tantrums, rage and meltdowns.* Shawnee Mission, KS: Autism Asperger Publishing Company.

Smith, N., & Tsimpli, I. (1995). *The mind of a savant: Language, learning and modularity.* Boston, MA: Blackwell Publishing Limited.

Smith, W.E. (2002). Reading readiness. In B. Guzzetti (Ed.), *Literacy in America: An encyclopedia of history, theory, and practice* (Vol. 2, pp. 526–527). Santa Barbara, CA: ABC-CLIO.

Sonnenmeier, R., Jorgensen, C., & McSheehan, M. (2005). A case study of team supports for a student with autism's communication and engagement within the general education curriculum. *Journal of Augmentative and Alternative Communication, 21*, 101–115.

Sorrell, A.L. (1990). Three reading comprehension strategies: TELLS, story mapping, and QARs. *Academic Therapy, 25*, 359–368.

Spandel, V. (2001). *Creating writers through 6-trait writing assessment and instruction* (3rd ed.). New York: Longman.

Stainback, S. & Stainback, W. (1996). *Inclusion: A guide for educators.* Baltimore: Paul H. Brookes Publishing Co.

Stanovich, K. (1986). Matthew effects in reading: Some consequences of individual differences in the acquisition of literacy. *Reading Research Quarterly, 21*, 360–407.

Stauffer, R.G. (1970). *The language-experience approach to the teaching of reading.* New York: Harper & Row.

Stokes, S. (2001). *Autism: Intervention and strategies for success.* Retrieved March 10, 2006, from http://www.cesa7.k12.wi.us/sped/autism/pdf

Street, B. (1995). *Social literacies: Critical approaches to literacy in development, ethnography, and education*. New York: Longman.

Strickland, D., & Schickendanz, J. (2004). *Learning about print in preschool: Working with letters, words, and beginning links with phonemic awareness*. Newark, DE: International Reading Association.

Strong, W. (2006). *Write for insight: Empowering content area learning, grades 6–12*. New York: Pearson Education.

Sweet, A.P., & Snow, C. (2003). *Rethinking reading comprehension*. New York: Guilford Press.

Tammet, D. (2007). *Born on a blue day*. New York: Free Press.

Tavalaro, J., & Tayson, R. (1997). *Look up for yes*. New York: Kondansha International.

Taylor, D., & Dorsey-Gaines, C. (1988). *Growing up literate: Learning from inner-city families*. Portsmouth, NH: Heinemann.

Temple University Institute on Disabilities. (1997). *What we are learning about autism/pervasive developmental disorder: Evolving dialogues and approaches to promoting development and adaptation*. New Cumberland, PA: Contract Consultants and Temple University Institute on Disabilities.

Tierney, R., Carter, M., & Desai, L. (1991). *Portfolio assessment in the reading-writing classroom*. Norwood, MA: Christopher-Gordon.

Tierney, R., & Clark, C. (2002). Portfolios. In B. Guzzetti (Ed.), *Literacy in America: An encyclopedia of history, theory, and practice* (pp. 443-445). Santa Barbara, CA: ABC-CLIO.

Tovani, C. (2000). *I read it but I don't get it: Comprehension strategies for adolescent readers*. Portland, ME: Stenhouse Publishers.

Udvari-Solner, A. (1997). Inclusive education. In C.A. Grant & G. Ladson-Billings (Eds.), *Dictionary of multicultural education* (pp. 141–144). Phoenix, AZ: Oryx Press.

Udvari-Solner, A. & Kluth, P. (2008). *Joyful learning*. Thousand Oaks, CA: Corwin Press.

Vacca, R., & Vacca, J. (2005). *Content area reading: Literacy and learning across the curriculum* (8th ed.). New York: Pearson Education.

Villa, R., & Thousand, J. (Eds.) (2005). *Creating an inclusive school* (2nd ed.) Alexandria, VA: Association for Supervision and Curriculum Development.

Vygotsky, L. (1978). *Mind in society: The development of higher psychological processes*. Cambridge, MA: MIT Press.

Wagstaff, J.M. (1999). Word walls that work. *Instructor, 110*(5), 32–34.

Waites, J., & Swinbourne, H. (2001). *Smiling at the shadows*. New York: HarperCollins.

Wallis, C. (2006). Inside the autistic mind. *Time Magazine, 167(20)*, 42–51.

Walpole, S., & McKenna, M. (2006). The role of informal reading inventories in assessing word recognition. *The Reading Teacher, 59*(6), 592–594.

Weaver, C. (1994). *Reading process and practice: From socio-psycholinguistics to whole language* (2nd ed.). Portsmouth, NH: Heinemann.

Weaver, H.R., Adams, S.M., Landers M.F., & Fryberger, Y.B. (1998). Meeting the life skill needs of students with developmental disabilities in integrated settings. In A. Hilton & R. Ringlaben (Eds.), *Best and promising practices in developmental disabilities*. Austin, TX: PRO-ED.

Wertsch, J. (1986). *Culture, communication, and cognition: Vygotskian perspectives*. Cambridge, MA: Harvard University Press.

Whalon, K. (2004). *The effects of a reciprocal questioning intervention on the reading comprehension of children with autism*. Unpublished manuscript. Florida State University, Tallahassee, FL.

Wilde, S. (1992). *You kan red this: Spelling and punctuation for whole language classrooms, K–6*. Portsmouth, NH: Heinemann.

Wilhelm, J., Baker, T., & Dube, J. (2001). *Strategic reading: Guiding students to lifelong literacy, 6-12*. Portsmouth, NH: Heinemann.

Williams, D. (1992). *Nobody, nowhere: The extraordinary autobiography of an autistic*. New York: Avon.

Williams, D. (1994). *Somebody, somewhere: Breaking free from the world of autism*. New York: Times Books.

Williams, D. (1996). *Autism: An inside-out approach*. London: Jessica Kingsley Publishers.

Wolf, D.P. (1989). Portfolio assessment. Sampling student work. *Educational Leadership*, *46*(7), 35–39.

Wormeli, R. (2006). *Fair is not always equal: Evaluation and grading in the differentiated classroom*. Portland, ME: Stenhouse Publishers.

LITERARY AND FILM REFERENCES

Blume, J. (1972). *Tales of a fourth grade nothing*. New York: Dutton Juvenile.

Brown, D. (Producer), & Reiner, R. (Director) (1992). *A few good men* [Motion picture]. United States: Castle Rock Entertainment, Columbia Pictures & New Line Cinema.

Canon, S. (1993). *Stellaluna*. New York: Harcourt.

Carle, E. (1969). *The very hungry caterpillar*. New York: Philomel.

Cherry, L. (1992). *A river ran wild*. New York: Voyager.

Curtis, C. P. (1997). *The Watsons go to Birmingham, 1963*. New York: Yearling.

Gibbons, G. (1989). *Monarch butterflies*. New York: Scholastic.

Hoyt-Goldsmith, D. (1998). *Lacrosse: The national game of the Iroquois*. New York: Holiday House.

Johnson, M. (Producer), & Levinson (Director). (1988). *Rain man* [Motion picture]. United States: MGM.

Lionni, L. (1963). *Swimmy*. New York: Alfred A. Knopf.

Martin, B., & Carle, E. (1991). *Polar bear, polar bear, what do you hear?* New York: Henry Holt and Company.

Mayes, F. (1996). *Under the Tuscan sun: At home in Italy*. New York: Broadway Books.

MacLachlan, P. (1985*). Sarah, plain and tall*. New York: HaperCollins.

O'Dell, S. (1960/1999). *The island of the blue dolphins*. New York: Yearling.

Peterson, J. (1969). *Mystery in the night woods*. New York: Scholastic.

Richter, C. (1963). *The light in the forest*. New York: Bantam Books.

Steinbeck, J. (2002). *Of mice and men*. New York: Viking. (Original work published 1937)

Taylor, M. (1976). *Roll of thunder, hear my cry!* New York: Puffin.

Wolff, V.E. (1993). *Make lemonade*. New York: Scholastic.

Wurtzburg, G. (Producer/Director). (2004). *Autism is a world* [Documentary]. United States: CNN Productions and State of the Art, Inc.

RECOMMENDED READING

Individuals with Autism

Undoubtedly, the best way to learn about autism is to learn from people with that label. Luckily, people on the spectrum are sharing their experiences in increasing numbers and today there are plenty of autobiographical accounts available to those wanting an insider's perspective on the autism label. We have personally enjoyed and learned from many such accounts but our recommendations here focus on those with the most information on literacy and learning.

Barron, J. & Barron, S. (1992). *There's a boy in here*. New York: Simon & Schuster.

Biklen, D. (2006). *Autism and the myth of the person alone*. New York: Teachers College Press.

Blackman, L. (1999). *Lucy's story: Autism and other adventures*. Brisbane, Australia: Book in Hand.

Gerland, G. (1997). *A real person: Life on the outside*. London, UK: Souvenir Press.

Grandin, T. & Scariano, M. (1986). *Emergence: Labeled autistic*. Navato, CA: Arena Press.

Grandin, T. (1995). *Thinking in pictures*. New York: Vintage Books.

Hall, K. (2001). *Asperger syndrome, the universe and everything*. London: Jessica Kingsley Publishers.

Jackson, L. (2002). *Freaks, geeks, and Asperger syndrome: A user guide to adolescence*. London: Jessica Kingsley Publishers.

Mukhopadhyay, T. R. (2000). *Beyond the silence*. London: National Autistic Society.

Nazeer, K. (2006). *Send in the idiots: Stories from the other side of autism*. New York: Bloomsbury.

O'Neill, J.L. (1999). *Through the eyes of aliens: A book about autistic people*. London: Jessica Kingsley Publishers.

Prince-Hughes, D. (2004). *Songs of the gorilla: My journey through autism*. New York: Harmony Books.

Sellin, B. (1995). *I don't want to be inside me anymore*. New York: Basic Books.

Shore, S. (2003). *Beyond the wall*. Shawnee Mission, KS: Autism Asperger Publishing.

Tammet, D. (2007). *Born on a blue day*. New York: Free Press.

Willey, L. (1999). *Pretending to be normal*. London: Jessica Kingsley Publishers.

Williams, D. (1992). *Nobody nowhere: The extraordinary biography of an autistic*. New York: Avon.

Williams, D. (1996). *Autism: An inside-out approach*. London: Jessica Kingsley Publishers.

Autobiographies of the Parents of Individuals with Autism

Another way to learn about autism from those "in the know" is to explore the many autobiographies now being written by the mothers and fathers of people with autism. While there are dozens (and maybe hundreds) of these accounts now available and they all have something to offer the field, we are recommending those we have found to be the most useful, interesting, and compelling as well as those with the most references to teaching, academic support, and literacy.

Cutler, E. (2004). *Thorn in my pocket: Temple Grandin's mother tells the family story*. Arlington, TX: Future Horizons.

Fling, E. (2000). *Eating an artichoke*. London: Jessica Kingsley Publishers.

Ginsberg, D. (2002). *Raising Blaze*. New York: Harper Collins.

Holland, O. (2002). *The dragons of autism: Autism as a source of wisdom*. London: Jessica Kingsley Publishers.

Hughes, R. (2003). *Running with Walker*. London: Jessica Kingsley Publishers.

Kephart, B. (1998). *A slant of sun*. New York: Norton.

LaSalle, B. (2004). *Finding Ben*. New York: McGraw-Hill.

Mont, D. (2002). *A different kind of boy*. London: Jessica Kingsley Publishers.

Waites, J., & Swinbourne, H. (2001). *Smiling at the shadows: A mother's journey through heartache and joy*. New York: Harper Collins.

Willey, L.H. (2001). *Asperger syndrome in the family: Redefining normal*. London: Jessica Kingsley Publishers.

Other Helpful Books on Disability and Literacy

As recently as the mid 1990s, few resources existed to help teachers support learners with labels of autism, cognitive disabilities, or significant disabilities. In the last few years, however, many researchers, teachers, and publishers have answered the call of educators seeking help for their students with autism and low-incidence disabilities. Here we recommend a few titles that we have found immensely helpful in our own teaching and research.

Copeland, S.R., & Keefe, E.B. (2007). *Effective literacy instruction for students with moderate or severe disabilities* (2nd ed.). Baltimore: Paul H. Brookes Publishing Co.

Downing, J. (2005). *Teaching literacy skills to students with significant disabilities: Strategies for the K–12 inclusive classroom* (2nd ed.). Thousand Oaks, CA: Corwin Press.

Erickson, K., & Koppenhaver, D. (2007). *Children with disabilities: Reading and writing the Four-Blocks® way.* Greensboro, NC: Carson-Dellosa Publishing Company, Inc.

Gregory, G.H., & Kuzmich, L. (2004). *Differentiated literacy strategies for student growth and achievement in grades K–6.* Thousand Oaks, CA: Corwin Press.

Gregory, G.H., & Kuzmich, L. (2005). *Differentiated literacy strategies for student growth and achievement in grades 7-12.* Thousand Oaks, CA: Corwin Press.

Keefe, C.H. (1996). *Label-free learning: Supporting learners with disabilities.* Portland, ME: Stenhouse Publishers.

Kliewer, C. (1998). *Schooling children with Down syndrome: Toward an understanding of possibility.* New York: Teachers College Press.

Parker, D. (1997). *Jamie: A literacy story.* Portland, ME: Stenhouse Publishers.

Rhodes, L., & Dudley-Marling, C. (1996). *Readers and writers with a difference: A holistic approach to teaching struggling readers and writers* (2nd. ed.). Portsmouth, NH: Heinemann.

Roller, C. (1996). *Variability not disability: Struggling readers in a workshop classroom.* Newark, DE: International Reading Association.

RECOMMENDED WEB SITES ON LITERACY, DIFFERENTIATED INSTRUCTION, AND DISABILITY

The Access Center
   http://www.k8accesscenter.org/default.asp
Center for Applied Special Technology (CAST): Universal Design for Learning
   http://www.cast.org/pd/index.html
The Center for Literacy and Disability Studies
   http://www.med.unc.edu/ahs/clds/index.html
Closing the Gap: Assistive Technology Resources for Children and Adults with Special Needs
   http://www.closingthegap.com/
Currents in Literacy [Lesley University]
   http://www.lesley.edu/academic_centers/hood/currentshome.html
Disability, Literacy, & Inclusive Education for Young Children
   http://www.uni.edu/inclusion/index.htm
Inclusion: School as a Caring Community
   http://www.ualberta.ca/~jpdasddc/inclusion/schoolcaring/intro.htm
Paula Kluth's web site
   www.paulakluth.com
TeachersFirst
   http://www.teachersfirst.com
Simplified Technology [Linda J. Burkhart's personal website]
   http://www.lburkhart.com/
Whole Schooling Consortium
   http://www.wholeschooling.net/

Index

Page references followed by *f* indicate figures; those followed by *t* indicate tables.